Praise for
The Number

"[One of the] Best Music Books of 2022"

"[The] Best Music Book of 2022" — *Pitchfork*

"A Pick to Bring on Weekend Travels" — *LitHub*

* * *

"Tom Breihan's *The Number Ones* is a glorious rabbit hole dive into the biggest hits in popular music, analyzing the very physics of how they became hits and taking a forensic look at what made them 'pop.' It's massively enjoyable when you love the song in question, and perhaps even more so when you don't. One of the most enjoyable books on pop to ever roar up the charts." — Edgar Wright

"Tom Breihan is an absolutely crucial chronicler of the hit parade, a madman scholar digging deep in the vaults. *The Number Ones* is a revelatory celebration of pop history in all its glorious weirdness, the way only Breihan could tell the tale. These are classic tunes that everybody knows, but Breihan brilliantly blows away the dust and makes them sound fresh and new. [Breihan is] a hell of a storyteller and a hell of a T-Pain fan." — Rob Sheffield

"[In] the engaging, illuminating, and exhilarating *The Number Ones*... Breihan brings a laser-like focus and fan's sensibility to stone-cold classic number one hits.... Perhaps nobody writing about music today is better equipped to grapple with those questions.... Whether in his column or [in] *The Number Ones*, Breihan unearths fascinating nuggets about even the most pedestrian songs. Like a Russian nesting doll, his writings contain multitudes.... Breihan has penned a work that resembles some of the indelible hits he spotlights: memorable, timeless, and worth revisiting again and again." — *The Los Angeles Times*

"Breihan displays a keen eye (and ear) for identifying landmark moments....Breihan will have you building out playlists and diving down new musical rabbit holes, but he will also leave you questioning how many times you've dismissed something as a passing trend."
—*The New York Times* (audiobook)

"A rich critical history of pop at its most universally revelatory."
—*Rolling Stone*

"Briskly written, a pleasure to read, *The Number Ones* is a musical treat."
—*The Wall Street Journal*

"For longtime readers of Breihan's work, the tone will be instantly familiar: affable, conversational, and always funny with surprising insights and ear-catching phrasings gliding in from every direction....The jokes, asides, and loping digressions all mimic the texture of conversation [and point] to Breihan's enduring strength as a critic. When you read him it feels like he's talking to you."
—*Pitchfork*

"Ripe with opinion and spiced by peppery humor....Breihan's book also lovingly looks into deserving artists (e.g., Bob Dylan, Bruce Springsteen, etc.) who have never topped the singles charts."
—*Variety*

"The book [is a] fascinating look at the last six-plus decades of popular music through the prism of *Billboard*'s signature songs chart, [and it also digs] into the nooks and crannies of both the music and the chart itself as the subject requires."
—*Billboard*

"*The Number Ones* is a tour de force of Breihan at his most nerdy, intricate, and enjoyable....No one parses the stories or puts the popular songs that have defined generations into perspective better than Breihan, [and he] has delivered on the promise of his crazy column idea."
—*The Aquarian*

THE
Number
Ones

TWENTY
CHART-TOPPING HITS
THAT REVEAL THE
HISTORY OF POP MUSIC

TOM BREIHAN

hachette
BOOKS
New York

Hachette Books
Hachette Book Group
1290 Avenue of the Americas
New York, NY 10104
HachetteBooks.com
Twitter.com/HachetteBooks
Instagram.com/HachetteBooks

First Trade Paperback Edition: October 2023

Published by Hachette Books, an imprint of Hachette Book Group, Inc. The Hachette
Books name and logo are trademarks of the Hachette Book Group.

The Hachette Speakers Bureau provides a wide range of authors for speaking events. To find
out more, visit hachettespeakersbureau.com or email HachetteSpeakers@hbgusa.com.

The publisher is not responsible for websites (or their content) that are not owned
by the publisher.

Print book interior design by Jeff Williams.

Library of Congress Control Number: 2022943895

ISBNs: 978-0-306-82653-5 (hardcover); 978-0-306-82654-2 (trade paperback);
 978-0-306-82655-9 (ebook)

Printed in the United States of America

LSC-C

Printing 1, 2023

For my wife, Bridget,
and my kids, Clara and Finn

Contents

Intro

THIS STORY, LIKE MANY, STARTS WITH A TEENAGE GIRL. Sharon Sheeley came from Newport Beach, California, and did a little modeling as a kid, but she really wanted to write songs. When she was seventeen, Sheeley had an affair with twenty-year-old Don Everly, the older of the two Everly Brothers, and it didn't end well. (He was married.) So Sheeley channeled some of her heartbreak into writing a song called "Poor Little Fool": "I'd played this game with other hearts, but I never thought I'd see / The day that someone else would play love's foolish game with me." It was the first song she'd ever written. Later, Sheeley claimed that "Poor Little Fool" started as an English-class assignment and that her teacher flunked her for it.

Ricky Nelson was a month younger than Sheeley. Nelson, one of the original teen idols, was probably the only fifties rock 'n' roll icon who'd been famous since before the birth of rock 'n' roll. Ricky's parents, Ozzie and Harriet Nelson, were the stars of *The Adventures of Ozzie and Harriet*, a radio sitcom that started in 1944, when Ricky was four. (Ozzie, a former college football star at Rutgers, had been a soft-jazz bandleader, and he'd created *The Adventures* after he and Harriet became regulars on Red Skelton's radio show.) Ricky was nine when he joined the show's cast. He was twelve when *The Adventures of Ozzie and Harriet* made the leap to television. And he was seventeen when he became a rock 'n' roll star.

Nelson recorded his first single, a cover of Fats Domino's "I'm Walkin'," in 1957. Nelson sang his version of the song on *Ozzie and Harriet*, and it became a hit. More hits followed. Sharon Sheeley lived pretty close to the Nelson family home in Laguna Beach. One night, Sheeley drove into the Nelsons' driveway and claimed that her car had broken down. When Ricky invited her inside, she told him that she had a song she'd written for Elvis Presley but that she really wanted him to record it. (According to some versions of the story, she told Nelson that her godfather had written "Poor Little Fool.")

Ricky Nelson didn't love "Poor Little Fool" at first, but he loved the idea of being offered a song that Elvis Presley wanted. He released "Poor Little Fool" as an album track on his self-titled 1958 LP, and when radio DJs started to play the song, Imperial Records, Nelson's label, released it as a single. Around the same time, the music-industry trade magazine *Billboard* combined its singles-sales and radio-play charts into one list, calling it the Hot 100. When *Billboard* ran its first Hot 100 list, "Poor Little Fool" happened to be the most popular song in the United States.

"Poor Little Fool" and the Hot 100 both arrived at a sort of changing-of-the-guard moment. A little more than two years earlier, a new hybrid sound called rock 'n' roll had captured young America's imagination. Bill Haley and the Comets had an international hit with "(We're Gonna) Rock Around the Clock," an anarchic frenzy of a song that combined country twang with rhythm-and-blues (R&B) push, both played at out-of-control speed. Soon afterward, Elvis Presley showed up, looking and acting like sex incarnate.

A small army of fired-up hornballs followed—Jerry Lee Lewis, Chuck Berry, Little Richard. Black music and white music were combining into strange new shapes. The sound was wild and caveman simple and nakedly sexual, and it ripped a hole in the space-time continuum. An instant generation gap was created. But that excitement couldn't last.

Six months before "Poor Little Fool" became the Hot 100's first #1 hit, Buddy Holly, Ritchie Valens, the Big Bopper (J. P. Richardson), and a pilot named Roger Peterson died in a plane crash. Three months before "Poor Little Fool" hit #1, Jerry Lee Lewis married his thirteen-year-old cousin, and the resulting scandal derailed his career. Four months after "Poor Little Fool" hit #1, Chuck Berry would be arrested for transporting a minor across state lines; his career would never recover. (Berry would eventually land one #1 hit of his own—fourteen years later, with a genuinely awful novelty song about his penis.) And two years after "Poor Little Fool," Elvis Presley, a man with plenty of #1 hits of his own, would join the army. (Presley would continue to make hits for a few years, but he would largely trade away sexed-up rock 'n' roll excitement for respectable B-movie irrelevance.) The same year that Presley joined the army, rockabilly star Eddie Cochran, who was engaged to Sharon Sheeley at the time, died in a car crash. (Sheeley was riding in the car, too. She broke her pelvis but survived.) Those losses and career cataclysms added up, and the sudden, violent, explosive energy of that first rock 'n' roll boom turned into something else.

Ricky Nelson was the new prototype of that something else. He was cute and friendly and approachable. Thanks to *Ozzie and Harriet*, he was familiar. With a song like "Poor Little Fool," Nelson could portray himself as a sensitive, heartbroken kid. Nelson's peers weren't Elvis Presley and Chuck Berry; they were clean-cut young rock 'n' roll crooners like Paul Anka and Pat Boone. Those singers became the prototypes for a wave of good-looking white boys who sang cute songs about crushes and breakups: Frankie Avalon, Fabian, Bobby Rydell. Like Ricky Nelson, many of those teen idols became familiar through the new medium of television; they cut their teeth on *American Bandstand*, the daily dance-party show that went national in 1957, hosted by the squeaky-clean former radio newscaster Dick Clark. With this new wave, rock 'n' roll became pop music. And in a way, that's where the story of pop music, in its modern form, begins.

For a long time, *Billboard* magazine has chronicled pop music, modern and otherwise. *Billboard* goes back more than a century. When the magazine began publishing in 1894, it covered the advertising industry. At that time, "advertising" meant "posters pasted up on walls," so that's why it's called *Billboard*. Before the new century started, *Billboard* began to pay attention to the glamorous world of entertainment: fairs, circuses, burlesque, vaudeville. When phonographs came into being, and then jukeboxes, *Billboard* was there. *Billboard* published its first chart, covering sales of 78-RPM singles, in 1940. When *Billboard* published its first weekly "Music Popularity Chart" in July 1940, the #1 single in America was Tommy Dorsey and His Orchestra's "I'll Never Smile Again." The chart listing didn't mention that song's vocalist, a young singer named Frank Sinatra.

By 1958, *Billboard* had a few different music charts going. One chart tracked radio play, and another followed record sales, while others kept track of the genres of country and R&B. (*Billboard* also tracked jukebox records, but that chart was discontinued in 1957.) In 1958, *Billboard* put its main charts together into the Hot 100, the one true chart that would keep a running tally of the most popular records in America, week in and week out. *Billboard* had good timing. The Hot 100 just missed the very beginning of the rock 'n' roll era, but the chart began at a moment of vast demographic change, a time when babyboomer children were starting to spend money on singles and a whole new cultural wave was gathering force.

In the years ahead, the Hot 100 would chronicle each new trend that would capture the collective imagination: the Beatles, Motown, psychedelia, disco, new wave, metal, rap. The Hot 100 has never been a perfect barometer for measuring the musical moment. *Billboard* uses a constantly shifting formula to measure all the different factors that decide a song's popularity, and the magazine still scrambles to keep up with the way people actually listen to music. There have always been rumors about corruption and bribery in the Hot 100 tabulation. For a whole stretch in the nineties, the Hot 100 was terribly misleading; at the time, *Billboard* would grant Hot 100 real estate only to songs that had been commercially released as singles, which ruled out a lot of the decade's biggest songs. Singles had once been the dominant format in the record business, but labels, capitalizing on the CD boom, were trying to push the public into buying full albums. It worked for a while.

But for more than sixty years, the Hot 100 has been there, charting every passing craze and every earthshaking revolution. It's the best way we have of scientifically, dispassionately watching the way popular music has fluctuated over the years, and it makes for a fascinating study. Over those decades, more than a thousand songs have hit #1 on the Hot 100. The Beatles have twenty #1 hits. Michael Jackson has thirteen. Drake, at the time of this writing, has seven. (If you count guest appearances, Drake has ten.) Bruce Springsteen, Bob Dylan, and James Brown all have zero.

There's something romantic about the idea of a #1 song—about the idea that, at any given moment, there's one song that's playing more than any other on our car radios, dancing through our brains, and shaping our memories. And because *Billboard* has been keeping its lists archived for more than sixty years, we can see how those songs reflect the way popular tastes have changed over time—sometimes incrementally, sometimes all at once.

This book looks at twenty game-changing singles that have hit #1 on the Hot 100 in the years after "Poor Little Fool." These aren't the *best* Hot 100 hits in history, though many of them, I'd argue, are great. Instead, these are the songs that marked new moments in pop-music evolution—the ones that immediately made the previous weeks' hits sound like relics. Some of these hits tell us a whole lot about where the world was and where popular tastes had shifted. Some of them show changes in recording technology or in the devices that people used to find the songs they loved. Some reflect the ways that a generation of Americans thought about sex, or drugs, or war.

Taken together, all of these songs paint a picture. They show us history through music. They chart a map of a changing culture—sudden moments of swift musical or technological advancement, of political thinking, of generational fears or fancies. Sometimes, the #1 song in the country might tell you more about a particular historical moment than anything else about the news of that day.

AT THE BEGINNING of 2018, I set myself a ridiculous task: I decided that I was going to review every single song that had ever occupied that #1 spot, starting with "Poor Little Fool" and plowing my way forward into the present. (In his column, "Popular," British writer Tom Ewing had been doing something similar with the UK charts for years, and his work served as a direct inspiration.) Stereogum, the website where I work, is mostly based around the music of the present—the songs and albums and news stories that matter in the moment, or the ones that might make for fun water-cooler conversations. But my boss, Scott Lapatine, the site's founder, allowed me to plow right into this absurd project. I started out writing quick, often snarky capsule reviews, but I eventually came to discover that virtually every #1 hit in Hot 100 history has a fascinating story of its own. I started to see the bigger picture laid out before me.

At the time of this writing, my column, "The Number Ones," has been running for years, and I've written about hundreds of past chart-toppers. The column has been more successful than I'd imagined. Other people, it turns out, are just as fascinated with the chart's twists and absurdities and sudden leaps forward. Some of them have started writing their own columns—covering things like the R&B charts, or the Australian singles charts, or whatever was happening in metal at that point—in the comments section of "The Number Ones."

A whole community has emerged in that comments section, and it's been wild and deeply gratifying to see it take shape.

In writing the column, I have learned that chart history is not particularly coherent, in the same way that American popular taste is not coherent. Plenty of the songs that have reached #1 are canonical classics, but plenty of them are also faddish little reminders of past cultural phenomena. (Studio musician Meco's disco version of John Williams's *Star Wars* score, for instance, was a #1 hit in 1977.) And plenty of other chart-toppers are also utterly forgotten trifles that now inspire complete puzzlement: *This* was a hit?

When you look at pop history exclusively through the lens of #1 hits, then you inevitably overlook some truly totemic records. The Miracles' "Shop Around" was the first national hit released under the Motown banner, and it introduced the world to the brilliance of Smokey Robinson, but that song peaked at #2 behind Lawrence Welk's chintzy easy-listening instrumental "Calcutta." Someone could probably write an entire book about the songs that couldn't get past #2 — the Kingsmen's "Louie, Louie," Bob Dylan's "Like a Rolling Stone," Madonna's "Material Girl," Dr. Dre and Snoop Doggy Dogg's "Nuthin' but a 'G' Thang," Kelly Clarkson's "Since U Been Gone" — and the singles that kept those songs out of the top spot. It's tempting to hold those #2 hits up as moments when America simply got it wrong, but the pop charts are not moral or meritorious. "Right" and "wrong" have nothing to do with it. Those charts simply record the winners and the not-quite-winners of their moments.

In limiting its focus to the Hot 100, this book also misses the sudden surge of rock 'n' roll in the midfifties. Fred Bronson's reference *The "Billboard" Book of Number 1 Hits*, a crucial resource for my whole project, begins in 1955 with Bill Haley and His Comets' "(We're Gonna) Rock Around the Clock," marking that record's success as the beginning of the rock era. By starting this book with the birth of the Hot 100, this book misses "Rock Around the Clock" and a few other crucial chart-topping hits of the early rock 'n' roll era: Elvis Presley's "Heart-break Hotel," Sam Cooke's "You Send Me," the Champs' "Tequila," the Everly Brothers' "All I Have to Do Is Dream." But starting at the dawn of the Hot 100 isn't arbitrary. There's been plenty written about the arrival of Elvis Presley and his contemporaries. This book looks at the many aftershocks that followed that first big bang.

The twenty songs in this book are all BC/AD moments. They're points where pop history pivoted—where new genres or technologies or cultural moments sent the pop charts off in a new direction. There aren't a lot of ballads in the book, mainly because most of the slow songs that have topped the Hot 100—and there have been hundreds of them—have gained steam precisely because they're reliable and familiar and comforting. These comforting songs, by and large, don't depend on the shock of the new, and this book is all about the shock of the new. (There are a few soothing songs in the book—the Byrds' "Mr. Tambourine Man," Fleetwood Mac's "Dreams," Mariah Carey's "Vision of Love"—but all of those songs found new ways to soothe.)

The Hot 100 is a funny thing. Sometimes, a new revolution in public taste will appear on the charts immediately; Beatlemania was a chart phenomenon before the Beatles themselves physically disembarked from their plane in New York. Rap music, on the other hand, existed within pop music for more than a decade before Vanilla Ice finally took "Ice Ice Baby" to #1. Some of the songs in this book, like the Beach Boys' "Good Vibrations," are here because they changed the scope of what a chart-topping pop song could even be. Some mark new technologies, or new applications of existing technology, as when T-Pain used the voice-warping effect of Auto-Tune to conquer the Hot 100 with "Buy U a Drank (Shawty Snappin')." A few, like Michael Jackson's "Billie Jean," changed the scope of pop dominance. Others reflect changes in the routes that a song could take to mass popularity. Soulja Boy's "Crank That (Soulja Boy)," for instance, showed how a teenager on his home computer could weaponize the Internet and transform himself, however briefly, into a full-on pop star.

In many cases, these songs mark moments where mass communication changed. The Human League's "Don't You Want Me," for example, reflected the new influence of MTV, the cable network that had launched the previous year. Rae Sremmurd's "Black Beatles," meanwhile, marks the moment when streaming services like Spotify and Apple Music became the main delivery system for pop music. Even the first chapter in this book, on Chubby Checker's "The Twist," tells a story about television, a relatively new invention, and about how that invention came to shape popular tastes.

Every hit song has a story. All those hits, taken together, tell a strange, twisty, self-contradictory epic tale about what America wants in a pop song. This book collects twenty important chapters in that story, but that story hasn't ended yet. Hopefully, it never will.

CHAPTER 1

Chubby Checker–
"The Twist"

Released June 1960	
Hit #1 September 19, 1960	
One-week reign	
Hit #1 again January 13, 1962	
Two-week reign	

"THIS ONE IS A GASSER," SAID DICK CLARK, SHAKING HIS head as if he couldn't believe what the world was about to see. "It's a pretty frightening thing. It's sweeping the country all over the place." Clark's eyebrows went up, as if to emphasize this next point: "Hottest dance sensation in the last four years, a thing called the twist."

Dick Clark was a pitchman, a guy who'd been an ad reader before becoming America's most successful teenage-dance-show host. He knew how to sell things. But Clark wasn't exaggerating about the twist. Clark had just turned thirty, and he'd already made a fortune, partly by recognizing the hottest dance sensations when they came along and by knowing how to present them to America. Clark knew that the twist was having its moment, and he knew exactly how to frame that moment.

As a phenomenon, the dance sensation is a whole lot older than rock 'n' roll. There's a direct line from jazz-age trends like the jitterbug to the televised contortions of the early rock 'n' roll era. Like most varieties of pop music since, swing was a crucial site of cross-racial conversation and appropriation in American life. In the twenties, young white adventurers would travel uptown, visiting hallowed Harlem institutions like the Savoy Ballroom. They would then attempt their own variations on the Black dances that they witnessed in those venues, and those dances would make their way into mainstream white culture— first bringing a whiff of sex and scandal, then slowly losing that vitality and turning into kitsch. That's more or less what happened with the twist when mainstream-entertainment purveyors like Dick Clark got hold of it, too.

The twist itself also predates rock 'n' roll. The Virginia Minstrels, a Black American vaudeville group, performed a song called "Grape Vine Twist" while touring England as early as 1844. On his 1912 ragtime number "Messin' Around," Black songwriter Perry Bradford admonished dancers to "twist around with all your might." Duke Ellington and Jelly Roll Morton recorded tracks with the word "twist" in their titles. In those songs, "twist" has a nebulously sexual meaning—part dance, part innuendo. But in the late fifties, the twist became something else. It became something you could watch on TV.

When it first exploded in the fifties, rock 'n' roll was really just a new name for rhythm and blues, the raw and insistent form of Black pop music that had already been evolving for years. Before white singers like Elvis Presley began doing their own variations of it, rhythm and blues was the dominion of Black stars like Hank Ballard, the Detroit-born singer and leader of a vocal group called the Midnighters. Ballard and the Midnighters first broke out with the 1954 single "Work with Me, Annie," a barely disguised sex song that topped *Billboard*'s R&B chart and crossed over into the top 40 of the magazine's pre–Hot 100 pop charts even though the magazine's writers referred to the song as "smut." "Work with Me, Annie," which Ballard wrote, inspired answer songs like "Work with Me, Henry," the hit that first put Etta James on the map, and it made Ballard a star on the so-called chitlin circuit of Black nightclubs.

One night in 1957, Ballard stayed at the same Florida hotel as the Sensational Nightingales, a gospel group whose members were big fans of the Midnighters. Some of them brought Ballard a blues song that was too secular for the Nightingales to record. Ballard rewrote the song, and he set it to a version of the melody from "What'cha Gonna Do," a 1955 R&B hit from Clyde McPhatter and the Drifters. (Five years later, after McPhatter had left the group, the Drifters and new leader Ben E. King would score their own Hot 100 chart-topper with the pop masterpiece "Save the Last Dance for Me.") Ballard had himself listed as the sole songwriter of this new track, and he released it as the B-side to the Midnighters' 1959 ballad "Teardrops on Your Letter." Ballard called that song "The Twist."

"Teardrops on Your Letter," released on the Cincinnati indie King Records, became an R&B hit, but its B-side hit even bigger when DJs started playing it at record-hop dances. "The Twist" is a simple, fast rumble of a song, built around Ballard's ecstatic exhortations. Ballard pleads, "Take me by my little hand, and go like this." Behind him, the Midnighters chant, "Round and round and round." When the Midnighters played a ten-night stand at Baltimore's Royal Theater, the young people in the predominantly Black crowd improvised their own dance to "The Twist." Soon after, the white teenage regulars on *The Buddy Deane Show*, a dance-party program that aired on TV, started doing that version of the twist on camera. (*The Buddy Deane Show*, the inspiration for John Waters's *Hairspray*, was canceled in 1964 because the station WJZ was unwilling to show Black and white kids dancing together.)

Before long, the twist made its way a hundred miles north, to the center of the teenage-dance-party universe. *American Bandstand*, the biggest of the dance-party TV shows, had begun broadcasting from Philadelphia in 1952. In 1957, original host Bob Horn was fired amid a string of underage-sex and drunk-driving scandals, and the boyish and smooth Dick Clark took over. That same year, Clark pitched *Bandstand* to the heads of ABC. The network, which originally saw *Bandstand* as cheap daytime programming, started broadcasting *Bandstand* nationally. The show became an immediate hit. Suddenly, kids across the country had a chance to hear records and see dances that might've been local phenomena in earlier years. Sales of 45-RPM singles exploded.

From the very beginning, Dick Clark put his considerable business instincts into making money from rock 'n' roll. Often, publishing companies, desperate to get their singles into *Bandstand* rotation, would give songwriting credit to Clark himself, which meant Clark had a financial stake in those songs' success. Clark even co-owned a label called Swan Records and a few publishing firms, and he'd reliably promote his own records. Amid the payola scandal of 1960, which took down pioneering rock 'n' roll DJs like Alan Freed, Clark had to drop all his investments in the record business. As Ballard's "The Twist" was starting to take off, Clark testified in front of a House subcommittee hearing on payola, and his respectful, professional manner may have saved his job and reputation.

Clark was always mindful of his image. Where rock 'n' roll had been a rebellious teenage phenomenon, Clark was quick to remove any sense of danger from *Bandstand*. The kids who danced on the show adhered to a strict dress code, and while the show's dancers and performers were integrated, they skewed heavily white. Sometimes, the white kids on the show would pass off dances that they'd learned from their Black classmates as their own inventions. Rather than relying on anarchic performers like early *Bandstand* guest Jerry Lee Lewis, Clark minted clean, approachable new teenage idols like his Swan Records protégé Freddy Cannon. Even after the payola scandal, Clark maintained close ties with Philadelphia labels like Cameo-Parkway, which made a lot of money by turning good-looking local teenagers such as Charlie Gracie and Bobby Rydell into heartthrob singers who played well on *Bandstand.* When Clark saw a new dance becoming popular, sometimes he'd call his friends in the business and tell them to put together a song to go along with the dance.

When Clark first heard "The Twist," he didn't hear money. Clark featured Ballard and the Midnighters on *Bandstand,* but he didn't push them hard. Some members of the Midnighters had been arrested for lewd acts like dropping their pants onstage. Radio stations had banned songs like "Work with Me, Annie" and the Midnighters' follow-up single, "Sexy Ways." Ballard himself claimed that the group's live act consisted of "doing dirty shit onstage." If Dick Clark was going to beam "The Twist" into American living rooms, he needed someone with a brighter, cleaner image than Hank Ballard and the Midnighters. Clark had to make sure that he could package and control "The Twist" on his own terms.

Freddy Cannon once claimed that Clark had deemed "The Twist" "too Black" to play on *Bandstand* and that he wanted Cannon to record it instead. But Cannon already had another single doing well at the time, and so the song went to another local teenager. Ernest Evans, a good-looking Black kid born in South Carolina, had spent his teenage years living in South Philadelphia public housing. He'd gone to high school with Frankie Avalon and Fabian, two white teen idols who became popular on *Bandstand,* and he wanted to be a singer like them. Evans would sing while plucking and cutting chickens at a local poultry market. Evans's boss became his manager, and he introduced Evans to Dick Clark.

Clark needed someone to record some tracks for a singing Christmas card that he'd made for his family. Evans was a gifted mimic, and he sang in a few different voices for Clark's card. He was so good at impersonating Fats Domino that Clark's wife, Barbara, gave him a new stage name: "You're Chubby Checker, like Fats Domino." His ability to do other singers' voices got the newly renamed Chubby Checker signed to Cameo-Parkway. On the novelty tune "The Class," his first single, Checker sang nursery rhymes in the voices of Fats Domino,

Elvis Presley, and the Chipmunks. Checker lip-synched "The Class" on *American Bandstand*, and the song became a minor hit. Soon afterward, the heads of Cameo-Parkway decided to record their own version of "The Twist." Cameo exec Dave Appell: "We figured we'd do [Ballard's] record with a kid, and then we would at least be on the Clark show." Chubby Checker was the kid.

The Chubby Checker version of "The Twist" is nearly identical to Hank Ballard and the Midnighters' original, right down to the note-for-note facsimile of the first song's honking saxophone solo. A local group called the Dreamlovers replicated the Midnighters' backing vocals, and Checker did his best version of Ballard's lead. In addition to *American Bandstand*, Clark had begun hosting a weekly prime-time series, *The Dick Clark Show*, from a New York studio. That's where Clark first showcased Chubby Checker's version of "The Twist." A grinning Checker mimed his way through both the song and a stiffer, less hump-heavy version of the dance. The audience in the theater shrieked its approval. (Those audience members were sitting down, so they couldn't really dance along with Checker, but at least a couple of them tried.)

Hank Ballard was relaxing in a Florida hotel pool when he first heard Chubby Checker's "The Twist" on his transistor radio. At first, Ballard thought he was hearing himself. Later, he told an interviewer about his reaction: "Wow, I'm finally getting some white airplay! I'm going to be a superstar!" Ballard's version of "The Twist," reissued as its own single, actually debuted on the Hot 100 two weeks before Chubby Checker's cover. But Ballard's original peaked at #28. Checker had *Bandstand* on his side, and his version went all the way to #1.

In both its Hank Ballard and its Chubby Checker versions, "The Twist" is a fast, energetic, extremely likable song. Ballard and Checker both deliver the lead vocal in charismatic bellows. Both versions of the song have propulsive backing vocals and fast, pounding beats. "The Twist" isn't an artistic masterpiece, but that was never the intent. It's a song that exists simply to get people moving, and it succeeds at that.

In its kinetic simplicity, "The Twist" set the template for decades of dance-craze hits that followed.

Clark may have resisted "The Twist" at first, but the song turned out to be perfect for *Bandstand*. As a dance, the twist was energetic and improvisatory enough that the show's teenage regulars could perfect their own personalized versions. The twist was adaptable enough that it didn't have to be sexualized, and it was simple enough that anyone could do it. Just as important, the twist didn't require a partner, so shows like *Bandstand* were never in danger of violating any morality codes. In 1957, ABC canceled *The Big Beat*, the dance show hosted by pioneering rock 'n' roll DJ Alan Freed, after its cameras showed Frankie Lymon, the young Black star, dancing with a white girl. Since the twist was a noncontact dance, Dick Clark didn't have to worry about anything like that happening.

"The Twist" was the first dance-craze record ever to top the Hot 100, and its success demonstrated the power of *Bandstand*. Many more dance-craze songs followed. A few months later, Checker followed "The Twist" up with "Pony Time," which topped the Hot 100 for three weeks early in 1962. Later that year, Checker made it to #8 with "Let's Twist Again," a single written by Cameo-Parkway execs Kal Mann and Dave Appell that capitalized on a sort of instant nostalgia: "Let's twist again, like we did last summer / Let's twist again, like we did last year."

The twist craze easily could've died down after "Let's Twist Again," but the dance took root in a place where nobody could've expected. Joseph DiNicola, an Italian kid from New Jersey, led a local nightclub act called Joey Dee and the Starliters. (Joe Pesci played in an early lineup of the band.) An agent caught a Starliters show in Lodi and offered them a gig at the Peppermint Lounge, a small Mafia-front bar on Forty-Fifth Street in Manhattan.

The Starliters became the Peppermint Lounge house band, and the club hired a publicist, who tipped off gossip columnists about the scene developing around the group's performances. Writers like Cholly Knickerbocker wrote in breathless tones about the working-class kids who came to the Peppermint Lounge to do the twist, and slumming celebrities like Marilyn Monroe and Judy Garland came to the club to take in the scene for themselves. Those appearances led to more gossip columns, which led to bigger and more excited crowds. Soon, the Peppermint Lounge was a New York–society destination, and the twist went from a teenage fad to a glamorous, slightly forbidden adult pastime.

With the success of the Peppermint Lounge, other twisting clubs opened up in New York, Los Angeles, and San Francisco. Advertising his Harlem club, Smalls' Paradise, for instance, NBA star Wilt Chamberlain said, "These white people come to twist. This is the best twist spot in town." Chamberlain's line illuminates one key aspect of the whole craze. It wasn't just adults doing a teenage dance. It was also rich white people doing a dance that had its origins in the Black community. But white consumers were taking part in Black culture in ways that often didn't advantage the Black creators of those sounds and dances.

Chubby Checker got paid, though. In 1961, as the twist revival continued, Thom McAn shoe stores started making a new line of shoes, Chubby Checker's Twisters, and Checker advertised them on TV. He also licensed twisting hats and dance mats. In January 1962, Checker's song "The Twist" returned to #1 on the *Billboard* Hot 100 for two weeks. It's the only time a non-Christmas song has landed at #1 years apart. The second time that "The Twist" topped the charts, the song that knocked it off its perch was another twisting song: Joey Dee and the Starliters' "Peppermint Twist—Part 1." Around the same time, both Chubby Checker and Joey Dee starred in twist-themed B movies. Nineteen years before his Oscar-nominated turn in *Raging Bull*, a teenage Joe Pesci made his big-screen debut as one of the Peppermint Lounge twisters in the Joey Dee vehicle *Hey, Let's Twist!*

Chubby Checker rode the twist wave as long as he could. Checker teamed up with Cameo-Parkway teen idol Bobby Rydell for the instructional song "Teach Me to Twist" and with sixteen-year-old singer Dee Dee Sharp on the #3 hit "Slow Twistin'." Checker wasn't the only one cashing in, either. Soul pioneer and former gospel great Sam Cooke had a #9 hit with "Twistin' the Night Away." The lo-fi R&B wailer Gary "U.S." Bonds made the top 10 with two different twist songs, "Dear Lady Twist" and "Twist, Twist Senora." Even the Isley Brothers' classic "Twist and Shout," famously covered by the Beatles a few years later, was originally intended as a cash-in on the craze—a twist-themed sequel to the Isleys' breakthrough, the 1959 wedding-reception perennial "Shout."

The popularity of "The Twist" led to a boom in dance-craze records, with *American Bandstand* showcasing both the dances and the songs that went with them. Chubby Checker's "Slow Twistin'" collaborator, Dee Dee Sharp, made it to #2 with "Mashed Potato Time." Sharp passed on recording "The Loco-Motion," a dance track written by married couple Carole King and Gerry Goffin, so Eva Boyd, the couple's teenage babysitter, recorded the song instead, taking it to #1 in the summer of 1962. That Halloween, Boris Karloff impersonator Bobby "Boris" Pickett reached #1 with the dancing-ghouls novelty "Monster Mash." In that song, an irate Dracula pokes his head out of his coffin to ask, "Whatever happened to my Transylvania Twist?"

The twist, Transylvanian or otherwise, kept hold over the American cultural imagination for about two years, but its popularity inevitably faded. The dance had saturated American life to the point where the Peppermint Lounge hired a dance troupe and rebranded itself as a tourist trap. By May 1962, the twist was so omnipresent that former president Dwight Eisenhower cautioned against its popularity while speaking at the dedication of his presidential library: "I have no objection to the twist as such, but it does represent some kind of change in our standards." When a former president is using a teenage fad as a symbol for what's wrong with America, it's a pretty good sign that the fad has run its course.

Chubby Checker's career never quite recovered after "The Twist" died down. Later in 1962, Checker had top-10 hits with follow-up dance-craze records like "Limbo Rock," which peaked at #2, and

"Popeye the Hitchhiker," which made it to #9. But after his early-sixties heyday, Checker has returned to the top 20 only once: a 1988 remake of "The Twist," recorded with joke-rap trio the Fat Boys, which reached #16.

Joey Dee and the Starliters broke up in 1962. A few years later, three former Starliters formed a new band, the Young Rascals, that played jangly R&B. Their cover of "Good Lovin'," a doo-wop song from the Black Los Angeles group the Olympics, hit #1 in 1966. As the sixties progressed, the band moved toward an easy-listening folk-rock sound, scored two more #1 hits, and dropped the "Young" from their group name. Hank Ballard's Midnighters broke up in 1965. Ballard went solo, but he scored only a few minor R&B hits in the years after. James Brown, who'd been massively influenced by Ballard, produced a few of those singles in the sixties and seventies. Ballard died of throat cancer in 2003.

In recent years, Chubby Checker has been lobbying the Rock and Roll Hall of Fame to induct him, arguing that he was "the Beatles before the Beatles." Thus far, the campaign has had no success. (Another member of Chubby Checker's family has had better luck with recognition; his daughter Mistie Bass won a WNBA championship with the Phoenix Mercury in 2014.) Joey Dee's not in the Hall of Fame, either, but the (Young) Rascals made the cut in 1997. Hank Ballard, meanwhile, was inducted in 1990, and the other Midnighters joined in 2002.

"The Twist"—both the song and the dance—is generally remembered as a flash-in-the-pan fad. But pop music history is built on flash-in-the-pan fads. Dance-craze records have never really left the charts in the years since "The Twist," and many of those records—Van McCoy and the Soul City Symphony's "The Hustle," Madonna's "Vogue," Los del Río's "The Macarena," Soulja Boy's "Crank That (Soulja Boy)"— have reached #1. As communications technology has evolved, teenagers have used that technology to show off their dances. In 1960, *American Bandstand* served that function. Today, dance crazes make their way out into the world as TikTok challenges. The medium has changed, but the basic urge behind it has not.

"The Twist" came along at a moment when rock 'n' roll was moving into a new era. Most of the genre's original stars were drafted, disgraced, or dead. The excitement behind the original explosion had died down, but its effects remained. This is when sales of 45-RPM singles had almost doubled, and America's baby-boomer teenagers had billions of dollars to spend. Businessmen like Dick Clark recognized that demand, and they found ways to supply it. TV shows like *American Bandstand* and record labels like Cameo-Parkway cashed in on rock 'n' roll, and they also tamed and professionalized it. But even in watered-down form, a song like "The Twist" had ripple effects that nobody could have foreseen.

"The Twist" crossed lines with unprecedented speed. In its two-year life span, the song and its attendant dance went from a Black teenage regional blip to a global phenomenon that captured the imaginations of people of all ages, races, and classes. Most of the people who benefited from this phenomenon were profiteers, not artists. But "The Twist" was also a cultural unifier—a song that got all kinds of people out on the floor at the same time. That's the kind of magic trick that only pop music can pull off.

CHAPTER 2

The Shirelles—
"Will You Love Me Tomorrow"

Released November 1960
Hit #1 January 30, 1961
Two-week reign

CAROLE KING WAS A NINETEEN-YEAR-OLD MOTHER WHEN her first big song hit #1. Three of the four members of the Shirelles, the New Jersey girl group who sang the song, were nineteen. Micki Harris, the oldest Shirelle, was about to turn twenty-one. Elder statesman Gerry Goffin, King's husband and cowriter, was twenty-one.

"Will You Love Me Tomorrow," the Goffin-King song that the Shirelles took to #1, is a song about teenage sex and anxiety. Maybe it took a teenager, or someone who had only just finished being a teenager, to write and sing meaningfully about those things.

A whole lot of rock 'n' roll was about teenage sex. This was part of the appeal. When he first showed up on *The Ed Sullivan Show*, Elvis Presley sent young hormones into overdrive, even though the show's cameras showed him only from the waist up. Little Richard may have originated the phrase "good booty" in 1955's "Tutti Frutti." Dick Clark did his level best to make *American Bandstand* into a clean, all-American spectacle, but a song like Chubby Checker's "The Twist" resonated in part because its accompanying dance involved a whole lot of vigorous hip action. Rock 'n' roll swiftly took over the music business because teenagers had money to spend. These teenagers were horny. Songwriters noticed.

By the early sixties, a whole industry had sprung up to sell music to those teenagers. Some of the best and biggest songs of that era are the songs that understood the urges of their listeners, that took them seriously. In New York, a remarkable clutch of young songwriters used teenage excitement and befuddlement and heartbreak as fuel for simple, direct, elegant songs. Those songs, often recorded by groups of young Black women, streamlined the noise and anarchy of early rock 'n' roll, giving it a sense of poise and sophistication that was altogether new.

The main songwriters of this era were teams of young New Yorkers, mostly Jewish and often divided into romantic couples. Carole King and Gerry Goffin maintained friendly rivalries with peers like Barry Mann and Cynthia Weil, a married couple who worked out of the same midtown Manhattan office space at 1650 Broadway, and Jeff Barry and Ellie Greenwich, who wrote across the street at the Brill Building. These young composers grew up steeped in New York songwriting traditions that predated rock 'n' roll by decades. They knew Cole Porter and George Gershwin and Broadway musicals, but they also grew up hearing Alan Freed play doo-wop, R&B, and early rock 'n' roll on New York radio. Together, working in close competition with one another, they found a sound that was steeped in both Black and white popular music—one that developed its own kind of harmony.

King and Goffin worked together at Aldon Music. Al Nevins, one of the founders of Aldon, had been a member of the Three Suns, a popular New York nightclub act in the forties, and he'd cowritten their 1944 easy-listening instrumental hit, "Twilight Time." The other cofounder was Don Kirshner, a former Tin Pan Alley song picker who was nineteen years younger than Nevins and who knew a great rock 'n' roll song when he heard one. (Aldon was named for its two founders.)

At Aldon's 1650 Broadway offices, songwriting teams would work in cubicles each just big enough to house one battered upright piano and one tiny writing desk. It's hard to imagine the cacophony of all these songwriting teams all working at the same time in the same office. Those teams couldn't help but influence one another, even as they all competed to get their songs recorded.

And Aldon had neighbors. Over at the Brill Building, the team of Jerry Leiber and Mike Stoller, who'd written hits for Elvis Presley and the Coasters, had already set up shop. In 1959, Leiber and Stoller wrote and produced the Drifters' "There Goes My Baby," which reached #2 and was among the first R&B singles ever to use a string section. Other Brill Building teams—Doc Pomus and Mort Shuman, Burt Bacharach and Hal David—would come up with lusher, more refined takes on R&B. The writers at Aldon were typically younger and less polished, but they loved strings, too.

Aldon's first real discoveries were composer Neil Sedaka and lyricist Howard Greenfield, two young Brooklyn natives who started out writing hits for country-pop star Connie Francis. Sedaka often recorded his own songs, too. In 1959, at the age of twenty, Sedaka reached #9 with "Oh! Carol," a lovelorn pop ditty that he and Greenfield wrote. Sedaka had been on at least one date with a high school classmate named Carol Klein, who'd taken the name Carole King when she wrote and recorded a few unsuccessful singles for the ABC-Paramount label. After those singles flopped, King dropped out of college, got pregnant, and married Gerry Goffin. Together, Goffin and King wrote and recorded the tongue-in-cheek answer song "Oh! Neil": "I'd even give up a month's supply of chewin' tobacky / Just to be known as Mrs. Neil Sedaky!" "Oh! Neil" didn't sell, but Sedaka thought it was funny, and he helped Goffin and King get a foot in the door at Aldon. Don Kirshner signed the couple to Aldon, paying them an advance of $1,000 a year.

Carole King loved R&B and show tunes equally. Goffin wanted to write for Broadway and didn't much like rock 'n' roll, but he came to understand the music more after he and King met and started writing songs together at Queens College. After the couple dropped out, Goffin found work as a chemist, and he kept his day job even after he and King signed with Aldon. Goffin would need to make some real money as a songwriter before he could think of it as a career.

Goffin and King needed a break. The Shirelles did, too. Three years earlier, the four Shirelles had been students at Passaic High School in suburban New Jersey. They'd gotten together to sing at a school talent show, and a classmate named Mary Jane Greenberg heard them and persuaded them to audition for her mother. Florence Greenberg, Mary Jane's mother, was a bored housewife who loved R&B and wanted to get into the music business. Greenberg's husband, a potato-chip executive, introduced her to some music-industry contacts, and she started a label called Tiara Records. Greenberg signed the Shirelles, and she licensed their debut single, 1958's "I Met Him on a Sunday (Ronde-Ronde)," to the larger label Decca Records. The song peaked at #49, and the Shirelles' next few singles failed to chart before Decca dropped them. So Greenberg started a new label called Scepter Records, and she rented an office space at 1650 Broadway— the same building where Aldon Music was based.

Shortly after founding Scepter, Greenberg hired songwriter and producer Luther Dixon to work with the Shirelles. Dixon had sung baritone in a Brooklyn doo-wop group called the Four Buddies, and he'd cowritten hits for pop singers like Perry Como and Bobby Darin. "Sixteen Candles," a single that Dixon cowrote for the mixed-race doo-wop group the Crests, reached #2 in 1958. Greenberg brought in Dixon after meeting in an elevator, and the two began an open-secret affair shortly afterward.

Despite their inconsistent track record, Dixon thought the Shirelles had potential, and he agreed to work with them. This was smart. With their early singles, the Shirelles had figured out a clean, warm, feminine take on doo-wop, the R&B subgenre built on simple melodies and intricate harmonies. All-female vocal groups had been around since the vaudeville era, and a few, like the World War II–era group the Andrews Sisters, had become major stars. In the fifties, all-Black girl groups like the Bobbettes and the Chantels landed major hits that combined doo-wop harmonies with bright, perky *American Bandstand*–ready pop sensibilities. The Shirelles had named themselves after lead singer Shirley Owens and, in a way, after the Chantels. But the Shirelles had a sexual directness that their predecessors lacked.

Shirley Owens and Luther Dixon cowrote "Tonight's the Night," the Shirelles' 1960 single. The song isn't exactly explicit, but when Shirley Owens sings about turning the lights down low and making her feel all aglow, its meaning isn't too hard to figure out. On "Tonight's the Night," Owens sounds breezy and confident, even as she acknowledges the possibility that the guy might tear her dreams apart. But she never sounds worried. Instead, she goes with her instincts: "I might love you so / Let's take a chance / Gonna be a great romance."

"WILL YOU LOVE Me Tomorrow" focuses on the same feelings that "Tonight's the Night" does; it's almost a sequel. On "Will You Love Me Tomorrow," Shirley Owens's narrator wonders what'll happen after she spends the night with the "you" of the title. The light of love is in his eyes, but will he love her tomorrow? She's nervous about where this is going and about what the guy thinks of her. But as on "Tonight's the Night," Owens's narrator is ready to go through with it. She just wants some reassurance: "Tell me now, and I won't ask again / Will you still love me tomorrow?"

Those lyrics are economical, but they're richer and more nuanced than what Owens sang on "Tonight's the Night." Carole King, a teenage girl herself, may have been intimately familiar with those feelings, but King has always been quick to credit Goffin with the song's lyrics. In her 2012 memoir, *A Natural Woman*, King writes that Goffin's "understanding of human nature transcended gender." Goffin was about the same age as the Shirelles, and he wasn't much older than the teenage girls who were the group's target market. In his lyrics, Goffin wove in sex without panicking radio programmers, and he wrote about teenage insecurity without infantilizing or condescending to his audience. Musically, King gave those lyrics a stately dignity that fitted the words beautifully. "Will You Love Me Tomorrow" is a small miracle of pop craftsmanship. It's the kind of thing that can happen when two young experts come up with the right song at the right time.

At first, Shirley Owens didn't agree. Owens thought the song wasn't R&B enough for the Shirelles, that it was too country. Groups like the Shirelles didn't have much creative freedom in those days. They sang what their labels wanted them to sing. But Owens had co-written "Tonight's the Night," and she evidently had enough authority to refuse the song. To placate Owens, King sped up the song's tempo and wrote a bright, romantic string arrangement. It was the first time King had ever arranged for strings. In her memoir, she writes that she used Lieber and Stoller's "There Goes My Baby" as her model and that she was "euphoric" when she heard the musicians in the studio playing the melodies she'd written.

Those strings add serious emotional weight to the song. The backbeat of "Will You Love Me Tomorrow" is a simple cha-cha, influenced, like so many Brill Building–era pop songs, by the mambo that was popular in New York's Latin communities. With Luther Dixon producing, the studio musicians laid that backing track in a half hour. The strings and backing vocals add layers of melody, bringing a sense of grandeur to the recording. Shirley Owens's lead vocal, graceful and innocent and almost conversational, floats above those sounds. She's the lead in a play that lasts less than three minutes.

"Will You Love Me Tomorrow" is the sort of song that could be possible only in an environment where cultures freely intermingle. A young Jewish couple writes a song for a young Black girl group, combining string orchestration with doo-wop vocals over a Spanish beat. A Black man produces it, and a middle-aged Jewish woman releases it on her label. The entire industry accepts the idea that the middle-aged Jewish woman, who is married, is sleeping with the Black producer. The lyrics address young women's feelings about sex, both the worry and the excitement, and the song reaches #1. The whole story feels almost utopian.

Of course, things were more complicated than that. When they signed with Scepter, for instance, the members of the Shirelles were allegedly led to believe that the label was putting their royalties into a trust and that they'd get paid when they turned twenty-one. After they left Scepter in 1963, the Shirelles learned that the trust was a fiction. They sued Scepter, and Scepter filed a countersuit. The parties settled out of court a couple of years later, but the legal battle kept the Shirelles from releasing any music for several years, and their careers never recovered. From then on, the Shirelles played the oldies circuit, and two of them died relatively young. At forty-two, Micki Harris succumbed to a heart attack in a hotel after a Shirelles show in Atlanta. Fellow Shirelle Doris Coley died of breast cancer at fifty-eight.

The New York record business of the early sixties wasn't remotely utopian, and plenty of the people who operated within it were predators. Yet some of those predators helped make great music. The success of the Shirelles and others led to a boom in early-sixties girl groups. Producer Phil Spector, a student of Lieber and Stoller, came up with a hugely influential sound, full of reverbed-out drums and crashing orchestrations. Working with Brill Building songwriters like the team of Jeff Barry and Ellie Greenwich, Spector made huge hits for girl groups like the Ronettes and the Crystals. Those songs have reverberated down through the ages, and they influenced later studio wizards like the Beach Boys' Brian Wilson. But Spector was also a notorious studio tyrant and an abusive husband to Ronettes leader Ronnie Spector. Later, Spector was convicted of murder, and he died in prison.

The girl-group boom of the early sixties was really possible only because of financial skullduggery and exploitation. But those songs! "Will You Love Me Tomorrow" was a blueprint, a Rosetta stone for how to take the emotional needs and dilemmas of teenage girls seriously. Some of the songs are dizzy with euphoria. The Ronettes' "Be My Baby" and the Crystals' "Then He Kissed Me," two 1963 hits that Phil Spector produced and cowrote with Jeff Barry and Ellie Greenwich, use all of Spector's operatic majesty to evoke the giddy feeling of young love. Others gesture at real social divisions in America—the boyfriend in the Crystals' "Uptown" who is treated like dirt at his job because of his economic standing and presumed race, the narrator of Lesley Gore's proto-feminist anthem "You Don't Own Me" who asserts her own personhood in the face of a controlling man.

In this early-sixties moment, most of the male pop idols—Bobby Vinton, Frankie Avalon, Pat Boone, even the post-army Elvis Presley—were smirky showmen who gave off the sense that they couldn't wait to join the pre–rock 'n' roll crooners as Vegas-revue entertainers and variety-show hosts. Plenty of those male singers also made use of the Brill Building and Aldon songwriters; Carole King and Gerry Goffin wrote big hits for people like Bobby Vee and Steve Lawrence. None were interested in depicting themselves as rebels in the mold of Chuck Berry or Jerry Lee Lewis or pre-army Elvis. Instead, rock 'n' roll rebels lived on in the lyrics of the girl-group songs. They're the mysterious, mercurial, doomed objects of affection on #1 hits like the Crystals' "He's a Rebel" or the Shangri-Las' "Leader of the Pack."

The boy in the Shirelles' second #1 hit, though, is no rebel. Instead, that song is dedicated to someone serving in the military overseas. Florence Greenberg and Luther Dixon cowrote "Soldier Boy," which finds Shirley Owens promising her love that she'll wait for him faithfully until he returns. "Soldier Boy" reached #1 in May 1962. Even with a song as conventional as that, there's some hint of a changing world. "Soldier Boy" and the Marvelettes' similarly themed 1961 smash, "Please Mr. Postman," are love songs for men far away, across the ocean. It's probably not a coincidence that both songs conquered the charts as the American government deployed more and more troops to Vietnam.

The early-sixties girl-group boom spanned only a few years, but it left a deep impact on the pop music that followed. The Beatles loved girl-group records, often playing their own versions in their nightclub residencies in Liverpool and Hamburg. Once the Beatles got famous, they kept playing girl-group songs. On *Please Please Me*, their 1963 debut album, the Beatles included their own version of "Chains," a song that Goffin and King had written the previous year for the girl group the Cookies, and "Boys," a Luther Dixon–written Shirelles song that had originally been a B-side of "Will You Love Me Tomorrow." In 1963, John Lennon said that he wanted himself and Paul McCartney to become "the Goffin-King of England."

The aforementioned "Please Mr. Postman," another song that the Beatles covered early on, was the first #1 hit for Berry Gordy's Tamla Records, the label that would soon become Motown. Gordy would establish his own version of the Brill Building–Aldon model, nurturing his own songwriting teams in-house. The girl-group model was good to Motown. Many of the label's early stars—the Marvelettes, Martha and the Vandellas, Mary Wells—followed that girl-group model. And then there were the Supremes, Motown's crown jewel. The Supremes outlasted the girl-group era, becoming the biggest non-Beatles pop-chart act of the sixties. Their hits, much like "Will You Love Me Tomorrow," usually told stories about young women facing dramatic moments in their love lives.

Once the Beatles and Motown changed the pop landscape, Goffin, King, and their Aldon contemporaries spent much of the sixties playing catch-up. Goffin and King wrote hits for the Monkees and for the Beatles' fellow British Invasion groups like Herman's Hermits and the Animals. They also wrote "(You Make Me Feel Like a) Natural Woman," a top-10 hit for Aretha Franklin, in 1967. But Goffin, who felt insecure about his own lyrics when compared with those of Bob Dylan and the Beatles, got heavily into LSD and mescaline, and the drugs took a toll on his mental health. He and Carole King divorced in 1969.

Goffin stayed busy after the divorce, and he wrote a few more big hits. In 1975, Goffin teamed up with Motown staffer Michael Masser to write the ballad "Do You Know Where You're Going To (Theme from *Mahogany*)," and Diana Ross, the former Supremes leader turned perennial solo star, took the song to #1. Masser and Goffin stayed together as a songwriting team in the seventies. In 1978, they wrote "Saving All My Love for You" for former Fifth Dimension members Marilyn McCoo and Billy Davis Jr. Seven years later, that song became the first-ever #1 hit for Whitney Houston.

Many of the Brill Building and Aldon veterans found ways to thrive after those early-sixties boom times. Burt Bacharach and Hal David, for instance, developed a reputation as sophisticated adult-contemporary craftsmen, and they wrote hits for Herb Alpert, B. J. Thomas, and especially Dionne Warwick, a former demo singer who'd occasionally served as a replacement Shirelle in concert. (The Shirelles reunited with Warwick in 1984, backing her up on a new version of "Will You Love Me Tomorrow.") Paul Simon and Tony Orlando, both of whom had recorded demos with Goffin and King, became big stars. So did Neil Diamond, an Aldon associate who rose to fame after writing "I'm a Believer," the Monkees' biggest hit.

And Carole King, who'd longed to become a pop star as a Brooklyn high school student, finally got her wish. After divorcing Goffin, King moved to Los Angeles, fell in with the Laurel Canyon folk-rock scene, and reinvented herself as a bohemian spiritual traveler. Her second solo album, *Tapestry*, released in 1971, became one of the biggest-selling albums of the seventies. King came out with *Tapestry* a week after her twenty-ninth birthday, and she tapped into a whole different pop zeitgeist, singing her own intimate and sensitive songs.

On *Tapestry*, King's voice is raw and raspy, and the album's instrumentation is loose and bluesy. But the album's songs address the same feelings of insecurity and heartbreak that animated so many of the Goffin-King songs of the early sixties. *Tapestry* was a personal artistic statement, but it was also a collection of hit singles. "It's Too Late," one of the songs on *Tapestry*, became a #1 hit for King. King's friend James Taylor covered another *Tapestry* song, "You've Got a Friend," and took it to #1. And one of the songs on *Tapestry* had already been a #1 hit. Near the end of *Tapestry*, King sings her own version of "Will You Love Me Tomorrow," with James Taylor and Joni Mitchell backing her up.

King's own version of "Will You Love Me Tomorrow" is slow and precise—a sly way to comment on her own romantic and professional past. King's life had changed in the eleven years since the Shirelles took "Will You Love Me Tomorrow" to #1, and so had pop music. But "Will You Love Me Tomorrow" still stood as a pop masterpiece—a monument to a moment and to a question that will never cease to be asked.

CHAPTER 3

The Beatles–
"I Want to Hold Your Hand"

Released December 26, 1963
Hit #1 February 1, 1964
Seven-week reign

E VEN WHEN THE PLANE WAS IN THE AIR, PAUL MCCARTNEY
was worried. In February 1964, McCartney was over the Atlantic,
on his way to New York for the first time. Six days earlier, "I Want
to Hold Your Hand," a song that McCartney had written with his
bandmate John Lennon, had made it to #1 on the American charts.
The Beatles had a busy week ahead of them: an engagement on *The Ed
Sullivan Show*; a show at the Washington Coliseum in Washington,
DC; and a pair of sets at Carnegie Hall in New York. Yet McCartney
just wasn't sure if the Beatles would work in America.

All through 1963, when the Beatles were becoming the biggest
musical act in the United Kingdom, none of their attempts to crack the
United States had worked. The Beatles were signed to EMI, the huge
British record label, but Capitol, the American subsidiary of EMI, had
refused to release any of the band's singles in the United States. Jay
Livingstone, an executive at Capitol, told Brian Epstein, the Beatles'
manager, "We don't think the Beatles will do anything in this market."

Instead, Epstein leased Beatles singles out to smaller American labels. Chicago's Vee-Jay put out "Please Please Me" and "From Me to You." Swan Records, the Philadelphia label that Dick Clark had cofounded, released "She Loves You." All three records died commercially; none of them even reached the Hot 100.

When "I Want to Hold Your Hand," a song specifically written to resonate in America, took off for Capitol, which had finally agreed to release a Beatles single, McCartney simply couldn't believe it. Crowds of screaming girls had waved good-bye to the Beatles at Heathrow, but the members of the group didn't know what would wait for them on the other side of the ocean. On the flight, McCartney sat next to American producer Phil Spector, the girl-group specialist who would later produce a few Beatles records that McCartney would hate. Talking to Spector, McCartney asked, "Since America has always had everything, why should we be over there making money? They've got their own groups. What are we going to give them that they don't already have?"

George Harrison felt the same way. A year earlier, Harrison had gone to Illinois to visit his sister, and he'd been to the local drive-in movie theater. The biggest English rock 'n' roll star in the pre-Beatles years was Cliff Richard, a grinning teen idol who sang in a fake American accent. The night that Harrison went to the drive-in, Richard's movie *Summer Holiday* ran as the second film in a double feature, and it played to an uninterested crowd. On the flight to New York, Harrison chatted with an older reporter who also happened to be named George Harrison. Years later, the less famous George Harrison remembered that conversation: "He mentioned all the big American stars who'd come across to Britain. He'd been across, unlike the others; he knew what the place was like. 'They've got everything over there,' he said. 'What do they need *us* for?'"

Hours later, the Beatles landed in New York and were greeted by a crowd of screaming teenagers even larger and more intense than the ones they'd left behind at Heathrow. When the Beatles played *Ed Sullivan* two nights later, seventy-three million Americans—34 percent of the entire population of the country—watched them. Throughout their week in the United States, the band caused mob scenes. New York's Plaza Hotel, where the band had booked rooms, begged them to stay anywhere else, since they couldn't keep order with all the throngs of fans outside. At the Washington show, the screaming got so loud that one of the police officers working security took two bullets out of his gun and stuffed them into his ears.

Two months later, the top five singles on the *Billboard* Hot 100 were all Beatles records. Vee-Jay and Swan had pressed more copies of those failed Beatles singles from the year before, and they all sold in the millions. No artist had ever occupied the entire top five in a single week. It would be nearly sixty years before anyone else pulled it off. (In 2021, the week after Drake released his much-hyped album *Certified Lover Boy*, he took up 9 spots within the top 10, including the entire top 5. It took a whole lot of *Billboard* rule changes to even make it possible for anyone to equal what the Beatles had done.) By the end of 1964, the Beatles had sent six different singles to #1, and the pop landscape had rearranged itself around them.

The Beatles' arrival in America was a perfect storm—the kind of pop cataclysm that simply couldn't be planned. The young Beatles had loved and studied American pop music from afar, but they'd developed their own version of it in relative isolation. In late-fifties England, American rock 'n' roll was an exotic import. In record stores, rock 'n' roll competed with skiffle, a fast and pop-friendly version of folk music, and trad jazz, an easy-listening mutation of New Orleans Dixieland. In 1957, a teenage John Lennon started the Quarrymen, a Liverpool band who played both skiffle and rock 'n' roll. Later that year, Paul McCartney joined. A year later, so did the younger George Harrison. The Quarrymen became part of a whole scene of Liverpool bands who gradually fell out of love with skiffle, getting more and more into American rock 'n' rollers like Little Richard and Buddy Holly.

Those Merseybeat bands, groups like Gerry and the Pacemakers and the Swinging Blue Jeans, were fast and crude and simple, entirely reliant on a big drum sound. The Quarrymen found themselves a drummer, Pete Best, and eventually renamed themselves the Beatles, partly in homage to Buddy Holly's Crickets. They started playing lunchtime shows at the Cavern, the one Liverpool club that booked rock 'n' roll bands, and then began setting up residencies in Hamburg, the German city where Merseybeat bands went to make money.

In Hamburg, the Beatles played frenzied, speed-fueled all-night shows in nightclubs. They had to get really good really quickly if they wanted to compete with other Merseybeat bands like Rory Storm and the Hurricanes. Playing those Hamburg shows, the Beatles learned to play every American rock record they could find, cranking up the songs' tempos to keep their rowdy audiences happy. They also adapted long haircuts that they'd seen on German bohemian kids, and they eventually switched out their jeans and leather jackets for skinny suits. They also fired Pete Best, their drummer, and replaced him with Ringo Starr, whom they'd recruited from Rory Storm's Hurricanes.

Brian Epstein, a Liverpool record-store owner, became the Beatles' manager after hearing them at the Cavern, and he shopped them around to record labels in England. Decca said no. EMI said yes. EMI producer George Martin, present for the band's audition, found the boys to be charming and funny, and he let them record the songs that Lennon and McCartney had written, even though most pop groups at the time relied on tracks from outside songwriters. The Beatles released "Love Me Do" in October 1962, and it made the top 20 in the United Kingdom. Their next single, "Please Please Me," reached #2. Then "From Me to You," the band's fourth single, topped the English singles charts.

In the United Kingdom, the Beatles were something new: a homegrown, provincial rock 'n' roll band who played with style and energy, adapting tricks from American forebears without pretending to be American. Early on, John Lennon mused, "Some of our songs are American, but when we sang them American, they just didn't come off. We learned you just can't be American." Lennon also said that Cliff Richard, the English star who *did* try to be American, was "everything we hated in pop." Other early-sixties British bands like the Rolling Stones and the Animals were in love with American blues records, but the Beatles were more concerned with pop—bright, up-tempo, melodic sounds like the ones coming from American song-writing factories such as Aldon. They covered dance songs and girl-group records. They adapted harmonies from the Everly Brothers and aggressive guitar stabs from Buddy Holly and Eddie Cochran. Their sound was fast and physical and immediate—a musical equivalent to the hysteria that they generated.

The Beatles also had personality, and that personality became star power. All four young men in the group were dashing and fashionable and good-looking, but they were also approachable. Their northern accents and working-class roots helped them radiate an everyman qual-ity. When they got famous, they seemed both humble and bemused about it. When clueless older reporters asked them about their haircuts or their yeah-yeah-yeah lyrics, they fired back with the sort of inscru-table playfulness that made those reporters want to ask more clueless questions. When crowds of screaming girls chased them, they seemed just about as excited as those girls were. On those early Beatles records, Lennon and McCartney both scream just like their fans. There's a ner-vous, wired energy to those early records that nicely complements the entire concept of Beatlemania.

Lennon later said that he and McCartney were "eyeball to eye-ball" when they wrote "I Want to Hold Your Hand." At the time, Mc-Cartney was dating actress Jane Asher. Lennon and McCartney would get together for songwriting sessions in Asher's parents' basement, with McCartney banging out tunes on their piano. When they wrote "I Want to Hold Your Hand," they did their best to give it what Brian Epstein called "a sort of American spiritual sound."

The final product doesn't sound a whole lot like an American spiritual. Instead, it's urgent and trebly and exuberant, an overcharged take on Brill Building pop music. Lennon and McCartney both sing

lead on the song, their voices blurring into one harmonic yelp. Everything on the song—the hand claps, the driving R&B riffage, jangly
guitar interplay on the twin bridges—serves the colossal beat. The
song is charged with adrenaline. It sounds like an endorphin rush, or
a panic attack.

Lennon and McCartney's lyrics are about as chaste as pop-song
lyrics can be, but they deliver those lyrics with a hormonal fire that
suggests that they want to do something more than hold your hand.
The excitement goes into the blackout zone on the bridge: "It's such a
happy feeling that, my love, I can't hide!" That last line could be about
a boner. When Lennon and McCartney bleat it again and again, "I
can't hide" also starts to sound a bit like "I get high." Those early Beatles songs weren't subversive, exactly. But if you wanted to, you could
hear something secret in all that noise.

In October 1963, Brian Epstein flew to New York to push, once
again, for Capitol to release a Beatles single in America. He also took a
few meetings, booking the Beatles on *Ed Sullivan* and accepting a promoter's offer to play Carnegie Hall. Sullivan, the TV host who'd first
introduced Elvis Presley to America, had just borne witness to Beatlemania himself. Sullivan had stopped by Heathrow with his wife on the
way back from a European trip just as the Beatles were coming back
from a tour of Sweden. By chance, Sullivan had seen the screaming
mobs that greeted the band, and that spectacle had roused his interest
enough to welcome the Beatles to his show. During that same New
York trip, Epstein finally convinced Capitol that "I Want to Hold Your
Hand" was worthy of an American release.

"I Want to Hold Your Hand" came out in England in October
1963, when Beatlemania was already in full swing. There, the song
vaulted straight to #1, knocking another Beatles record, "She Loves
You," out of the top spot. Capitol made plans to give the single a January release, but circumstances intervened. A radio DJ in Washington, DC, started playing a copy of "I Want to Hold Your Hand" that
he'd gotten from a British Airways stewardess. Stations in Chicago and

St. Louis also put import copies of the single into rotation. In response, Capitol rush-released the single, keeping three different pressing plants open on Christmas Day, manufacturing a million copies of the single and shipping it to stores the next day.

Brian Epstein persuaded Capitol to spend unprecedented amounts of money, tens of thousands of dollars, on publicity for the Beatles' arrival in America. The same Capitol execs who'd refused to release the band's earlier singles posed for pictures in Beatle wigs. The label printed up five million stickers that said "The Beatles are coming," putting them up on telephone poles and bathroom walls. Somehow, the label persuaded movie star Janet Leigh to get a Beatle haircut. Michael Braun, an American journalist who accompanied the band on their first British tour and their first American visit, claimed that Capitol "tried, unsuccessfully, to bribe a University of Washington cheerleader into holding up a card reading 'The Beatles Are Coming' to the television cameras at the Rose Bowl." Nicky Byrne, the man who made a fortune by licensing Beatles merchandise, enlisted two New York radio stations to play an announcement, promising a free T-shirt to any young person who went out to the airport to greet the Beatles' plane.

But the Beatles' arrival wasn't just a manufactured cultural event. It immediately took on a life of its own. Timing has something to do with this. Mere weeks before the Beatles landed in New York, President John F. Kennedy was assassinated in Dallas. (November 22, the day of Kennedy's death, was also the day that EMI released *With the Beatles*, the group's second album, in the United Kingdom.) Kennedy had made himself into an embodiment of young American optimism, and the young Americans who'd believed in him were in shock. At the time, American pop was dominated by the canned pleasantries of teen idols like Bobby Vinton. When Kennedy was killed, the #1 song on the Hot 100 was Nino Temple and April Stevens's chipper version of the sentimental 1933 ballad "Deep Purple." A song like that couldn't hope to embody the chaos and uncertainty of that moment. When the Beatles arrived, though, they brought their own kind of optimism. They showed up just in time.

Lester Bangs once described that moment: "We were down, we needed a shot of cultural speed, something high, fast, loud, and superficial to fill the gap; we needed a fling after the wake." In his 1964 book, *Love Me Do! The Beatles' Progress*, Michael Braun included a letter from a fan, one Sharon Flood, who thanked the Beatles for showing up when they did: "Perhaps you are not aware of this fact, but you are the first happy thing that has happened to us since the tragedy on November 22. You are the first spot of joy to come to a nation that is still very much in mourning."

Timing in pop music is a funny thing. There's no direct cause-and-effect correlation between the Kennedy assassination and the Beatles' conquest of the American charts. But American kids were primed for something to happen, and the Beatles were that thing. The Beatles' takeover of America was swift and overwhelming. On the last night of their first New York visit, three Beatles visited the Peppermint Lounge, hoping to see the home of the twist for themselves. Instead, the band playing at the club that night was a group of Beatle imitators who'd learned the band's whole repertoire that week. (Ringo Starr's review: "It wasn't much like us. The music was too good.")

Former pop critic Neil Tennant, whose group the Pet Shop Boys once scored a #1 American hit of their own in 1985 with "West End Girls," coined the phrase "the imperial phase" to describe what happens when an artist reaches an absolute peak. When an artist is in their imperial phase, they have an absolute chokehold over the popular imagination. An artist in the imperial phase of their career can release just about anything, and the public will happily accept it. The Beatles' imperial phase started the week that "I Want to Hold Your Hand" hit #1, and it didn't end until Paul McCartney announced the group's breakup in 1970. Over a seven-year period, the Beatles went on artistic journeys, from the frantic pop of their early days into strange new directions. They made mutant music-hall oompah. They made flowery orchestral psychedelia. They made angry, guttural hard rock. Sometimes, they did all these things in the space of a single song. But even at their most experimental, the Beatles never lost the American public.

Between 1964 and 1970, the Beatles took twenty different singles to #1. As I write this, that's the most any artist has ever pulled off. (Mariah Carey, who has nineteen, is the only artist who's remotely close to catching them.) In their seven years of existence, the Beatles notched fifty-nine weeks—more than a year—at #1. After the band's breakup, all four Beatles went solo, and all of them made multiple #1 hits. Even Ringo! Ringo Starr has two #1 hits! Guesting on "Going Bad," the 2018 Meek Mill single that peaked at #6, Drake claims that he has "more slaps than the Beatles." That's a great line, but it's empirically, demonstrably untrue. Drake has nowhere near as many slaps as the Beatles. Nobody does.

In terms of pop-music impact, the Beatles' arrival was a comet striking the earth. If "I Want to Hold Your Hand" merely announced the band's American arrival, it would be one of the most important hit singles of all time. But "I Want to Hold Your Hand" did more than that. It opened floodgates. Five months after "I Want to Hold Your Hand" hit #1, the first of the ersatz Beatles arrived. Peter Asher, the brother of Paul McCartney's girlfriend Jane, had an Everly Brothers–style folk-pop duo with his school friend Gordon Waller. McCartney had written a song called "A World Without Love," but John Lennon thought the lyrics were stupid, and he vetoed the idea of the Beatles recording it. So McCartney gave his song to the duo of Peter and Gordon, and they took it to #1 on the Hot 100 in June 1964. Even the Beatles' throwaways were smashes. (Years later, Peter Asher became a hitmaking producer for Californian folk-pop artists like James Taylor and Linda Ronstadt.)

All through 1964, American artists—whether it be Berry Gordy's exploding Motown stable, up-and-coming rock 'n' roll acts like the Beach Boys and the Four Seasons, or heritage artists like Louis Armstrong or Dean Martin—found occasional pop-chart success. But they had an uphill battle. They had to contend with the Beatles and with the parade of British rock bands who followed in their wake. After Peter and Gordon came Manchester's Animals, whose drawling, gothic take on the blues standard "House of the Rising Sun" hit #1 in September. Then came Manfred Mann, a London band who covered "Do Wah Diddy Diddy," a song from the Brill Building songwriting duo of Jeff Barry and Ellie Greenwich. The previous year, "Do Wah Diddy Diddy" had been a flop for the Exciters, a Black American girl group. In giving the track a revved-up big-beat Brit-rock makeover, Manfred Mann turned it into a #1 hit in America.

Before the Beatles hit in America, the Animals and Manfred Mann thought of themselves as blues, jazz, and R&B purists, not rock 'n' rollers. The same was true of the Rolling Stones, the young London band who broke out with the 1965 chart-topper "(I Can't Get No) Satisfaction" and who promptly became one of the decade's—and music history's—biggest acts by styling themselves as the Beatles' sex-drunk, droogy bad-kid counterparts. Early on, the Stones, the Animals, and Manfred Mann—as well as plenty of other British acts, like the Yardbirds, the Spencer Davis Group, and John Mayall & the Bluesbreakers—tried to make versions of blues that didn't deviate too far from the genuine American article. But after the Beatles exploded, America was only too happy to accept those bands' records as pop music anyway.

Even as the British rockers exoticized American bluesmen, American teenagers exoticized the British rockers. Before the Beatles, most American teenagers generally didn't even know that British rock 'n' roll existed. So even when the British groups were singing American songs, American record buyers loved it—a two-way pop-music lovefest. There's a similar dynamic at work in America's recent embrace of South Korean pop music—K-pop artists internalizing the gestures and styles of the era of *Total Request Live* American boy bands and then selling that stuff back to America.

But plenty of the British bands who followed in the Beatles' wake didn't present themselves as serious musicians or as blues enthusiasts.

Instead, plenty of them were hard, exciting big-beat thumpers, an approach that scored #1 hits for the Dave Clark Five with "Over and Over" and for Wayne Fontana and the Mindbenders with "The Game of Love." Others worked straight-up pop gimmicks. Freddie and the Dreamers—a group led by a giggling nerd with a trademark high-kicking dance move—managed one #1 hit with "I'm Tellin' You Now." Herman's Hermits—grinning moppets with old-timey music-hall leanings who weren't too proud to work with America's pop-factory songwriters—managed two, but the song you most likely remember best because it's been featured on several film and television soundtracks in the decades since, the Goffin-King composition "I'm into Something Good," reached only #13.

These pop-chart success stories wouldn't have been possible without the Beatles. The Beatles loomed over virtually everything that hit in America in the midsixties. In December 1964, for instance, *Bonanza* actor Lorne Greene hit #1 with a rumbling country story-song. Greene's single didn't have anything to do with the Beatles, but the song happened to be titled "Ringo." There's at least some chance that Greene's one hit snuck to the top of the charts because it shared a name with a Beatle.

Within a couple of years, the biggest act in America was the Monkees, a Beatles-style cute-moptop act assembled to star in a network sitcom. Davy Jones, the Monkees' lead singer, was British, and he'd actually performed on the same episode of *The Ed Sullivan Show* in which the Beatles made their debut. That night, the Broadway cast of *Oliver!* shared the stage with the Beatles, and Davy Jones, two years younger than the youngest Beatle, played the Artful Dodger. That must've been a lightbulb moment for Jones.

The success of the Monkees shows just how much the Beatles permeated popular culture, and so does the Monkees' downfall. After their first few albums, the Beatles stopped covering the songs of the American bands they admired. Instead, they focused on the songs that they wrote for themselves. Before the Beatles, plenty of American pop acts—Buddy Holly, Sam Cooke, the Beach Boys—wrote their own songs, but it wasn't the norm. The Beatles changed that. They became a force so relentlessly creative that their American competitors had to scramble to keep up.

The Monkees sold records, but Aldon Music cofounder Don Kirshner forced them to record tracks from songwriters like Neil Diamond and the team of Goffin and King. The Monkees didn't want to be pop puppets. They figured that they could become serious artists like the Beatles. In a power play, the members of the band had Kirshner fired, and they seized control of the group's musical direction, moving it away from pop and toward pastoral psychedelia. As a result, the Monkees disappeared from the pop charts before breaking up in 1971. Kirshner, meanwhile, went on to mastermind the Archies, the cartoon band who, being entirely fictional, could not rebel against his dictates. *Billboard* named the Archies' "Sugar, Sugar," a song cowritten by Brill Building veteran Jeff Barry, the #1 single of 1969.

The success of a song like "Sugar, Sugar" goes to show that the Beatles' arrival didn't change *everything*. But it did change the calculus. In their six years in the American spotlight, the Beatles took advantage of new advances in recording technology and in the autonomy that their astronomical success had bought them. They pushed their music in different directions, taking inspiration from Motown and Bob Dylan and Indian ragas and British music-hall oldies. Within a few years, they stopped playing concerts entirely—partly because the screaming hordes of girls made it impossible for them to hear themselves—and devoted themselves to making records full-time.

Through the sixties, the artists who continued to thrive—the Rolling Stones, the Beach Boys, the Supremes, and the rest of the Motown roster—were the ones who understood the challenge that the Beatles represented. Like the Beatles, those acts pushed themselves, incorporating new sounds and ideas and aesthetics. They made themselves competitors. All these acts influenced one another, and they all spurred each other to new heights, while most of the pre-Beatles rock 'n' rollers and British Invasion bands fell away. The Beatles weren't just a pop event. They were an unrelenting driving force.

As soon as the Beatles broke up, Beatles nostalgia took hold. The solo Beatles themselves remained pop stars for years afterward. As a solo artist and as the leader of his band Wings, Paul McCartney couldn't maintain the creative intensity of his Beatles years, but he still managed eight more #1 hits. Ringo Starr had two, both released in 1973, with "Photograph" and "You're Sixteen." In 1974, John Lennon scored his only #1 solo hit in his lifetime with "Whatever Gets You Through the Night," on which Elton John sang backup. Lennon returned the favor when Elton John coaxed him into playing guitar and singing backup on a version of the Beatles' "Lucy in the Sky with Diamonds," which became another Hot 100 chart-topper. At the very end of 1980, in the wake of Lennon's murder, his recently released single "(Just Like) Starting Over" ascended to the top for five weeks. And later in 1981, the Dutch novelty-pop act Stars on 45 went to #1 with a disco-fied medley of old pop songs, mostly Beatles numbers, sung by Beatle impersonators. George Harrison still had enough juice in 1988 to push his third #1, "Got My Mind Set on You," to the top—eighteen years after the Beatles' breakup.

All through the seventies, sloppily assembled Beatles collections and live albums sold millions. In the nineties, a three-volume best-of called *Anthology* became a pop event, taking the #1 spot away from contemporary chart juggernauts like Garth Brooks and Mariah Carey. In 2000, thirty years after their breakup, the Beatles released *1*, a collection of all their #1 singles. In its first two weeks, that collection sold more than a million copies in America. It went on to move ten million more. As I write this, *1* remains the biggest-selling album of this century. The Beatles could probably release another greatest-hits collection tomorrow, full of nothing but songs that had been compiled dozens of times on previous records, and it could outsell virtually anything from any contemporary act. The Beatles still moved the needle in the fall of 2021, when the release of *Get Back*, Peter Jackson's six-hour documentary about the Beatles' final days, became a massive Disney event. In the decades since their breakup, the Beatles have practically become bigger than pop music itself.

The Beatles' real legacy isn't in all the records that they've sold over the decades. Instead, it's in the explosion of excitement and creativity that they brought to popular culture—and the mad rush to cash in and to keep up. Nobody can truly compete with the Beatles, but plenty of people try, and those attempts sometimes become their own kinds of explosions.

CHAPTER 4

The Supremes—
"Where Did Our Love Go"

Released June 17, 1964
Hit #1 August 22, 1964
Two-week reign

SHOES SLAP ON A WOODEN FLOOR. IT'S THE FIRST THING you hear. For the first few seconds, before the bass and the piano and the languid Diana Ross vocal come in, those feet are the only things on the song. The song "Where Did Our Love Go" never gets too complicated: a softly plinking piano, a brushed snare, a burbling bass, a tootling and blatting saxophone solo, a few incandescent voices. After that stark opening, though, the track sounds symphonic. And all throughout "Where Did Our Love Go," those shoes remain in the mix, slapping away.

The shoes belonged to Mike Valvano, a young white guy who worked in the Motown studio as an all-purpose gofer. Early on, Motown had only one studio. That one studio was in high demand. If you were there, you helped out. This was how things were done. Before the Supremes broke out with "Where Did Our Love Go"—before they even signed to Motown—they were part of that process. A lot of people at Motown were. Before he made hits of his own, Marvin Gaye played drums on Martha and the Vandellas and Little Stevie Wonder records. Berry Gordy, the label's founder and owner, found the time to write songs for his acts. And the young Supremes were once high school kids hanging around the studio, adding backing vocals or hand claps whenever anybody needed them.

This tiny organization figured things out. Motown was not the first small label to make an impact on the pop charts. It wasn't even the first small Black-owned label to make hits. Other operations, like Houston's Duke-Peacock and Chicago's Vee-Jay, predated Motown and scored early successes. (Vee-Jay was the first US label to release a Beatles single.) But Motown became a self-contained, sui generis entity in the way that those other labels did not. Against all possible odds, Motown built both an empire and an era-defining sound. The Supremes were the towering stars who made Motown what it was, but they couldn't have become that if Gordy's organization hadn't put them in a position to succeed.

For years, Motown operated as a creative community. Gordy used the same musicians, a crew of hard-drinking regulars from the local jazz scene who called themselves the Funk Brothers, on just about every record. He had his artists writing songs for one another or producing for one another. Every Monday morning, Gordy would bring together his core songwriters for quality-control meetings, where they'd decide which songs would be released and which ones wouldn't. Gordy's employees weren't shy about spiking even the songs that Gordy himself had written and submitted for consideration. Gordy once held a staff-wide songwriting competition to see who could come up with the single that would make the Temptations into stars. At the end, Gordy had to concede that he'd lost; the song he'd written wasn't as good as Smokey Robinson's "The Way You Do the Things You Do." (Gordy's song was called "Just Let Me Know," and it became the B-side for "The Way You Do the Things You Do.")

Gordy sent his acts out on the road together, booking Motown Revue shows that would showcase his entire roster. He hired key behind-the-scenes figures like choreographer Cholly Atkins and charm-school teacher Maxine Powell, ensuring that his acts would represent themselves in public in the ways that he wanted. Gordy kept the members of his songwriting teams in constant competition with one another. Gordy streamlined the process of making hit records. He ran Motown, in effect, more like the old Hollywood studio systems, with their in-house ecosystems of stars and screenwriters and directors, than like a record label. Gordy built this system more or less from scratch. Big companies, like South Korea's thriving K-pop entertainment conglomerates, are still trying to re-create what Gordy put together in that one Detroit house.

Motown started from almost nothing. Berry Gordy's father, the grandson of a slave and a slave owner, had moved to Detroit from Georgia to work on the city's assembly lines, and his family had gradually pushed its way into the city's nascent Black middle class. Gordy himself had a tumultuous professional life before he became a music mogul. Gordy dropped out of high school to go pro as a boxer. When that career stalled, he served briefly in the army, getting himself discharged as quickly as possible. He spent time working in his family's printing press. After becoming besotted with the local jazz scene, he borrowed money from his father to start a record shop called the 3-D Record Mart. The store went out of business after a couple of years. Working-class Black people in Detroit wanted to buy blues, not jazz. At the time, Berry Gordy didn't understand what kind of music people wanted to hear. But Gordy would later work hard to correct that mistake—to meet the listening public where it was.

After his store failed, Gordy worked at a local Lincoln-Mercury plant, installing chrome and upholstery. He made up melodies while he worked. After two years, Gordy quit to start a new career as a full-time songwriter. "Reet Petite," a song that Gordy wrote for electric young Detroit singer Jackie Wilson, became a minor national hit in 1957. Gordy went on to write more songs for Wilson, a rising star of the era. "Lonely Teardrops," a 1958 Wilson single that Gordy cowrote and produced, was a full-on crossover hit, peaking at #7. Being associated with Jackie Wilson gave Gordy confidence and credibility, and it drew other Detroit musicians into Gordy's orbit.

Jackie Wilson had a long and successful career, but he's also a sort of unsung hero in Motown's history. Gordy knew Wilson before either broke into music; as teenagers, they'd trained as boxers together. Wilson's style—bright, up-tempo, doo-wop-influenced R&B that foregrounded the singer's voice over strings and hand claps—evolved into the Motown sound. But when Motown was taking off, Brunswick Records, Wilson's label, pushed him toward easy-listening balladry. (Wilson's biggest hit, the 1960 slow-dance number "Night," peaked at #4.) Later, Wilson did what he could to replicate the Motown sound that he'd helped establish, scoring a late-career top-10 hit with the 1967 Motown-copycat smash "(Your Love Keeps Lifting Me) Higher and Higher," which he recorded with Motown's house-band musicians. But because of his Brunswick contract, Wilson never had a chance to fully take part in the Motown phenomenon that he'd helped make possible.

While he was working with Wilson, Gordy met the Miracles, the singing group led by the teenage Smokey Robinson, and took them under his wing. Robinson would soon become Gordy's biggest early star and his most important staff songwriter. Gordy didn't think he was making enough money from songwriting royalties, so in 1959 he borrowed another $800 from his father. Acting partly on Smokey Robinson's advice, Gordy invested the money in starting Tamla, the label that would become Motown. Within a year, the label had a #2 hit in the Miracles' sticky, driving "Shop Around," a love-advice R&B anthem. Gordy himself played piano on the record.

Even after the early success of "Shop Around," it took time for Gordy to develop Motown. For a few years, he recruited the best local singers, songwriters, and musicians, bringing them into his orbit. Mary Wells was a seventeen-year-old nightclub singer who wanted to write songs for Jackie Wilson. The Contours were a local vocal group led by

Jackie Wilson's cousin. Marvin Gaye was a new-to-town session singer who'd been in a few failed groups. Within a few years, Gordy turned all of them into stars.

But the Supremes were Berry Gordy's ultimate achievement. Diana Ross, Florence Ballard, Mary Wilson, and Betty McGlown were four girls from the Detroit housing projects. They started singing together as the Primettes, the sister group of local stars the Primes. (Two of the Primes would later become Temptations.) Smokey Robinson, who once lived in the same project building as Ross, helped the Primettes get an audition at Motown in 1960. At that first audition, Berry Gordy turned them down, telling them to finish high school.

Even after their rejection, the Primettes visited the Motown studios every day after school, until Gordy finally agreed to bring them aboard a year later. When he signed them, Gordy demanded that they change their name. Florence Ballard—a younger cousin of the R&B star Hank Ballard, who'd written "The Twist"—was the one who decided to call them the Supremes. Before the Supremes signed to Motown, Betty McGlown got engaged and left the group. The Supremes replaced her with Barbara Martin, but then Martin left the group after getting pregnant in 1962. So the Supremes carried on as a trio, and they got to work right away.

For two years, the Supremes cranked out singles for Motown, and those singles went nowhere. Starting with "I Want a Guy" in 1961, the Supremes released six Motown singles in the early sixties. Half of them only scraped the bottom of the *Billboard* Hot 100; the other half didn't chart at all. But Berry Gordy had a vision for the Supremes. Gordy made Diana Ross the trio's leader, which didn't sit well with Mary Wilson or Florence Ballard, both of whom were better-trained singers with more powerful voices. Gordy thought Ross—ambitious and effete, with gigantic eyes—had a certain star quality. History has proved him correct.

The Supremes were getting songs from the best songwriters that Motown had to offer. Gordy himself wrote their 1962 single "Let Me

Go the Right Way." Smokey Robinson wrote "A Breathtaking Guy" the next year. But the Supremes didn't find their sound until Gordy teamed them up with the songwriting and production team of Eddie Holland, Lamont Dozier, and Brian Holland. "It was incredible," Brian Holland wrote in the Holland brothers' 2019 memoir, *Come and Get These Memories*. "All these great writers, the biggest and most successful names in the building, and not one of them could get a hit on the Supremes." The Holland-Dozier-Holland (H-D-H) team broke that string of failure.

Eddie Holland had been one of Motown's early stars. In 1958, before he founded Motown, Gordy had written and produced "You," a single that a nineteen-year-old Holland released on Mercury. Holland was one of the first artists on Motown; his 1959 single "Merry-Go-Round" was only the third record that the label released. Holland was a handsome, charismatic kid with a voice that could be forceful or dreamy. He sounded a lot like Jackie Wilson, and since Wilson couldn't record for Motown, Gordy had use for a singer like that. Holland's gently up-tempo 1961 single "Jamie," one of Motown's early successes, made it to #30 on the Hot 100. But Holland figured out that songwriters tended to earn more money than performers, and he decided he was in the wrong racket.

Eddie's brother, Brian Holland, had already joined Motown's stable of songwriters; he was one of the five writers credited for the Marvelettes' 1961 smash, "Please Mr. Postman," Motown's first #1 single. Berry Gordy paired Brian with Lamont Dozier, another former singer who'd recorded for a few local Detroit labels in the late fifties. Eddie had to lobby the other two to join the songwriting team. Eddie argued that, with him writing lyrics, they'd be able to crank out songs more quickly and be better able to compete with Motown songwriters like Smokey Robinson and Gordy himself.

The Holland-Dozier-Holland team quickly found a knack for writing direct, propulsive songs like Martha and the Vandellas' "(Love

Is Like a) Heat Wave," a naggingly catchy horn-driven dance track that peaked at #4 in 1963. The writers had an easy chemistry with the Supremes, too. They had such good chemistry, in fact, that Eddie Holland, then unhappily married to someone else, started an affair with Diana Ross. In 1963, the Holland-Dozier-Holland team wrote the Supremes a brassy, hand-clap-driven tune called "When the Lovelight Starts Shining Through His Eyes," which reached #23, finally giving the Supremes their first hit.

That hit granted the Supremes the opportunity to join the Caravan of Stars, Dick Clark's touring revue. Every night, Clark would send a whole crew of unformed young hitmakers out on stages at high school gyms and National Guard armories across the country, all of them backed by a house band. Clark would have a Brylcreemed idol, a Gene Pitney or a Brian Hyland, as headliner, and he'd fill the rest of the bill with acts who had a recognizable song or two. Clark wanted Mary Wells, one of the bigger Motown stars at the time, for the tour, but Motown wanted too much money for her. They offered up the Supremes as a cheaper alternative, and the Supremes became the tour's opening act that summer.

The Supremes needed a new single to promote on that tour, and Holland-Dozier-Holland wrote "Where Did Our Love Go," a simple lilt of a song about the unraveling of an unstable affair. The Supremes themselves didn't much like the song; Mary Wilson has said that she wanted songs like the ones that H-D-H were writing for Martha and the Vandellas, not "teeny-bop songs" like "Where Did Our Love Go." H-D-H themselves weren't sure which of the Supremes should sing lead on it; Eddie Holland, who didn't think Ross could sing softly enough, pushed for Mary Wilson, but his two collaborators voted for Ross instead. Yet the song took off so quickly that the Supremes climbed up the Caravan of Stars bill as the summer went on.

"Where Did Our Love Go" was not Motown's first smash. The Miracles' aforementioned "Shop Around" got as high as #2 in the early weeks of 1961, blocked from the top only by Lawrence Welk's "Calcutta." Later in 1961, the Marvelettes' yelpy, up-tempo "Please Mr. Postman" made it all the way to #1.

"Please Mr. Postman" was the first true Motown victory, the song upon which an empire was built. Musically and culturally, though, "Please Mr. Postman" was a song for its moment, not a sign of an impending future. The Motown machine was still getting up and running, and it wasn't yet operating at peak capacity. "Please Mr. Postman" is a girl-group song not unlike the ones that were coming out of New York's Brill Building around the same time. It's a catchy number—bright and chirpy and a bit slight. Lead Marvelette Gladys Horton has a tugging ache in her voice, an early echo of the elegant sweep that would later animate the best Motown songs. But in its brittle brightness, "Please Mr. Postman" is a mere echo of what would come.

Motown's second #1 was a glorious fluke. Little Stevie Wonder was a thirteen-year-old blind multi-instrumentalist prodigy who'd released a couple of albums of elegant but aimless jazz-pop. Before his one euphoric early hit, Wonder had found no pop success whatsoever. But Wonder was a scene-stealing dynamo onstage at Motown's touring package shows. The year 1963's "Fingertips (Pt. 2)," the first live recording ever to hit #1, is a document of Wonder dizzily and joyously vamping, wailing improvisations and tootling a harmonica, for a raucous crowd at Chicago's Regal Theater.

"Fingertips (Pt. 2)," which ascended the Hot 100 in 1963, is a live version of an instrumental that Wonder had already released, but it's more of a free-form jam than anything. On the recording, we can hear the live Motown band (including drummer Marvin Gaye) working hard to follow Wonder's lead. There's an amazing moment at the end of the song where Wonder simply refuses to leave the stage without giving an encore, returning to bask in the audience's adoration. The band has to scramble to keep up with him. Deep in the mix, you can hear bassist Joe Swift frantically asking what key the song is in.

That unplanned encore was a playfully rebellious move. Wonder would indulge that same impulse again and again over the course of his long and massively successful career, playing around with song structures and experimenting in the studio. That impulse would make Wonder Motown's key figure a decade later, and it would earn him a great many #1 singles. But Wonder didn't become a reliable pop success until years later. At the time, "Fingertips (Pt. 2)" was a one-off. The single's success helped lift Motown's pop profile, and it also worked as a powerful advertisement for those live shows. But "Fingertips (Pt. 2)" had nothing to do with Berry Gordy's songwriting assembly line. It almost existed as a rebuke to Gordy's whole model.

Mary Wells's "My Guy," Motown's third #1, comes a little closer to the classic Motown sound and methodology. The song, a zippy rejection of a flirty casanova, is straight from the Motown system. Smokey Robinson, Wells's regular songwriter, wrote and produced it. The musicians who played on the track—Earl Van Dyke, Robert White, James Jamerson—already made up the core of Motown's killer house band. And the song draws on Black blues and R&B traditions while jacking up the tempo, turning those sounds into something bright and sparkly enough to attract white audiences.

"My Guy" hit #1 at the height of early-1964 Beatlemania—a tremendous achievement at a time when Americans weren't having a whole lot of success on the American pop charts. The Beatles themselves, vocal Motown admirers, invited Wells to tour the United Kingdom with them. Back then, Mary Wells was in position to become Motown's biggest star. "My Guy" was a coup for Motown, but Wells never became a big star. Instead, she struggled to land another big hit. She wasn't happy with the contract that she'd signed at seventeen, and she wasn't happy with the way that Motown used the "My Guy" money to promote newer stars. A year after "My Guy," Wells left the label. She never got anywhere near the top 10 again, and she spent her later years locked in a legal battle with Motown over royalties. Wells died of cancer in 1992, when she was just forty-nine. Hers is a tragic story and an old one: a talented young artist butts heads with her label, demands the money that she's owed, and sees her career destroyed as a result. Mary Wells symbolizes Motown's failures more than its successes.

But even taking into account all the complications built into the Motown dynamic, the Supremes were, for years, an unqualified success story and a pop-music juggernaut. Where Mary Wells stalled, the Supremes went into overdrive. That ascension begins with "Where Did Our Love Go," a brilliant piece of songcraft and persona building that immediately announced the Supremes as a cultural force.

For such a simple song, "Where Did Our Love Go" sure is complicated. Diana Ross sings to a lover, sensing the oncoming end of the relationship and doing everything she can to stop it. She appeals to his empathy. She sings of a "burning, burning, yearning feeling" inside her—something that could be sadness or need or some combination of the two. And she accuses him of changing on the fly, wrongfooting her: "Now that you got me, you wanna leave me behind."

Those lyrics are direct and economical, laser-focused on a specific emotional situation. The words leave room to maneuver. Another singer might've taken advantage of that room, bringing the showy vocal theatrics that stood as a shorthand for heartbreak even in the early sixties. That's how Ross wanted to sing it. In the Holland brothers' memoir, Eddie writes that he had a hell of a time teaching Diana Ross to sing the song in the quiet, murmuring way he wanted. Ross wanted to sing R&B riffs, but Eddie wanted something that was "soft and innocent" but also "sensuous and seductive." When she finally recorded the song, Eddie says that she did it in a sarcastically blank-faced deadpan, locking eyes with him the entire time. That attempt at pissed-off provocation translated into an iconic pop vocal.

On "Where Did Our Love Go," Ross sounds like she's doing everything she can to maintain her composure, to hold herself together. Ross is playing a character, and her character wouldn't scream at the guy. She's not trying to accuse the guy of letting their love die; she's trying to coax him back. It's a plea, and it might also be a seduction. She's restrained, austere, almost sleepy. She turns her voice into an invitation.

The music is an invitation, too. "Where Did Our Love Go" isn't a ballad; it's a four-four pulse. Most of the arrangement is fast and simple, anchored to that foot-stomping beat. The song even has the honking saxophone solo that practically every early-sixties up-tempo pop song had to have. But there's also a tingly vibraphone in there, lending an extra layer of warmth and dimension to the sound. (Later, Holland-Dozier-Holland would recruit the Detroit Symphony Orchestra to add elegant sweep to Supremes songs. On "Where Did Our Love Go," the vibraphone does all that work by itself.) Mary Wilson and Florence Ballard gently circle Diana Ross's voice, murmuring "baby, baby" languidly in the background. The spartan melody, and the lost feeling that it conveys, was potent enough that it still worked as pop music years later. In 1981, UK synthpoppers Soft Cell added a bit of "Where Did Our Love Go" to the end of their version of Gloria Jones's "Tainted Love." The ensuing single made it into the American top 10, peaking at #8.

"Where Did Our Love Go" might be a song about a desperate romantic situation, but it's light and fun, built for dancing. There's a deep longing in Ross's voice, but audiences could still hear it as a simple, fizzy love song. In the even-keeled poise of her delivery, Ross shows the facility to communicate emotion that she'd eventually turn into an acting career. In the way she radiates delicate warmth even on a jumpy beat, Ross also brings the adaptability that would serve her for years to come. In the early eighties, long after most of her Motown contemporaries had faded away, Ross was still making disco-pop chart-toppers. Nobody could've predicted that based on what Ross did with "Where Did Our Love Go," but all that potential is right there in the song.

"Where Did Our Love Go" established a blueprint for the Supremes, and Holland-Dozier-Holland quickly turned that blueprint into a formula. When "Where Did Our Love Go" took off, Berry

Gordy went to H-D-H and told them that they needed to keep the Supremes' momentum going. In a single evening, the trio wrote three more Supremes singles: "Baby Love," "Come See About Me," and "Stop! In the Name of Love." All three songs went to #1. All three sounded a whole lot like "Where Did Our Love Go."

"Baby Love," which hit #1 just two months after "Where Did Our Love Go," is almost a clone. Diana Ross sings understatedly about a dissolving relationship over a simple stomping beat. Vibraphones shimmer. A saxophone bleats. The other two Supremes repeat the word "baby" again and again. And while "Baby Love" was almost certainly a cynical attempt to replicate a past success, it's also a gorgeous song in its own right. "It's the Motown way," Mary Wilson explained to the *Guardian* years later. "The music is beautiful, but the words are stories about love and hurt, which reflect the way life is. The combination of the two made the music last."

The Motown way served the Supremes insanely well. "Where Did Our Love Go" was the first of five consecutive #1 singles, a streak that not even the Beatles had equaled. Those songs all represented minor tweaks on the original formula. Holland-Dozier-Holland slowly brought in grander melodic ideas, and the Funk Brothers added more of their own instrumental flourishes, but the near-mathematical precision was always the same. Over the years, the Supremes played around with delicate orchestration ("I Hear a Symphony"), psychedelic electronic bleepage ("Reflections"), and even the pointed social commentary that Berry Gordy was reluctant to allow onto Motown records ("Love Child"). Even after Holland-Dozier-Holland left Motown in 1967 and stopped working with the Supremes, the group remained on top by sticking to the formula that those songwriters had established.

But as the Supremes' music kept its continuity, their persona evolved. As Motown's crown jewel, the group shouldered the responsibility of making the label as friendly and approachable as possible. They didn't spend long touring the Dick Clark teeny-bop circuit. Soon enough, Gordy had them outfitted in ball gowns and long silk gloves.

The Supremes' stage choreography became graceful and almost exaggeratedly feminine. Gordy also worked to get the group booked at the Copacabana, the mob-controlled New York nightclub that he saw as a symbol of the white pop establishment. In getting the Supremes into the Copa, Gordy fancied that he was presenting the trio as a down-the-middle adult pop act.

Amid those subtle musical and presentational maneuvers, the Supremes continued to adapt, becoming pop survivors. They remained huge throughout the sixties. Before Diana Ross left the trio at the end of the decade, they notched twelve #1 singles, more than anyone other than the Beatles. Indeed, the Supremes were the only true contenders to the Beatles' pop dominance, and there's some strange symmetry in the way the two groups came apart within a few months of each other at the end of the sixties. Like the Beatles, the Supremes found ways to stay on top of the changing cultural tides. But unlike the Beatles, the Supremes always presented themselves as pop musicians rather than as artists. Throughout that entire run, the Supremes kept doing things the Motown way. Even the 1969 chart-topper "Someday We'll Be Together," the final single that Diana Ross recorded with the group, still seems spun off from the DNA of "Where Did Our Love Go."

The DNA of "Where Did Our Love Go" wasn't just in the music that the Supremes released. It existed in practically everything that Motown did over the course of the sixties. "Where Did Our Love Go" was a sincere, genteel, dramatic R&B song—an R&B song that drew as much from the up-tempo white pop coming out of the Brill Building as from the blues or gospel roots of the genre. Berry Gordy, gambling on the notion that white baby boomers cared less about racial division than any previous generation in American history, aimed to sell his music to both Black and white teenagers. "Where Did Our Love Go" was proof of concept.

Other labels had experimented with soft, orchestral soul records, and they'd had real success with that sound. Atlantic Records, for instance, hit #1 in the fall of 1960 with the Drifters' "Save the Last

Dance for Me" and with Ray Charles's "Georgia," two pop master-pieces that influenced the Motown sound. But by marrying the soft-focus sophistication of those records to brisk, up-tempo finger snappers that early-sixties teenagers demanded, Motown's musicians found a down-the-middle sweet spot and created a brand name. They inspired brand loyalty beyond what any other American record label could hope to achieve.

By the end of the sixties, Motown's roster was lousy with stars. The Temptations, the Four Tops, and Marvin Gaye had all made singles that topped the pop charts. The Miracles and Stevie Wonder were consistent hitmakers. The Jackson 5, signed in 1969, were primed to explode. And just as much as any of the artists on its roster, Motown itself became a star.

The label had a signature sound, and anyone who bought a record with that logo could be sure of a few things: big beats, propulsive bass, sweetly sung lyrics about romantic dilemmas, choruses that would get stuck in your head all day. Motown's signature sound took shape around the time "Where Did Our Love Go" hit #1. It was partly a function of the way the records were made: the same musicians, play-ing songs written by the same songwriters, in the same studio. But this was also an intentional move on Berry Gordy's part. If he had some-thing that worked, he kept doing that thing until that thing no lon-ger worked. In Motown, Berry Gordy created his own assembly line. For a while, everything that rolled off of it was shiny and inviting and irresistible.

Gordy's own narrative was irresistible, too. He was a Black man who'd founded and owned a fabulously lucrative cultural enterprise, which made him a quintessential American success story. By most esti-mates, Gordy became one of the wealthiest Black American entrepre-neurs of his day—perhaps behind only John H. Johnson, the founder of the *Ebony* and *Jet* magazine-publishing empire. Within Motown's offices, Gordy inspired loyalty by pushing the idea that he was beating white executives at their own game. Gordy insisted that Motown's music should be seen as pop, not as Black-specific R&B music. As the Holland brothers write in their memoir, "It was one of the reasons that [Gordy] was so keen to break into the pop market. Not for the money, although of course that was part of it, but to try and break down the barriers between 'us' and 'them.'"

America was changing around Motown. About six weeks before "Where Did Our Love Go" hit #1, Lyndon Johnson signed the Civil Rights Act into law. Motown was in the business of making feel-good music. Its bright, optimistic sound was playing out of transistor radios and jukeboxes, filling the air during some great victories in the struggle for racial equality in America. But Gordy was also careful not to let his label's music be drawn into that struggle.

Berry Gordy was not an idealist or a crusader. Motown, Gordy had decreed, was not in the business of message music. In their book, the Hollands write, "Berry was devoted to the civil rights cause. But what he didn't want us doing—any of us—was anything that could be perceived as protest music." When Marvin Gaye made his near-perfect protest-music opus *What's Going On* in 1971, he had to fight bitterly with Gordy to bring the album to market.

In retrospect, it's striking how forcefully anodyne Motown's lyrics were in the sixties. In times of great American tumult and rupture, Motown's musicians sang songs about matters of the heart. They didn't even hint at any greater sense of sadness or longing, as Ray Charles had done on "Georgia." There were exceptions, like Stevie Wonder's wonderful hit 1966 cover of Bob Dylan's "Blowin' in the Wind," but they were rare. Gordy even coached his acts not to say anything of substance in interviews. Motown's artists were inoffensive by edict.

Gordy's controlling arm took a heavy toll on the Supremes. Florence Ballard suffered from depression and alcoholism, and she was always angry at being relegated to background-singer status in her own group. In 1967, Berry Gordy fired Ballard from the Supremes, replacing her with Cindy Birdsong, a member of the Patti LaBelle–fronted group the Blue Belles. (Birdsong looked a lot like Ballard, which helped her get the job.)

For a little while, Ballard was allowed to return to the Supremes on a probationary basis. Ballard was hoping to win her position back permanently, but Gordy was only stalling. He needed to buy Birdsong out of her old Blue Belles contract. Once Birdsong was free, Gordy kicked Ballard out for good. Ballard lost a lawsuit against Motown and fell into poverty, splitting with her husband and losing her home to foreclosure. A solo deal with ABC Records didn't pan out. In 1976, when Ballard was thirty-two, she went into cardiac arrest and died. Without the system that Gordy built, Florence Ballard probably would've never become a star. But Ballard's dismissal, decline, and death tell a story of how cold and exploitative Gordy could be.

Even after Gordy fired Ballard, the Supremes continued to thrive until 1969, when Diana Ross announced her departure. Motown gave a grand red-carpet rollout to Ross's solo career, putting the label's entire machinery behind her. For a while, the entire label was built around Diana Ross; even the label's newest stars of the seventies, family-act sensation the Jackson 5, were initially presented as Diana Ross protégés. The Jackson 5's 1969 debut album was titled *Diana Ross Presents the Jackson 5*, even though Ross had nothing to do with discovering them. Without Ross, the Supremes continued on but became an afterthought, fading away from the charts entirely in the first few years of the seventies.

Ross kept making hits into the early eighties, when she teamed up with the disco group Chic to make the album *Diana* and scored the triumphant late-career smashes "Upside Down" and "I'm Coming Out." Ross had left Motown, signing a record-breaking $20 million deal with RCA in 1981. By that time, Motown's once-impeccable assembly line had broken down. The label still scored hits with artists like the Commodores, whose leader, Lionel Richie, knew how to write a slick middle-of-the-road ballad. But Motown was no longer a central-ized system. It had become a record label like any other.

There's beauty in the Motown narrative—in this Black-owned enterprise coming out of nowhere, showcasing genius, and conquer-ing the pop charts. But there's darkness, too. Berry Gordy was a ruthless capitalist. He kept a tight grasp on his royalties, he fought to main-tain control over the images and public statements of his artists, and he worked every Motown act hard. Berry Gordy exploited the artists on Motown, and he did that in ways that went beyond the financial. Gordy, for instance, was the father of Diana Ross's oldest daughter, Rhonda Ross Kendrick, born in 1971. Gordy and Ross kept their affair secret, and Ross married her manager, Robert Silberstein, before Rhonda was born. Rhonda didn't learn that Gordy was her biological father until she was thirteen.

Gordy's hubris eventually became Motown's downfall. By mid-1972, Gordy had moved all of Motown's operations from Detroit to Los Angeles. Gordy wanted to move into film, and he had early success in that arena. Diana Ross made her screen debut in *Lady Sings the Blues*, a 1972 Billie Holiday biopic that Gordy produced, and Ross earned an Oscar nomination for her lead role. But Gordy's movie hopes crashed spectacularly with the 1975 film *Mahogany*, another Diana Ross vehi-cle. Gordy took over as the film's director after firing British filmmaker Tony Richardson. *Mahogany* was a critically savaged flop, and Gordy never directed again.

In its move to Los Angeles, Motown lost its identity, its sense of internal cohesion. Stevie Wonder, the Motown artist who thrived the most in the seventies, wrote and produced and played all the instru-ments on many of his own records. He moved beyond the Motown assembly line and became a complete enterprise unto himself. Over the course of the decade, most of Motown's biggest stars either faded or, in the case of the Jackson 5, left the label. In 1988, Gordy sold Motown to MCA for $61 million.

It's remarkable that Diana Ross continued to score #1 hits even sixteen years after "Where Did Our Love Go"—after the Motown system had become a distant memory. In retrospect, Motown's boom period lasted only a few years, but it changed pop music irrevocably. In its salad days, Motown streamlined R&B music, made Black artists into towering monocultural stars in a racially divided America, and perfected a precise and resonant sound that never hinted at the cynicism of the commercial process behind it. "Where Did Our Love Go" had soft sweep and energetic vitality, and it pointed to a future where a truly on-fire pop machine could serve its audience without condescending to it.

"Where Did Our Love Go" hints at a kind of utopian pop-music vision. It's a bittersweet jam that gestures at shared experiences and universal yearning. It transcends and it promises. Motown, itself, couldn't live up to the promise, but the craft and optimism of "Where Did Our Love Go" still changed the pop landscape. All through the sixties, the sleek and dependable sound of Motown, in general—and the Supremes, in particular—moved to the center of the American pop mainstream. "Where Did Our Love Go" changed what was possible. For years afterward, Motown took full advantage of that new sense of possibility.

CHAPTER 5

The Byrds—
"Mr. Tambourine Man"

| Released April 12, 1965 |
| Hit #1 June 26, 1965 |
| One-week reign |

ROCK 'N' ROLL, IN ITS EARLIEST FORM, WAS NOT COUNTER-
culture music. It was rebellious music, but that's not necessarily
the same thing. Rock 'n' roll was teenage-freak-out music, music about
falling in love and dancing and driving fast cars and getting your heart
broken. It wasn't music about making sense of an incoherent world or
attempting to reshape that world into something more humane. In the
late fifties and early sixties, that was folk music's job.

If rock 'n' roll was teenage music, then folk was collegiate music.
Starting in the thirties, ethnomusicologists such as John Lomax and
his son Alan combed the southern states, looking for undiscovered
working-class musicians and songwriters. Leadbelly, for instance, became a blues legend after the Lomaxes found him in a Louisiana
prison. The songs from those Lomax recordings became popular
among certain circles within the intelligentsia. Leftist intellectuals like
Harvard dropout Pete Seeger started playing those songs, using them to
highlight issues such as racism and inequality. This wasn't pop music,

but sometimes it led to commercial success. Seeger was a member of a group called the Weavers, who had a massive 1950 hit with their pop-friendly version of "Goodnight Irene," a traditional song that they'd learned from Leadbelly.

But the Weavers' leftist inclinations made sustained pop stardom impossible. During the McCarthy era, the Weavers were blacklisted because of suspected ties to the Communist Party. Seeger, testifying before the House Committee on Un-American Activities in 1955, refused to answer questions about his politics. He was found guilty of contempt of Congress and sentenced to a year in prison. That sentence was later overturned, but the Weavers broke up in the wake of their blacklisting. With television and the radio unavailable, Seeger and his contemporaries played colleges, finding a following and rekindling interest in these old songs among many young people.

From the very beginning of the Hot 100 era, folk music was part of the pop ecosystem. In November 1958, a few months after the chart was introduced, the Kingston Trio, a clean-cut and approachable California group, hit #1 with their version of the old Appalachian murder ballad "Tom Dooley." While that song's lyrics were bleak and intense, the group sang it like a hymn, or a lullaby. The Kingston Trio never made another #1 hit after that, but they sold vast numbers of albums in the early sixties. In the years that followed, other folk groups also scored occasional crossover successes with traditional songs. A few even made it to #1: the Highwaymen with "Michael" in 1961, the Rooftop Singers with "Walk Right In" in 1963.

But most of the real action in folk music wasn't happening anywhere near the singles chart. Instead, the music lived in coffeehouses, nightclubs, and college auditoriums, where a whole circuit was taking shape. Jim McGuinn, a young guitarist who'd learned his instrument at Chicago's Old Town School of Folk Music, was a creature of that scene. A teenage McGuinn, who would later change his name to Roger, started out as a sideman for the Limelighters, a Kingston Trio–style group that had some success in the early sixties. From there, McGuinn found work as a session musician. He arranged versions of the Pete Seeger songs "Turn! Turn! Turn!" and "The Bells of Rhymney" for folk singer Judy Collins, and he also played guitar for the genre-agnostic pop star Bobby Darin, who had worked a few folk songs into the middle of his live sets.

Bob Dylan followed a different trajectory. Like McGuinn, the young man born Robert Zimmerman was a midwestern teenager who'd arrived in New York after inhaling the folk-music songbook. But where McGuinn was a young professional working within a system, Dylan was a self-made character. Dylan started out playing traditional songs, but he saw himself as being within the tradition of itinerant thirties songwriter Woody Guthrie. Shortly after he came to New York, Dylan visited an ailing Guthrie in Brooklyn, looking for his blessing. Dylan sang in a ragged, nasal bleat, which made old folk traditionals sound rough and urgent. After a couple of years of playing Greenwich Village coffeehouses, Dylan signed with Columbia Records and released his first album. Before long, Dylan was writing his own songs—a bold step in a genre that revolved almost entirely around the perceived authenticity of old handed-down folk songs.

Unlike the Kingston Trio and their successors, the young Dylan wasn't making the kinds of records that would make any kind of impact on the radio. But he wrote resonant, poetic protest songs, and some of those songs did well in other singers' hands. In 1963 the New York trio Peter, Paul and Mary recorded a softened, prettified cover of Dylan's "Blowin' in the Wind," and it peaked at #2 on the Hot 100, behind Little Stevie Wonder's "Fingertips (Pt. 2)." (Three years later, Wonder would take "Blowin' in the Wind" to #9 on the Hot 100 and #1 on the R&B chart.) "Blowin' in the Wind" helped make Dylan a key figure in the folk-music revival. Dylan famously sang at Martin Luther King Jr.'s March on Washington in 1963, and he also backed out of a booking on *The Ed Sullivan Show* when the show wouldn't let him play his song "Talkin' John Birch Paranoid Blues," a move that only burnished his legend. But Dylan soon grew alienated with his role as a topical songwriter in the folk movement, and he took to writing elliptical, impressionistic songs instead.

Both Dylan and McGuinn had loved rock 'n' roll before finding folk music. Dylan had idolized Little Richard and Buddy Holly. At a few shows in 1959, Dylan had even played piano for Bobby Vee, the teen idol who had a #1 hit in 1961 with the Goffin-King song "Take Good Care of My Baby." Later, both Dylan and McGuinn tentatively toyed around with rock 'n' roll. In 1962, Dylan used electric instrumentation on a 1962 single called "Mixed Up Confusion," but Dylan didn't like how it turned out, and Columbia quickly withdrew the record. In the early sixties, McGuinn had a short stint as a Brill Building songwriter, working for Bobby Darin's publishing company. But only one of the songs that McGuinn cowrote ever even came out as a single: "Beach Ball," a forgettable surf-pop track from a group called the City Surfers.

In those pre-Beatles years, some pop stars showed interest in the folk underground. The Tokens, a New York doo-wop group that had once included Neil Sedaka as a member, hit #1 with their 1961 version of "The Lion Sleeps Tonight," an old South African song that Pete Seeger had popularized. Rock 'n' roll stars like the Everly Brothers and Chubby Checker released quickly forgotten folk albums. The Four Seasons, the New Jersey doo-wop stars, covered a song from Bob Dylan's protest-song contemporary Phil Ochs. But that appreciation went only one way. Folk musicians almost never used drums or electric guitars, and when they made reference to rock 'n' roll, they were generally mocking it. (Dylan did something like that when he and Ramblin' Jack Elliott parodied doo-wop on a 1961 song called "Acne.")

But the folk scene couldn't maintain that aloofness when the Beatles showed up. McGuinn, in particular, fell in love with the British group. McGuinn thought he heard some folk in the Beatles' chord changes. (In their time as the Quarrymen, the Beatles had played skiffle, a fast form of pop-folk popular in England; maybe that's what McGuinn recognized.) The Beatles opened their 1964 chart-topper

"A Hard Day's Night" with the smeary, ringing sound of a twelve-string Rickenbacker, an instrument that George Harrison had bought during the Beatles' first visit to New York. The guitar had been on the market for only a few months when Harrison got hold of it. McGuinn had already mastered the acoustic twelve-string, and he picked up the electric version immediately after hearing what Harrison had done with it. McGuinn started growing his hair out, too. He wanted to be a part of whatever the Beatles were doing.

McGuinn had relocated to Los Angeles, another city with a bustling folk scene, and he started playing "I Want to Hold Your Hand" on an acoustic twelve-string at the Sunset Strip club the Troubadour. Gene Clark, a member of a folk group called the New Christy Minstrels, had also fallen for the Beatles, and he loved McGuinn's folk take on their sound. Clark approached McGuinn about forming a duo. David Crosby, another local folk singer, heard McGuinn and Clark harmonizing in a nightclub stairwell, and he joined in. Crosby brought his manager, Jim Dickson, into the mix. Before long, McGuinn, Clark, and Crosby were a trio.

Jim Dickson heard money in those three voices together. Capitalizing on the fascination with all things British, Dickson named the group the Beefeaters, and they released one single on the folk-centric label Elektra. When that record didn't sell, Dickson recruited a rhythm section: Chris Hillman, a teenage bluegrass mandolinist who'd never picked up a bass before the band's first practice, and Michael Clarke, a drummer who had a great shaggy Beatles-style haircut but who didn't own a drum set. (At early rehearsals, Clarke would bang on cardboard boxes.)

Dickson changed the Beefeaters' name, going with the Beatles' misspelled-animal-name strategy and calling them the Byrds. Dickson also got the Byrds a contract with Columbia, the major label that also put out Bob Dylan's records. Another Columbia artist, jazz great Miles Davis, helped set up the Byrds' audition. At the time, Columbia had no interest in becoming a rock 'n' roll label; former easy-listening star

Mitch Miller, who'd become Columbia's head of A&R (artists and repertoire), famously referred to rock as "musical baby food." But the label was intrigued enough to offer the Byrds a single deal. If the band's first record didn't sell, they wouldn't have a future at the label. Fortunately, the Byrds found the right song.

Bob Dylan wrote "Mr. Tambourine Man" early in 1964, pecking out the lyrics on a typewriter in the backseat of a station wagon while on a cross-country road trip. The song is a product of the moment when Dylan consciously walked away from protest songs, moving toward more personal and abstract fare. Dylan himself has never been too forthcoming regarding what "Mr. Tambourine Man" is about. He's said that the song was inspired by the Fellini film *La Strada* and by the sight of his friend guitarist Bruce Langhorne playing a gigantic tambourine. He's also claimed that the song has nothing to do with drugs, though you could forgive anyone for feeling otherwise.

Lyrically, "Mr. Tambourine Man" is a hallucinatory ramble. Dylan's narrator wants the tambourine man to take him on a trip in his magic swirling ship, to take him disappearing through the smoke rings of his mind and down the foggy ruins of time. Dylan's words are vague and precise at the same time—a poetic evocation of longing and wanderlust. In every version of the song, Dylan sings "Mr. Tambourine Man" as a warm incantation. It's a strange, inviting piece of work.

In June 1964, Dylan recorded his fourth album, *Another Side of Bob Dylan*, in one marathon twelve-hour recording session. That day, Dylan laid down a raw, sloppy seven-minute version of "Mr. Tambourine Man," with fellow Village folkie Ramblin' Jack Elliott adding harmonies. Dylan didn't include "Mr. Tambourine Man" on *Another Side*, but a Columbia promotions man handed an acetate recording of the song to Jim Dickson, the Byrds' manager. Dickson brought the song to the band, who didn't like it. David Crosby wasn't impressed with Dylan's singing style. Roger McGuinn had seen Dylan early and decided that he was "basically a Woody Guthrie imitator." But Dickson insisted, telling the band that "Mr. Tambourine Man" had a depth that their other songs lacked. Eventually, the band caved.

The Byrds radically reworked "Mr. Tambourine Man," doing everything in their power to turn Dylan's original demo into a pop song. They cut three of the song's four verses, layered their harmonies over Dylan's chorus, and used the track as a vehicle for McGuinn's chiming, droning guitar sounds. Ultimately, those harmonies and guitar sounds would be the only things that the actual Byrds recorded on the song. Columbia had paired the Byrds up with producer Terry Melcher, and Melcher decided that, McGuinn aside, the Byrds weren't good enough musicians to actually play on their own record.

Melcher was the youngest producer at Columbia and the only one who had any affection for rock 'n' roll. Melcher was also show-business royalty. His mother was movie-musical star Doris Day, Columbia's biggest-selling artist at the time. Melcher had been in an early-sixties surf-rock group called the Rip Chords, and they'd made it to #4 with the Beach Boys–style drag-racing ditty "Hey Little Cobra." (Another Rip Chord, Bruce Johnston, would later join the Beach Boys, and Melcher would produce the Beach Boys' widely reviled 1988 comeback #1 smash, "Kokomo.") Melcher caught some early Byrds rehearsals and decided that most of the players in the band were too rough and unpolished to play on their own single. McGuinn had done session work before, so he was seasoned enough, but the others were too raw. Instead, Melcher replaced them with Los Angeles session-player aces—members of the team that later came to be known as the Wrecking Crew.

Much like the Funk Brothers, Motown's unshowy but brilliant house band, the musicians of the Wrecking Crew were workhorses. Their names usually didn't appear on the credits of records, but they still found ways to add their touch to dozens of hits. Drummer Hal Blaine played on forty different singles that went to #1. Melcher brought in Blaine, bassist Larry Knechtel, guitarist Jerry Cole, and keyboardist

Leon Russell to play on the Byrds' version of "Mr. Tambourine Man." All four of those Wrecking Crew musicians had already played on early Beach Boys hits, and they'd helped producer Phil Spector devise his ringing, echoing sound.

Not all the Byrds were thrilled with the idea of having other musicians on their single. In his memoir, bassist Chris Hillman later wrote that watching the recording session was "a great experience," but Melcher threatened to kick drummer Michael Clarke out of the studio after he complained about being replaced. Melcher also reportedly considered using Wrecking Crew guitarist Glen Campbell, who knew his way around a twelve-string. (Later, Campbell would become a solo star, recording a couple of his own country-pop chart-toppers in the seventies.)

In any case, the decision to use session musicians wasn't up to the Byrds. There was money on the line, and Melcher and Columbia weren't willing to indulge the members of the group. Ultimately, Columbia made the right decision. The Byrds' own demo of "Mr. Tambourine Man," released decades later, doesn't have the warm punch of the single that Melcher recorded that day. Melcher still captured the key elements of the band's sound. McGuinn's sparkling, intricate guitar dominates the track. McGuinn, Clark, and Crosby sing hazy, bittersweet harmonies. The crisp propulsion of the Wrecking Crew's backbeat puts muscle behind their voices.

By the time the Byrds recorded "Mr. Tambourine Man," folk and rock were already starting to intermingle. The Beatles had become besotted with Dylan. In August 1964, Dylan met the Beatles and introduced them to marijuana. The Animals, another British Invasion band, had an American #1 hit that year with their fearsomely gothic take on "House of the Rising Sun," an old blues traditional that Dylan had recorded on his first album. And on half of his own 1964 album, *Bringing It All Back Home*, Dylan himself played with an electric rock band. The chaotic, wordy blues-rock single "Subterranean Homesick Blues" peaked at #39, giving Dylan his first appearance on the Hot 100. Dylan had even tried out an electric arrangement of "Mr. Tambourine Man," though he didn't like the result. Instead, Dylan included an acoustic version of the song on *Bringing It All Back Home*. Dylan's album came out just two weeks before the Byrds' single.

The Byrds' big innovation wasn't turning a Bob Dylan song into pop music; Peter, Paul and Mary had already done that. And their innovation wasn't combining folk with rock; that combination was already in the air. Instead, the Byrds' real accomplishment was in pulling all these sounds that were floating around in the air and combining them into a fully formed head-blown space-age whole—a sound that captured a young generation's questioning imagination.

While all of the Byrds had come from folk music, McGuinn thought of them as futurists, not traditionalists. At first, McGuinn wanted to call the band the Jet Set. McGuinn would rhapsodize possibilities of the twelve-string electric guitar, a brand-new piece of technology at the time: "You can do anything on it—Bach organs, harpsichord, jet plane whining turbine engines, air raid sirens, kittens, a baby crying, anything." Just as much as the decision to cover Bob Dylan, that ringing, spinning, brain-expanding guitar tone was what set the Byrds apart. Decades later—long after folk-rock had faded from the charts—acts like Tom Petty, U2, and R.E.M. would cite that guitar sound as a major inspiration.

The voices mattered, too. McGuinn, Clark, and Crosby sang in harmony, but their harmonies didn't sound like the Beach Boys or the Everly Brothers or even the Beatles. Instead, their searching tone came from their shared folk background. Later, McGuinn said that his lead vocal on "Mr. Tambourine Man" was his attempt to sound like a combination of Bob Dylan and John Lennon. That's a tall order, but McGuinn's voice fills it. McGuinn sounds lost but euphoric, caught up in the magic of whatever's happening in those words. In the hands of the Byrds and the Wrecking Crew, Dylan's song becomes a woozy, ecstatic pop reverie. The Byrds' version of the song tidies and sweetens Dylan's version, but it also syncs up with the astral surreality of Dylan's lyrics. Along the way, the song finds its own pulsating electric bliss.

Melcher and the Byrds recorded "Mr. Tambourine Man" in January 1965, but the single didn't come out for another three months. In that span of time, the Byrds came close to breaking up more than once. McGuinn even temporarily fired Crosby, not for the last time. But the band jelled after Jim Dickson found them a steady gig at Ciro's, a small supper club on the Sunset Strip. Within weeks, the Byrds' sets at Ciro's became a bohemian sensation in Los Angeles. The band played loud and ferocious, covering folk songs but also Chuck Berry and the Beatles. Actors and musicians showed up to dance, and Jane Fonda hired the Byrds to play at her birthday party. (Henry Fonda, Jane's father, repeatedly asked the band to turn it down. They ignored him.) While playing at Ciro's, the band also figured out their shaggy, ornate look. By the time "Mr. Tambourine Man" came out, the Byrds were ready-made stars. Thanks to those gigs at Ciro's, they'd even cohered as musicians to the point where Melcher decided not to use the Wrecking Crew on any of the Byrds' records after "Mr. Tambourine Man."

Of course, the fact that "Mr. Tambourine Man" became a chart-topping smash probably had something to do with Melcher's decision. "Mr. Tambourine Man" was an explosive game changer of a hit—a song that offered up a fully formed combination of rock 'n' roll and folk music that ultimately didn't sound much like either. The Byrds' timing was perfect. Marketed as America's answer to the Beatles, the band tapped into the mania of the moment, figuring out their own American strain of big-beat rock 'n' roll. But while the Beatles' influence was the catalyst for the Byrds' success, the Byrds also turbocharged the literary discontent of the folk revival, helping establish the idea that rock 'n' roll could work as deep, exploratory music that wasn't necessarily about teenage love. They latched onto the rising star of Bob

Dylan, a generational figure, but they also put Dylan into a whole new context and helped him along his own way to pop stardom.

Dylan loved the Byrds' version of the song; he was amazed by the idea that you could dance to it. During one set at Ciro's, Dylan joined the Byrds onstage. The band used a photo of Dylan playing with them on the back cover of their debut album, *Mr. Tambourine Man*, which came out in June, the same week that their single topped the charts. Dylan's approval was hugely important for the Byrds; it gave them a stamp of credibility. On their *Mr. Tambourine Man* album, the Byrds covered four different Dylan songs. But the influence went both ways. Later, Dylan sideman Mike Bloomfield claimed that Dylan had been trying to re-create the Byrds' sound on *Highway 61 Revisited*, the folk-rock album that he released that August.

The first single from *Highway 61* would become Dylan's biggest hit. The scrambled, mythic six-minute internal travelog "Like a Rolling Stone" came out in July and quickly became the biggest hit of Dylan's career. That summer, the song peaked at #2 behind the Beatles' "Help!"—a song that might've harbored some folk influence of its own. That summer, Dylan also caused a huge rift in the folk scene when he played a loud, messy three-song rock set with the Paul Butterfield Blues Band at the Newport Folk Festival. To this day, nobody has quite managed to agree whether the crowd at Newport was furious, excited, or bemused over Dylan's electric set. (Pete Seeger admitted that he was angry over not being able to hear Dylan's words, but he denied rumors that he tried to cut the electricity with an ax.)

Dylan wasn't the only one who saw an opportunity in the Byrds' folk-rock fusion. Less than two months after "Mr. Tambourine Man" fell from #1, Phil Spector associate Sonny Bono and his young girlfriend, Cher, topped the charts with their lush, chiming folk-rock love song "I Got You, Babe." Sonny and Cher had seen the Byrds at Ciro's, and Cher quickly came out with her own version of Dylan's "All I Really Want to Do." (Cher's cover of the song was a direct copy of the Byrds' arrangement, which Bono may have learned by secretly taping the Byrds' live set. Cher's version peaked at #15 and probably stalled the momentum of the Byrds' own cover of the same song, which made it to only #40.)

In September, Barry McGuire, a folk singer who'd been in the New Christy Minstrels with Gene Clark, hit #1 with "Eve of Destruction." This was a straight-up protest song, the same kind that Dylan had been writing a few years earlier. "Eve of Destruction" songwriter P. F. Sloan, a teenage session guitarist and part-time Wrecking Crew member, had cowritten a few songs for the surf-pop duo Jan and Dean. Sloan wasn't a crusading folksinger; he was part of the pop machine. Sloan was certainly imitating Bob Dylan's early protest anthems when he wrote "Eve of Destruction," but it was still a radical decision to vent rage about segregation and the Vietnam War on a pop song—or, for that matter, to give that song to a gravel-voiced singer like McGuire. (Sloan first offered "Eve of Destruction" to the Byrds, but they passed on it.) "Eve of Destruction" was a pop product, and the members of the Wrecking Crew, including Hal Blaine and Larry Knechtel, backed McGuire up on the record. But it was also an intense, fatalistic political broadside. "Eve of Destruction" was the first protest song ever to hit #1. Before the Byrds came along, a hit like that would've been impossible to imagine.

The Byrds themselves hit #1 once more. Pete Seeger had written "Turn! Turn! Turn!"—adapting the lyrics from the book of Ecclesiastes—in the late fifties, and he'd recorded the first version of the song in 1959. McGuinn had arranged Judy Collins's cover of "Turn! Turn! Turn!" in 1963. The Byrds' electrified, kaleidoscopic take on "Turn! Turn! Turn!" reached #1 in December 1965.

In the few years after "Mr. Tambourine Man" hit #1, folk-rock dominated the pop charts. Consider the case of Paul Simon and Art Garfunkel, two high school friends from Queens. As teenagers, they'd called themselves Tom and Jerry, and they'd recorded a silly 1957 rock 'n' roll single called "Hey Schoolgirl." "Hey Schoolgirl" charted on the Hot 100, and Simon and Garfunkel lip-synched the song on *American Bandstand*. But in the early sixties, the duo had turned toward the Greenwich Village folk scene.

Simon & Garfunkel's debut album, *Wednesday Morning, 3 AM*, had come out on Columbia in 1964 and sold almost nothing. The duo had effectively broken up after the album's failure, and Simon had moved to England. But producer Tom Wilson, an early Dylan collaborator, had noticed that some college-radio stations were playing the duo's song "Sound of Silence." So Wilson brought in some studio musicians, overdubbing Byrds-style folk-rock guitars onto the song. Columbia rereleased Wilson's remix of "Sound of Silence." Simon said that he was "horrified" when he first heard Wilson's remix of the song, but that remix reached #1 in January 1966, and a reunited Simon & Garfunkel went on to become one of the biggest acts of the late sixties.

The Lovin' Spoonful and the Mamas & the Papas, two rock acts composed of former Village folkies, also racked up huge hits in the years after "Mr. Tambourine Man." Donovan, a Scottish balladeer who never shook his image as a Dylan acolyte, notched four top-10 hits, including the chart-topper "Sunshine Superman." The Turtles, a band who started out as Byrds imitators, took "Happy Together" to #1 in 1967. The psychedelic rock of the late sixties and the singer-songwriter pop of the early seventies were both direct outgrowths of folk-rock, and that whole story hinges on the Byrds.

The chaos of the psychedelic era had its own impact on the people who made "Mr. Tambourine Man." Producer Terry Melcher is now probably most famous as a footnote to a tragedy. Melcher is the man who decided not to offer Charles Manson a recording deal in 1969. In retaliation, Manson sent some of his followers to the house where Melcher had met with Manson. Manson's followers may have been under orders to murder Melcher and his actress girlfriend, Candice Bergen, but Melcher and Bergen were no longer living in that house, and so the Manson family butchered the five people they found in the house, including movie star Sharon Tate.

The story of the Byrds themselves isn't quite as dark, but it's not bright, either. After "Turn! Turn! Turn!" the Byrds never made it into the top 10 again. The rest of the band's tenure was messy. The Byrds experimented musically, veering off into psychedelia and then into country-rock. Those later records would prove nearly as influential as their folk-rock beginnings, but those records didn't sell as well. By 1967, the Byrds were bitter enough to release "So You Wanna Be a Rock 'n' Roll Star," a song that sneered at teen idols like the Monkees: "With your hair swing right and your pants too tight, it's gonna be all right." The song is full of the sound of screaming girls—a sound that, just a few years earlier, had helped motivate the Byrds to become a band in the first place.

Over the next few years, the Byrds clashed with one another relentlessly, and they fell apart in slow motion. Within three years, Gene Clark and David Crosby were out of the band. By 1970, everyone but McGuinn had left. The original Byrds reunited for one album in 1973, but they didn't get the reception that they wanted, and the band soon broke up for good.

Former Byrds David Crosby and Chris Hillman did well for themselves. After leaving the Byrds in 1968, Crosby went on to tremendous success with Crosby, Stills, Nash, and sometimes Young. Gram Parsons replaced Gene Clark on the great 1968 Byrds album *Sweetheart of the Rodeo*. Soon afterward, Parsons and Hillman left the Byrds and formed the Flying Burrito Brothers, the short-lived but massively influential country-rock band. The Flying Burrito Brothers included guitarist Bernie Leadon, who went on to cofound Eagles, arguably the most successful band of the seventies. In the eighties, Hillman became a country star with the Desert Rose Band.

The other Byrds had a harder time. Roger McGuinn's and Gene Clark's solo careers never took off. Both Gene Clark and Michael Clarke struggled with serious addiction problems. The Byrds reunited to play their Rock and Roll Hall of Fame induction in 1991. Later that year, Gene Clark was dead at age forty-six. Two years later, Michael

Clarke died at forty-seven. Crosby had serious addiction and health problems, too, but he survived them.

Bob Dylan's career took some dark turns, too—like the 1966 motorcycle crash that sent him into seclusion for a few years, when his career was at its peak. Dylan reemerged, and he's had plenty of artistic triumphs since then. But Dylan, unlike so many of his disciples and imitators, never made a #1 hit. Dylan got as high as #2 twice—with "Like a Rolling Stone" and with the playful 1966 drug song "Rainy Day Women #12 & 35." "Monday, Monday," a song from fellow folk-scene veterans the Mamas & the Papas, kept "Rainy Day Women" out of the #1 spot.

Bob Dylan's voice has appeared on only one #1 single: "We Are the World," the 1985 all-star charity sing-along credited to USA for Africa. Oddly enough, the exact same fate has befallen Bruce Spring-steen, maybe Dylan's greatest rock-star-poet successor. With 1984's "Dancing in the Dark," Springsteen reached #2 on the Hot 100. (In an echo of Dylan and "Mr. Tambourine Man," another artist has covered a Springsteen song and taken it to #1—Manfred Mann's Earth Band cover of "Blinded by the Light" went to the top in 1977.) And, yes, Springsteen sang on "We Are the World," too.

It goes to show: Pop charts don't measure the importance of an artist over time. *Billboard* success won't cement a legacy. Pop charts are all about timing—capturing the ear of the masses at the exact right moment. The Byrds did that. Their success didn't last long, but the Byrds still sent the Hot 100 spinning off in bold new directions.

CHAPTER 6

The Beach Boys–
"Good Vibrations"

Released October 10, 1966
Hit #1 December 10, 1966
One-week reign

F OR A FULL YEAR, THE AMERICAN EXECUTIVES AT CAPITOL
Records didn't think they needed the Beatles. Part of that was pure
blinkered obliviousness, the old story of a big company not realizing
what it had on its hands. But part of it was probably also hubris. Capitol
already thought it had the new sound of American pop music locked
up. After all, Capitol had the Beach Boys.

In the early sixties, the Beach Boys were a shimmering vision of
American prosperity: five bright, handsome, presentable young men
singing in pinched, nasal harmony about sun and surf and cars and
girls. The Beach Boys had taken their inspiration from what was already
becoming classic American rock 'n' roll. For their breakthrough single,
the 1963 #3 hit "Surfin' USA," bandleader Brian Wilson had swiped
the melody from "Sweet Little Sixteen," a Chuck Berry song from
five years earlier. (Berry's publisher quickly sued, and the Beach Boys
awarded Berry a songwriting credit.)

But Brian Wilson was also besotted with the prim, sterile, extremely white vocal layering of the Four Freshmen, a vocal group popular in the pre–rock 'n' roll era. With their glee-club harmonies, the Beach Boys presented an overwhelmingly white version of rock 'n' roll, which, just a few years earlier, had been a predominantly Black art form. On their earliest records, the Beach Boys used the speed and excitement of early rock 'n' roll to present an idyllic, dreamlike take on teenage life in the Californian promised land. In the years ahead, though, Brian Wilson would push the group into wilder, more expressive territory.

The Beach Boys were a family band. Growing up in the Los Angeles suburb of Hawthorne, Brian Wilson had learned to sing with his younger brothers, Dennis and Carl. Their overbearing father, Murry, was a machine-shop owner who'd been through a bitter experience as a failed pop songwriter. Brian was a tall, good-looking, athletic kid who played quarterback on his high school's football team, but he was also sensitive and shy. His father berated him and ground him down. As a young child, Brian went mostly deaf in one ear, and he blamed his father, thinking that his condition might've been caused by being hit as a small child. Regardless of the cause, Brian Wilson would never be able to hear again in stereo.

But Brian remained fascinated with music, excelling at piano as a kid and singing in harmony with his brothers and his cousin Mike Love at family functions. In 1961, Love and the three Wilson brothers sang in public for the first time, at a high school talent show. At the time, Brian was already in junior college, studying psychology, but he still came back to his old high school. To coax the shy and reluctant Carl to take part, the quartet called themselves Carl and the Passions.

In college, Brian became close friends with Alan Jardine, a former high school classmate who was trying to make it as a folk songwriter. Jardine suggested that he and Brian start a singing group, and an enthusiastic Brian agreed, recruiting his brothers and his cousin. Calling themselves the Pendletones, the new group auditioned for music publishers Hite and Dorinda Morgan, a married couple who had published a couple of Murry Wilson's songs in the fifties. Dennis, the mischievous and energetic middle brother of the Wilson family, had enthusiastically taken up surfing, and he loved the growing culture around the Southern California beaches. In the audition for the Morgans, Dennis mentioned that the group had started to write "Surfin'," a song about the craze, and the Morgans were interested to hear it. The boys spent some grocery money on rented instruments, and they quickly finished the song.

Surfers had their own music: fast and reverb-heavy instrumental rock 'n' roll from groups like the Ventures and Dick Dale and the Del-Tones. On "Surfin'," the young group took that sound and added tight harmonies that drew on both doo-wop and barbershop. Brian Wilson wasn't a surfer, but he and Mike Love still wrote lyrics about the joys of the ocean: "Surfin' is the only life, the only life for me." The Morgans liked the boys' song, and they took it to the local indie Candix Records. The label changed the group's name to the Beach Boys to better capitalize on the surfing trend. "Surfin'" came out in November 1961 and became a hit, first locally and then nationally, where it reached a peak of #75.

Murry Wilson, ecstatic over the Boys' success, took over as their manager and sold them relentlessly, getting them a contract at Capitol. Al Jardine, disappointed over the unimpressive royalties that the Beach Boys had earned from "Surfin'," left the group to finish dental school, and Murry recruited a replacement: David Marks, a thirteen-year-old kid who lived across the street. Marks couldn't sing as well as the others, but the inclusion of an actual child helped the group's wholesome image. A year later, when Jardine decided that he was interested in becoming a Beach Boy again, Murry pushed Marks out. (Marks went on to become a session guitarist, and he rejoined a couple of different Beach Boys lineups over the years.)

Once the Beach Boys were on Capitol, Murry relentlessly criticized the group's work and pressured them to record the songs he'd written. He also pushed them to record more, and faster. The Beach

Boys struggled with Murry's domineering management; after one bad fight, for instance, Murry temporarily kicked Dennis Wilson out of the family home. But partly because of Murry's disciplinarian approach, the Beach Boys quickly became a hit machine, cranking out single after single and selling the Californian dream of beaches and waves. Early on, most of their songs were about surfing: "Surfin' Safari," "Surfin' USA," the ballad "Surfer Girl." They also started writing about fast cars: "409," "Little Deuce Coupe." Brian Wilson, who quickly took over as the group's lead songwriter and producer, would add his own sound effects, lugging his tape recorder out into the world to capture the crash of waves or the revving of engines.

The surf sound came easy to Brian, and it took on a resonance that went way beyond California. On a song like "Surfin' USA," Brian imagined a utopian America where everybody had an ocean, and he sold an idealized sense of high school glamour. Imitators sprang up, and other groups had hits with the surf sound. Brian gave an unfinished tune called "Surf City" to Jan and Dean, a duo who'd been around before the Beach Boys and who sang in a similar sort of crystalline harmony. In the summer of 1963, Jan and Dean's "Surf City" became Brian's first #1 single, and Murry Wilson was furious that Brian had given what could've been the Beach Boys' first chart-topper away to another group. (Two years later, Jan and Dean's Dean Torrence joined Brian to sing lead on "Barbara Ann," the Beach Boys' cover of the Regents' 1961 doo-wop hit. The Beach Boys' version of the song peaked at #2.)

Brian Wilson didn't really indulge in the Californian life that he wrote about. Instead, he was a withdrawn, fragile young man who didn't know how to surf and never bothered to learn. Slowly, Brian found ways to work his personality into his music. "In My Room," which peaked at #23 in 1963, is a beatific ode to solitude. A year later, the group made it to #9 with "When I Grow Up (to Be a Man)," a song about the anxieties of aging beyond teenage life. Certain lyrics from hits like "Surfer Girl" and "Don't Worry Baby" gestured at frustration and insecurity, but they did so within the context of the Beach

Boys' shimmering, idealized sunshine pop. That slight hint of melancholy added a subtle depth to the Beach Boys' singles, but the group's public image never reflected it. Instead, they posed for album covers with surfboards and striped shirts and mile-wide smiles. They sold the image.

When the Beatles arrived in America in February 1964, the Beach Boys quickly recognized their new Capitol labelmates as an existential threat. The Beach Boys had been Capitol's hottest young act, but they'd never gotten the kind of promotional push that the label gave to the newly arriving Beatles. In February 1965, the Beach Boys released their single "Fun, Fun, Fun," and it reached #5, but it would've presumably done better if it hadn't come out the same day that "I Want to Hold Your Hand" first reached #1. Later in 1964, the year of rampant Beatlemania, the Beach Boys ascended to #1 for the first time with "I Get Around." But Brian Wilson could tell that the Beatles were eclipsing his group, and he struggled to respond. He stopped writing songs about surfing.

In December 1964, during a flight to a show in Houston, Brian suffered a debilitating panic attack and barely made it to the stage. Soon afterward, he told the rest of the band that he wouldn't and couldn't perform anymore. Instead, he would stay at home in Los Angeles and work on records while the other Beach Boys took those records on the road. At first, the Beach Boys replaced Brian with Wrecking Crew session guitarist and future solo star Glen Campbell before bringing in Bruce Johnston, who'd been in the surf-pop soundalikes the Rip Chords with Byrds producer Terry Melcher, as a permanent new member.

Brian was more at home in the studio anyway. Early on, Brian used his considerable sway to move the Beach Boys recording sessions out of the Capitol studios, which he didn't like. Instead, in an unusual arrangement, Brian preferred to record in a series of more expensive outside studios. The Beach Boys played their own instruments in concert, but on records, Brian preferred to use the members of the Wrecking Crew, including many of the same musicians who'd played on the Byrds' "Mr. Tambourine Man."

Brian was a huge admirer of Phil Spector, the domineering pop producer who had figured out how to, in Brian's words, "play the studio." In the early years of rock 'n' roll, singers and bands had to record in the same room at the same time, and technology didn't allow for much sonic experimentation. But as technology improved, some producers figured out new ways to play around with sound. In 1962, for example, British pop mastermind Joe Meek used electronic hums and echoes on "Telstar," a sci-fi-influenced rock 'n' roll instrumental credited to the Tornados. "Telstar" made it to #1 in both the United Kingdom and the United States, and it pulled off that feat during the pre-Beatles era when American charts acknowledged few British artists. But even more than Meek, it was Phil Spector who discovered ways to use new studio techniques to enhance the pure sound of pop production.

Spector would use vast ensembles of Wrecking Crew studio musicians, creating orchestral effects with reverb and echo, compulsively fussing with his layers of sound. He'd record singers and instrumentalists separately, dubbing the vocals over the music in ways that wouldn't have been possible a few years earlier. Brian would listen obsessively to Spector-produced singles like the Ronettes' "Be My Baby," a #2 hit in 1963. For a while, Spector let Brian sit in on his recording sessions, though he played mind games with the young man—inviting him to play piano on one single, then rescinding the invitation. After quitting the road, Brian worked obsessively to create his own version of Spector's sound, using the musicians from Spector's stable to achieve it.

For reasons that are virtually impossible to understand, the main forces behind that kind of experimental pop production often turned out to be mentally unwell. Joe Meek suffered from bipolar disorder and schizophrenia, as well as the mental strain of living as a closeted gay man in the early sixties. In 1967, Meek murdered his landlady with a shotgun and then turned it on himself and committed suicide. Phil Spector, meanwhile, also had bipolar disorder, and he was a notoriously nasty and combative figure even at the peak of his fame. Spector repeatedly threatened to kill his second wife, Ronettes lead singer Ronnie Spector, and he later became notorious for pulling guns on collaborators like John Lennon, Leonard Cohen, Blondie, and the Ramones. In 2003, Spector murdered Lana Clarkson, an actress he'd met earlier that night, with a revolver. He died of COVID-19 in prison in 2021. Brian Wilson never shot anyone, but his own mental health problems got worse even as his production became more adventurous.

With Brian working in the studio, the Beach Boys' records became increasingly ornate and introspective. Brian started to record with strings, harpsichords, and sleigh bells. In Los Angeles, Brian, never much of a bohemian, met glamorous new people in the Hollywood record business, and he started smoking weed and dropping acid. (The other Beach Boys, spending most of their time on tour, remained ignorant of California's growing drug culture, though Dennis Wilson certainly took to it quickly enough.) During the tense process of recording 1965's "Help Me, Rhonda," the song that would become the Beach Boys' second #1 hit, Brian fired Murry as the band's manager. Meanwhile, the Beach Boys hired former Beatles publicist Derek Taylor, who also worked with the Byrds and consistently pushed the narrative that Brian Wilson was a musical genius.

When the Beatles released 1965's *Rubber Soul*—an album partially inspired by both Motown and the Byrds—Brian felt a new sense of pressure. Before *Rubber Soul*, Brian had mostly seen the Beatles as commercial competitors, not artistic equals; he preferred the ornate thump of Phil Spector's productions. *Rubber Soul* changed that. In his 2016 memoir, *I Am Brian Wilson*, Brian wrote, "*Rubber Soul* came out in December of 1965 and sent me right to the piano bench. It's a whole album of Beatles folk songs, a whole album where everything flows together and everything works." Brian had to see if he could make something that good—something better, even.

Brian spent $70,000 of Capitol's money recording 1966's *Pet Sounds*. None of the Beach Boys played instruments on *Pet Sounds*.

Instead, Brian found new ways to layer sounds and melodies, building new arrangements and chord structures. The members of the Wrecking Crew, arriving in the studio, would be shocked to learn that Brian wanted them all to play in different keys. Working with lyricist Tony Asher, Brian wrote *Pet Sounds* as a lush, sweeping, melancholy song cycle about longing and isolation. The album still used the Beach Boys' high, pristine harmonies, but it sounded nothing like the surf-pop that made them famous. Capitol executives were nervous, and so were Brian's Beach Boys bandmates, but Brian was convinced that he'd made his masterpiece.

Today, critical consensus sides with Brian Wilson. At the time, though, *Pet Sounds* was considered an indulgent commercial disappointment. Two months after *Pet Sounds* came out, Capitol released a Beach Boys greatest-hits collection that outsold *Pet Sounds*. Two of the singles from *Pet Sounds* made the top 10: the Beach Boys' baroque take on the folk traditional "Sloop John B," which reached #3, and the extravagantly melancholy "Wouldn't It Be Nice," which peaked at #8. But the album simply didn't make the impact that Brian had wanted so badly. To Brian's bandmates and label, *Pet Sounds* was proof that Brian was losing touch—that the public just wanted to hear Beach Boys songs about being boys at the beach.

Overseas, *Pet Sounds* sold well, thanks in part to critical raves and to the enthusiasm of the Beatles. Paul McCartney and John Lennon both attended a *Pet Sounds* listening party staged for the British press. At the event, McCartney immediately said that "God Only Knows," a single that peaked at #39 in the United States, was the greatest song ever written. After the party, Lennon and McCartney immediately returned to the studio to keep working on their album *Revolver*—a true vote of confidence from Brian Wilson's peers and competitors. With the clash between the acclaim for *Pet Sounds* and the album's American sales, Brian had something to prove. "Good Vibrations" became his focus.

Brian had already been working on "Good Vibrations" for months. He'd been drawn to the idea of extrasensory perception. In *I Am Brian*

Wilson, Brian writes, "I was thinking of how people sense instinctively if something is good news or bad news—sometimes when the telephone rings, you just know—and I was thinking of how my mom used to say that dogs could read a situation or person immediately." Brian found that concept both terrifying and alluring. The song didn't have lyrics yet, but Brian was consumed with capturing that *idea*, sonically.

Working on "Good Vibrations," Brian wrote fragments of music and recorded them at different studios, with different groups of musicians. He added more and more sounds and ideas: flute, clarinet, bongo drums, jaw harp. For stretches of the song, the rhythm section is nothing but cellos sawing away. Paul Tanner, a professor and session trombonist who'd played in the Glenn Miller Orchestra, came in to play the Electro-Theremin, an instrument that he'd invented. The Electro-Theremin produced a high, eerie, otherworldly whine. Tanner had played it on things like the score for the sitcom *My Favorite Martian*, but nobody had ever used the instrument on a pop song. For Brian, that sound was simply part of the sonic landscape of "Good Vibrations."

In an era when pop acts were expected to crank out multiple singles in marathon studio sessions, Brian Wilson couldn't stop working on "Good Vibrations." Wilson tinkered and rewrote and recorded new parts in four different studios. Some days, Brian would walk into a session, decide that the feeling wasn't right, and cancel immediately. In his book, Brian writes, "I didn't know what I was in for. I didn't know until I got into it, and then I got so far into it that I got lost in it. There are more than 80 hours of tape if you add up all the parts and all the takes. And I didn't even play on the tracks. I sang. I directed. I wrote. I produced. The whole thing took about seven months, and the cost was gigantic, more than $50,000. At the time, a Cadillac DeVille cost around $5,000." In its day, "Good Vibrations" was the most expensive single ever made.

"Good Vibrations" is not a verse-chorus-verse pop song. Instead, Brian structured the track as a series of mini-suites that he called "modules." Splicing together tapes of different sessions, Brian edited all the music that he'd recorded into one three-and-a-half-minute song. Talking to *Rolling Stone* years later, Brian said, "I saw it as a totality piece." But Brian's bandmates weren't sure about the totality. While the other Beach Boys were in Fargo for a show, Brian called his younger brother Carl and played him the edited-together instrumental over the phone. Later, Carl remembered that phone call, describing what he'd heard as "this really bizarre-sounding music . . . A real funky track."

But "Good Vibrations" wasn't a case of one lone genius taking on the world. Later, Brian credited Carl with suggesting the use of cellos on "Good Vibrations." And Mike Love, generally remembered as the Beach Boy most opposed to Brian's far-out ideas, wrote the "Good Vibrations" lyrics, coming up with most of them while driving to the studio to record the song's vocals. In his book, Brian writes that Love "went from room to room talking out the idea of good vibrations— what it meant, that it was connected to the peace and love happening in San Francisco and everywhere else." (A year later, Love, along with the Beatles, would begin studying transcendental meditation under Maharishi Mahesh Yogi.)

Love wrote the "Good Vibrations" lyrics in a hurry, not over the course of months of studio experimentation, but those lyrics are still key to the power of "Good Vibrations." So is Carl's warm, tremulous lead vocal. "Good Vibrations" is a song exploding with ideas, but it still works as pop music, as a Beach Boys song about a crush on a girl. Carl delivers the opening line in a choirboy sigh: "I, I love the colorful clothes she wears / And the way the sunlight plays upon her hair." Later, Carl sings that when he looks in her eyes, she goes with him to a blossom world. Other than that, though, "Good Vibrations" is a song light on psychedelic imagery. From a certain perspective, all of Brian Wilson's elaborate orchestration could be an attempt to mimic the excitement and vulnerability of a crush's early stages. Mike Love's lyrics aren't exactly great literature, but they give tangible stakes to the song's astral drift.

"Good Vibrations," then, is not merely Brian Wilson's psychedelic masterpiece. It has at least a few things that were perfectly calibrated toward the 1966 pop marketplace. Like many other Beach Boys songs, "Good Vibrations" has a massive chorus. Even though the song ventures far afield, the chorus always comes back, and everything always seems to snap back into focus when it returns. The song is a balancing act, and that big central hook helps all the sonic experimentation work as well as it does.

Still, "Good Vibrations" worked as proof that Brian Wilson's wildest ideas could grab the mass imagination. Upon its release, "Good Vibrations" sold hundreds of thousands of copies in the first few days, and it quickly became the biggest-selling single of the Beach Boys' career. The song set new benchmarks for playful ambition in American pop music—for producers who used the studio as a site of experimentation, or as an instrument itself. If a song like "Good Vibrations" could go to #1, then nobody else had any excuse for holding back.

"Good Vibrations" came about, at least in part, because Brian Wilson wanted to make pop music as grand and ambitious as what the Beatles were doing. Brian's innovations pushed the Beatles to continually reinvent their own sound, as well. In 1966, while Brian Wilson was working on "Good Vibrations," the Beatles, like Brian before them, decided to stop touring, to devote themselves to working as a full-time studio act instead. The Beatles came out with *Sgt. Pepper's Lonely Hearts Club Band* in 1967, and their producer, George Martin, later claimed that the Beatles' opus "was an attempt to equal *Pet Sounds.* . . . Brian confirmed it. We really could do what we liked, and that was liberating." The success of "Good Vibrations," then, helped spur on a tremendously exciting late-sixties arms race, with the Beatles, the Rolling Stones, and the artists at Motown, among others, rearranging the sound of pop music.

In March 1967, three months after "Good Vibrations" topped the Hot 100, the Beatles returned to #1 with "Penny Lane," a similarly bright and daring work of orchestral pop; Paul McCartney modeled its sound, at least in part, on that of *Pet Sounds*. The Turtles' "Happy Together," another dizzily layered single, replaced "Penny Lane" at #1. Within a year, psychedelic imagery was appearing in even the silliest hits—proto-bubblegum chart-toppers like the Strawberry Alarm Clock's "Incense and Peppermints" or the Lemon Pipers' "Green Tambourine."

A few years after the Beach Boys, the starry-eyed and multiracial San Francisco group known as Sly and the Family Stone went through a similar evolution. Like Brian Wilson, Family Stone leader Sly Stone was a troubled sonic traveler who led a band partly composed of his family members. Like the Beach Boys, the Family Stone started out making good-time Californian pop music, and they landed on the charts with party songs like "Dance to the Music" and the 1968 chart-topper "Everyday People." Later, Sly Stone, affected by drugs and mental illness, alienated his bandmates while creating rich, experimental studio masterworks. As successful as those experimental records were, Sly Stone eventually disappeared into drug-fueled seclusion.

Sly Stone was part of a new generation of studio wizards who took over R&B in the late sixties and early seventies. Temptations producer Norman Whitfield found great success with what he called psychedelic soul—squelching wah-wah guitars, pulsing bass, cascading layers of sound. Marvin Gaye and Isaac Hayes worked with orchestral arrangements, fuzzed-out guitars, and cutting-edge electronics. In the early seventies, new multitrack recording techniques made it possible for people like Paul McCartney and Stevie Wonder, Motown's former child star, to play every instrument on their albums themselves. That allowed Wonder, in particular, to take complete artistic control of his music and to enter his greatest period of productivity and popularity.

Looking back, "Good Vibrations" stands out as a psychedelic turning point—the moment where the pop charts opened up and allowed
a certain level of freakiness in. These new sounds—wilder, freer, more
lyrically obtuse—were part of a generational shift. The music resonated with emerging cultures around drugs and protest. But if this was
rebellion, it was rebellion that could be sold. Some record-label execs,
like Motown's Berry Gordy, resisted pop music's shift toward free-form
wooziness, but they still profited mightily from it. New pop figures like
the Doors' Jim Morrison had their own sense of glamour, which fitted just fine with established Hollywood structures. The psychedelic
era didn't collapse the pop order, but it did represent an exciting new
mutation of it.

The Beach Boys did not capitalize on this new moment that they'd
helped usher in. Brian Wilson had big plans to follow *Pet Sounds* and
"Good Vibrations" with *Smile*, an album that he called his "teenage
symphony to God." But Wilson had become increasingly withdrawn
and paranoid. Drugs played a role, and so did mental health problems. Wilson's bandmates lost faith in him, and so did his label. Mike
Love objected to the surreal imagery in the lyrics that Van Dyke Parks,
Brian's newest collaborator, had written. After the "Good Vibrations"
follow-up "Heroes and Villains" stalled at #12, Capitol abandoned
its plans for *Smile*, and the album went unfinished. The Beach Boys
released parts of it on an album called *Smiley Smile*, which came and
went quickly. (Decades later, Brian Wilson went back and rerecorded
a finished version of *Smile*, releasing it as a solo album in 2004.)

At the last minute, the Beach Boys also backed out of plans to
headline the Monterey International Pop Festival, one of the most
important rock events of the late sixties. The Beach Boys were widely
mocked and derided for their decision. From the stage, Jimi Hen-
drix told the Monterey crowd that they'd "heard the last of the surfing
music."

Instead of riding this new wave that they'd helped start, the Beach
Boys played a role in the darkest moment of the psychedelic era. One

night in 1968, Dennis Wilson picked up two girls who were hitchhiking. He took both of them to his house, showed them his gold records,
and had sex with them. Those two girls later introduced Dennis to
Charles Manson, and Dennis fell in with Manson and his cult, taking
part in their orgies and letting them move into his house. Dennis was
also impressed with the songs that Manson had written. Dennis tried
to help Manson land a record deal, and Brian and Carl Wilson coproduced some demos for Manson. The Beach Boys even recorded one of
Manson's songs, "Cease to Exist," retitled "Never Learn Not to Love,"
releasing it as a B-side, though Dennis took songwriting credit.

It was after Dennis's friend Terry Melcher opted not to sign Manson to a recording contract that Manson sent members of his cult—
including Patricia Krenwinkel, one of the girls whom Dennis had
picked up hitchhiking the previous year—to the house where Melcher
had previously been living, and Manson's followers massacred five people that night and two more the next night. After the murders, Manson
himself showed up at Dennis's house, demanding money, and Dennis
gave it to him. (Manson and his Family weren't arrested until months
later.) Dennis's behavior grew increasingly erratic in the years afterward. In 1983, an extremely drunk Dennis went diving in a Pacific
Ocean marina, looking for things his ex-wife had thrown off their yacht
years earlier. He drowned at the age of thirty-nine.

By the time Dennis died, the Beach Boys had long since lost rel-
evance as a pop act. In the years after "Good Vibrations," the group
increasingly sidelined Brian Wilson, who went into seclusion and
was eventually institutionalized. An opportunistic psychiatrist named
Dr. Eugene Landy took complete control of Brian's life for years.
Mike Love took over leadership of the Beach Boys and essentially
remade them as an oldies act. In the twenty years after "Good Vibrations," the Beach Boys made the top 10 only once more: a 1976 cover
of Chuck Berry's "Rock and Roll Music," which peaked at #5. The
Beach Boys remained a lucrative touring act, and they scored one
more fluke hit in 1988, when "Kokomo," a song that they recorded

for the soundtrack of the Tom Cruise vehicle *Cocktail*, took them all the way back to #1. Brian Wilson was not involved in the whole "Kokomo" enterprise, and the Beach Boys never recorded another significant hit afterward.

Carl Wilson died of lung cancer in 1998. Mike Love kept the Beach Boys going as a touring institution, and he was usually the sole original member involved. He filed multiple lawsuits against ex-bandmates Brian Wilson and Al Jardine. In 2010, Brian Wilson, Al Jardine, and early-sixties Beach Boy David Marks rejoined Mike Love and Bruce Johnston for a fiftieth-anniversary tour and album. But once the tour wrapped up, Mike Love kept going without them. Love claimed that he hadn't fired Brian Wilson; Brian wrote that it felt like being fired.

The Beach Boys' legacy is a messy and sordid one, and there have been many arguments, legally and otherwise, over who deserves credit for what. But none of that can dim the luster of "Good Vibrations," an elaborate head rush of a song. With that song, the Beach Boys made a miracle. For years afterward, even as the Beach Boys themselves fell out of the race, the world scrambled to catch up.

CHAPTER 7

George McCrae–
"Rock Your Baby"

Released April 1974
Hit #1 July 13, 1974
Two-week reign

DISCO HAD A WILD RIDE. AT THE BEGINNING OF THE SEVENTIES, disco wasn't even a genre. Instead, it was a loose underground network of clubs and parties in New York—rooms where people, mostly Black and gay, would dance all night to anything with the right kind of beat. By the end of the decade, disco was a pop-culture phenomenon that had hit its sell-by date and become a loaded punch line, and former hitmaking monsters like the Bee Gees and Chic watched as their records failed to chart at all. In between, disco absolutely dominated the Hot 100 for a few years, upending the pop-music ecosystem and introducing new approaches that would reverberate down through the decades.

In the beginning, disco was a tiny phenomenon, one that existed almost entirely outside of pop music. In early-seventies New York, gay bars were functionally illegal. In 1969, a police raid of the Stonewall Inn spurred on the nascent gay-liberation movement, but the laws against gay bars remained. Gay clubs, banned from serving alcohol, went private, becoming semiclandestine invite-only affairs. Instead of serving drinks, those clubs brought in money by charging membership fees, and they attracted crowds by hiring DJs. Some of those DJs— people like David Mancuso, Francis Gallo, Nicky Siano, and David Rodriguez—took pride in their ability to find exciting records and to take dancers on emotional journeys.

Those club DJs found that certain sounds worked best. In particular, rhythmic and orchestral R&B music—like the sophisticated and luxurious soul music coming out of Kenny Gamble and Leon Huff's Philadelphia International label—could trigger moments of mass dance-floor euphoria. A textured, panoramic soul record like "Girl, You Need a Change of Mind," a 1972 solo single from former Temptations singer Eddie Kendricks, barely made a dent on the pop charts, peaking at #87, but it was a smash in the clubs. As club culture spread from New York to other cities, radio programmers and record buyers started to pick up on some of those records. In 1973, Kendricks made it all the way to #1 with the thumping, strutting eight-minute track "Keep on Truckin'."

Eddie Kendricks was not making records for nightclubs. Instead, he was doing his best to make wide-appeal pop music. Kendricks himself once said that he knew "Keep on Truckin'" would be a hit because "the trucking industry would support the record." The seventies fascination with truckers and CB radios really did drive hits, like C. W. McCall's 1975 country-novelty smash "Convoy," but that's not why "Keep on Truckin'" hit #1. In Tim Lawrence's great disco history *Love Saves the Day*, Kendricks's producer Frank Wilson says, "When I began hearing reports about what was happening with the record in the New York disco clubs, I was shocked. That was not what we were going for. We were after radio."

In 1973, the deep-voiced Texan producer Barry White recorded "Love's Theme," a lush and symphonic instrumental that was credited to the Love Unlimited Orchestra. The song went nowhere at first, but New York disco DJs started playing it, and promotional people at

White's 20th Century label noticed. The label started handing out free copies of "Love's Theme" to more and more DJs, and those DJs played it. Radio programmers in New York caught on and added "Love's Theme" to rotation. "Love's Theme" became a snowballing hit, reaching #1 in February 1974.

A few months later, another accidental disco hit topped the Hot 100. In Los Angeles, songwriter Wally Holmes had put together the vocal trio known as the Hues Corporation as a vehicle for his own tracks. Holmes figured, best-case scenario, a bright and friendly and up-tempo Fifth Dimension–style R&B group could potentially become a lucrative Las Vegas act. The Hues Corporation's excellently titled 1973 album, *Freedom for the Stallion*, didn't leave much of an impression, and its title track topped out at #63 on the Hot 100. But disco DJs discovered "Rock the Boat," a percolating deep cut from the album. Holmes himself admitted that "Rock the Boat" was "an afterthought" and that he hadn't even thought about releasing it as a single. But when RCA realized that "Rock the Boat" was resonating in clubs, the label released a remixed version of the song, boosting the bass and drums so that they'd sound better on club speakers. The tactic worked. In July, "Rock the Boat" reached #1. Down in Florida, Henry Wayne Casey and Richard Finch were watching.

Casey and Finch were two white kids who grew up in South Florida and loved R&B music. As teenagers, they would hang around the studios of TK Records, an R&B indie label based in Hialeah, just outside Miami. TK was a relatively new operation. One of its two cofounders was Steve Alaimo, a former singer who'd been a moderately successful teen idol in the early-sixties *American Bandstand* era. The other, Henry Stone, was a veteran R&B promoter and producer who'd recorded some of the earliest music from Ray Charles and James Brown, as well as Hank Ballard and the Midnighters' original version of "The Twist." Stone and Alaimo launched TK Records in 1972, and they almost immediately found success with "Why Can't We Live Together," a single from Miami-based soul singer and keyboardist Timmy Thomas.

"Why Can't We Live Together," which Thomas wrote, is a stark, wounded plea for peace, a classic protest song of the civil rights and Vietnam era. Thomas found a clear inspiration in Marvin Gaye's sweeping 1971 anthem "What's Going On," but "Why Can't We Live Together" is a lot chillier and more minimal than anything Motown would've ever even considered releasing. Thomas recorded the entire thing himself, and the only sounds on the single are his voice, an organ, and a primitive drum machine.

Thomas recorded "Why Can't We Live Together" on a Lowrey organ, an elaborate keyboard that sounded thinner than the industry-standard Hammond B-3. (It was also a lot less expensive than the Hammond.) The Lowrey came with a series of preset electronic drum tracks—clicking loops that sounded cold and alien when compared with what flesh-and-blood drummers could do. A lot of Lowrey players probably used those drum presets as metronomes, but Thomas built the entire song on its built-in beat, and the hollowed-out emptiness of that drum loop makes Thomas sound more and more desperate and fervent. At the end of the song, an eruption of clicks mimics the sound of gunfire. "Why Can't We Live Together" struck a chord, topping the R&B charts and reaching #3 on the Hot 100 early in 1973. That hit helped TK Records become an independent commercial powerhouse. Decades later, Drake sampled the skeletal drum loop and the organ blurts from "Why Can't We Live Together" on "Hotline Bling," a 2016 single that reached #2.

Drum machines were still a strange new novelty in the late sixties and early seventies. In 1968, during the brief period when folk-rock hitmakers the Bee Gees were broken up, Robin Gibb used a drum machine on "Saved by the Bell," a ballad that reached #2 on the UK charts. Sly and the Family Stone also used one on much of their classic 1971 album *There's a Riot Goin' On*, including on the #1 hit "Family Affair." That machine's rigorous and unchanging beat is part of what makes the album sound so strange and messy. In disco, a genre that used a steady rhythmic pulse to keep dancers moving, the drum machine would prove massively important. Henry Wayne Casey and Richard Finch figured that out early.

As teenagers, Casey and Finch were both low-level staffers at the TK studios. Casey worked for free, answering phones and pulling records from the distributor warehouse. Finch was a part-time recording engineer. Casey had been to a wedding at TK star Betty Wright's house, and he'd fallen in love with what he'd heard there: Junkanoo, a Bahamian genre of party music. In 1973, Casey and Finch started KC and the Junkanoo Sunshine Band. (Casey was KC.) For a while, Casey and Finch were the only two members. Eventually, they put together a full band lineup, mostly using the Black studio musicians who played on TK's records. Before long, Casey and Finch dropped the word "Junkanoo" from the group's name, and the newly rechristened KC and the Sunshine Band released their debut single, a giddy party-funk record called "Blow Your Whistle," on TK. The single did pretty well on the R&B charts, but it didn't cross over to the Hot 100.

In the early seventies, Miami had a thriving disco scene. Gay clubs in Miami weren't subjected to the same police harassment as the ones in New York, and dance floors flourished. Casey and Finch were too young to get into those clubs; Finch was still in high school. But some establishments wouldn't check IDs, and Casey and Finch would hit those clubs, taking note of which sorts of sounds were moving dancers. Both of them had noticed that up-tempo R&B records were doing well in the clubs and on the charts, and they paid close attention as "Rock the Boat" scaled the Hot 100.

Inspired by what they heard in those clubs, Casey and Finch wrote a sparse but slinky R&B song called "Rock Your Baby." Timmy Thomas had left his Lowrey organ at the TK studios, and that's the instrument that Casey and Finch used to write "Rock Your Baby." Casey programmed in a samba beat, and then Finch played drums along to that beat. "Rock Your Baby" is about sex, not about violence, but it has the same kind of otherworldly empty-space minimalism as "Why Can't We Live Together." Two of the first big hits to use drum machines, it turns out, probably used the exact same drum machine.

Thanks to that samba preset, "Rock Your Baby" doesn't have the same four-four pulse as most of the disco hits that would come later, but it does have the mechanical insistence that would become key to the genre's appeal. Casey and Finch worked in a small studio with only a few instruments, but they still managed to conjure some of the layered splendor that disco fans associated with Philadelphia International Records and Barry White. Casey played smooth, pillowy melodies on that Lowrey organ, while session guitarist Jerome Smith, who would soon become a member of the Sunshine Band, added a tricky, jittery groove. Smith got paid fifteen dollars for playing on "Rock Your Baby."

Casey was already singing with the Sunshine Band, but he knew he was a limited vocalist and that the song needed a singer who could work in a higher register. When Casey and Finch finished recording their demo, they played it for TK Records boss Henry Stone. At the time, Stone was recording some songs with a Miami singer named Gwen McRae, who'd made a few minor R&B hits. McRae's husband, George, was a singer himself. When Henry Stone heard the demo, George happened to be at the studio to pick Gwen up.

George McRae, the son of a police officer, came from West Palm Beach, and he'd been singing for years, though his career had never taken off. In the early sixties, before he joined the navy, George led a local group called the Jivin' Jets. George married Gwen in 1963, the same year he enlisted. After his discharge, George found work singing in lounges and nightclubs, and George and Gwen recorded a few songs together. Betty Wright helped get Gwen signed to TK, and George added occasional backing vocals to her records. By the time he recorded "Rock Your Baby," George was studying law enforcement at college and managing Gwen's career. He was in his thirties, and his career was mostly over.

Henry Stone had heard George McRae singing backup on a few records, and he knew that George had a high singing voice, and so Casey and Finch spent about an hour recording George singing "Rock Your Baby." George delivered Casey's simple, repetitive "Rock Your Baby" lyrics in a feathery falsetto, making the robotically insistent track sound loose and seductive. McRae's raspy coo showed the clear influence of Al Green, who was near the peak of his career at that point. ("Let's Stay Together," Al Green's sole Hot 100 chart-topper, had hit #1 in 1972.) McRae didn't have the same easy, charismatic presence as Green, and he sounded a little more anonymous. But in club-friendly R&B, sounding anonymous wasn't really a problem. The emphasis was on the beat, not on the lyrics or the voice. McRae was smooth and tender and euphoric, and his voice was exactly what the song needed.

"Rock Your Baby" was the song that knocked the Hues Corporation's "Rock the Boat" out of the #1 spot, and there's something deliciously poetic about disco, a genre that seventies rock fans would come to despise, having its big pop-chart takeover moment with two consecutive hits that had the word "rock" in their titles. "Rock the Boat," like "Keep on Truckin'" and "Love's Theme" before it, was an accidental disco hit. McRae's "Rock Your Baby" intentionally imitated "Rock the Boat," but the song was a different beast. McRae's song was the first crossover hit written and recorded with club DJs in mind. It's the first truly intentional disco hit.

Henry Stone called himself "the king of payola," but he later wrote, in a self-published book called *The Stone-Cold Truth on Payola*, that "no payola was involved in this record at all. . . . I didn't need to promote it. They came to me, everybody came to me." Stone made sure club DJs got copies of "Rock Your Baby," and radio picked up on the song soon afterward. As the song took off in the United States, Stone quickly made international deals to distribute "Rock Your Baby." The single also went to #1 in the United Kingdom, Canada, Germany, and all around Europe. Stone later bragged that "Rock

Your Baby" cost him only the fifteen dollars that he had to pay to guitarist Jerome Smith.

Henry Stone also avoided handing out much money even after "Rock Your Baby" topped the Hot 100. Fredric Dannen's book *Hit Men* includes an anonymous story about Stone. McCrae hadn't seen any money from "Rock Your Baby," and he didn't have enough to pay his rent. McCrae came to threaten Stone over money. Stone handed McCrae a wad of bills and the keys for a Cadillac that was sitting in the parking lot. Stone didn't mention that the Cadillac was rented.

By the end of 1974, *Billboard* launched a new chart to keep track of which singles were getting play in clubs, and three more club hits made it to #1: Barry White's "Can't Get Enough of Your Love, Babe," the Spinners and Dionne Warwick's "Then Came You," and British singer Carl Douglas's gloriously silly fluke "Kung Fu Fighting."

If the summer of 1974, with the one-two punch of "Rock the Boat" and "Rock Your Baby" was the beginning of the disco takeover, 1975 was really the year that disco broke through in a huge way. In 1975, club records crowded out the sincere, folky soft rock that otherwise dominated the charts in that era. Many of 1975's biggest hits were unashamedly silly novelties from acts that would quickly disappear: Van McCoy and the Soul City Orchestra's "The Hustle," Silver Convention's "Fly, Robin, Fly," Bazuka's "Dynomite." But that year, KC and the Sunshine Band matured into full-on stardom, cranking out a series of bone-shakingly simple party-starter songs. The Sunshine Band landed their first #1 hit with "Get Down Tonight" in August, and they returned to the top spot three months later with "That's the Way (I Like It)." By the time their run was over, the Sunshine Band had five #1 singles—or, if you count "Rock Your Baby," six.

Around the same time that KC and the Sunshine Band were exploding, another white Miami-based group turned toward disco and became the biggest stars of the era. The Bee Gees, three British brothers who'd been raised in Australia, sang eerie melodies in high, pinched harmonies. In the late sixties, the Bee Gees became massively successful with stately pop ballads that carried a clear Beatles influence. The early Bee Gees had their greatest success in the United Kingdom, but they made hits in America, as well. Their single "How Can You Mend a Broken Heart" topped the Hot 100 in 1971. By 1975, though, the Bee Gees were struggling. At the advice of their friend Eric Clapton, they relocated to Miami. Once settled in Florida, the Bee Gees began to embrace the sound of American soul music. In August, the thumping dance track "Jive Talkin'" became the Bee Gees' second American chart-topper.

The Bee Gees and the Sunshine Band insisted that they didn't make disco music, that their sound was just R&B. But both groups made sense in the context of disco. They both thrived on repetitive grooves and chest-puffed lyrical confidence. The Bee Gees, in particular, were made for that moment, especially when disco hit the movies. The group's manager, Robert Stigwood, optioned a *New York* article about the scene surrounding a Brooklyn club. The resulting film, *Saturday Night Fever*, featured young sitcom star John Travolta playing a peacocking disco dancer named Tony Manero. *Saturday Night Fever* came out at the end of 1977 and became a huge hit, grossing hundreds of millions and earning Travolta an Oscar nomination for best actor. Its soundtrack was even more of a blockbuster than the film itself.

For a few years, the *Saturday Night Fever* soundtrack album, which was dominated by Bee Gees tracks but also featured the Sunshine Band, was the best-selling album of all time. Thanks to that soundtrack, the Bee Gees lorded over the 1978 Hot 100 like nobody since the Beatles in 1964. Three different Bee Gees singles from the soundtrack went to #1, and the Gibb brothers also wrote and produced #1 singles for Yvonne Elliman, Frankie Valli, and their baby brother, Andy Gibb. Songs written by the Gibb brothers spent more than half the year at #1 on the Hot 100.

The Bee Gees' take on disco was its own idiosyncratic beast—built on the Gibb brothers' pinched falsetto harmonies and on the newest studio gadgetry. When they were working on their 1978 smash "Stayin'

Alive," one of the #1 hits from the *Saturday Night Fever* soundtrack, Bee Gees drummer Dennis Bryon couldn't make it to the session. Rather than using another drummer or even a drum machine, the Bee Gees and producer Albhy Galuten used the drums that Bryon had played on the previous Bee Gees hit "Night Fever," using that recording to build an endless tape loop. That loop gave "Stayin' Alive" its own steady mechanical thump, and that thump became the center of the song. "Stayin' Alive" topped the charts for four straight weeks in 1978, and it became one of six consecutive #1 hits for the Bee Gees.

After the success of the Bee Gees and *Saturday Night Fever*, it was impossible to think of disco as a gay underground phenomenon anymore. By that point, disco was the de facto sound of American pop music. Dance clubs opened in suburban strip malls across the country. In New York, the midtown nightclub Studio 54, which had opened in 1976, had become a new locus for celebrity culture, famous itself for its haughty and exacting admission policies. Chic, the great New York dance group, originally wrote their first #1 hit, 1978's "Le Freak," as an angry response to being denied entry to Studio 54. At first, they called it "Fuck Off."

Plenty of silly cash-in disco songs topped the charts in those years: Walter Murphy and the Big Apple Band's "A Fifth of Beethoven," Meco's disco take on the *Star Wars* theme music, snarky radio DJ Rick Dees's execrable joke-song "Disco Duck." Established stars also turned toward disco and made chart-topping hits: Diana Ross with "Love Hangover," the Four Seasons with "December 1963 (Oh, What a Night)," the Rolling Stones with "Miss You," Rod Stewart with "Da Ya Think I'm Sexy?"

But disco also opened the pop charts up to lush, thumping soul anthems from singers who might've otherwise never had a chance on the pop charts: Gloria Gaynor, Thelma Houston, the Emotions. The genre also brought new sounds into the mainstream. Donna Summer and producers Giorgio Moroder and Pete Bellotte, for instance, developed a pulsating, electronic Euro-disco style that drew on the synthetic art-rock of Kraftwerk more than the soulful swirl of Philadelphia International. This was a fully mechanical take on the sound—an evolution of the drum machine that sat at the heart of George McRae's "Rock Your Baby." On twelve-inch singles, Moroder and Bellotte would stretch Summer's voice out to psychedelic lengths. One version of Summer's orgasmic odyssey "Love to Love You Baby" lasted seventeen minutes. That length was no commercial obstacle; "Love to Love You Baby" reached #2 in 1975 and became Summer's breakout hit. With that sound, Donna Summer reached #1 four times in the late seventies.

For about four years, disco, in its various guises, held sway over the Hot 100—its dominance so complete that soul veteran Johnnie Taylor topped the chart for a month in 1976 with "Disco Lady," which wasn't even a disco song. Then the backlash came quickly. In 1979, Chicago radio DJ Steve Dahl—incensed after the station where he'd been working switched over to a disco format and fired him—launched a snarky months-long campaign against disco. This culminated with Disco Demolition Night in July 1979. The White Sox announced the night as a promotion: if anyone brought a disco record to be destroyed at the ballpark, they'd get in for ninety-eight cents. The event sold out, and thousands more crashed the gates. In between games at a doubleheader, Dahl blew up a huge box of records, leaving a smoking hole in center field. Thousands of fans immediately rushed out of the stands, pulling down the batting cage and stealing the bases from the field and the bats from the dugout. The White Sox had to forfeit the second game.

Disco Demolition Night did not immediately end the commercial prospects of disco in America, but it marked a shift in American tastes. Disco faded from the charts soon afterward. A month and a half later—after a summer when the Bee Gees, Chic, and Donna Summer had traded off the #1 spot—the Knack's retro, riff-happy new-wave rocker "My Sharona" began a six-week stay atop the Hot 100, and *Billboard* later named it the year's #1 song. The success of "My Sharona" was, at least in some ways, a reaction against disco. Chic, Summer, and the Bee Gees all struggled to chart afterward, and Chic and the Bee Gees never reached #1 again. (Summer got there once more, a couple of months later, with the dramatic Barbra Streisand duet "No More Tears [Enough Is Enough].")

Even though many of its biggest stars were white guys like Henry Wayne Casey and the Bee Gees, disco never really lost its reputation as music associated with Black and gay cultures. Rock fans like Steve Dahl claimed they were angry that disco had displaced rock, but hard rockers like Led Zeppelin weren't singles acts, and they had never been much of a factor on the pop charts. Instead, disco really pushed out sleepy folk-rockers like John Denver and soft-pop balladeers like the Carpenters. Proponents of the Disco Sucks movement complained that the music was vapid and repetitive, but disco was really reaching its creative peak in 1979, thanks to impeccably funky hits like Gloria Gaynor's "I Will Survive" and Chic's "Good Times."

That creative energy didn't disappear after 1979. It merely changed. The members of the Bee Gees and Chic became hugely successful pop producers and songwriters in the eighties. Their own records didn't do well, but the brothers Gibb wrote and produced #1 hits for Barbra Streisand and for Kenny Rogers and Dolly Parton. Chic's Nile Rodgers and Bernard Edwards made hits with Diana Ross, David Bowie, Madonna, and Robert Palmer, among others. Donna Summer collaborator Giorgio Moroder won three Oscars and crafted chart-toppers like Irene Cara's "Flashdance . . . What a Feeling" and Berlin's "Take My Breath Away."

In the eighties, disco simply became a part of the pop-music language. Michael Jackson and Madonna became dominant pop stars with club-centric dance-pop hits that were disco in all but name. Both stars worked with disco veterans and sang over drum machines, just as George McRae had done years before.

Drum machines were also key to the sound of new wave and synthpop, which colonized the American charts after the launch of

MTV. Blondie, the first true new-wave stars, had their breakthrough with 1979's "Heart of Glass," a disco song. Duran Duran, the biggest stars of the second British Invasion, claimed that they wanted to sound like a cross between the Sex Pistols and Chic—and by working with Nile Rodgers and Bernard Edwards, they came a lot closer to the latter than the former. Disco's drum-machine thump also moved from new wave to house music—which, like disco, started out in Black and gay clubs. (Frankie Knuckles, a DJ from the New York underground, moved to Chicago and became the star attraction at a Chicago club called the Warehouse. House music got its name from the music— a combination of disco, R&B, and new wave—that Knuckles would play.) In the early 2000s, electronic dance music, a distant descendant of disco, once again dominated the Hot 100.

Rap music also owed its existence to disco. Early rap thrived at New York clubs with names like Disco Fever, and it nurtured its own star DJs. Towering figures like Grandmaster Flash and Afrika Bambaataa had the same exploratory sensibilities as their disco predecessors. On their 1979 single "Rapper's Delight," the Sugarhill Gang rapped over the replayed groove from Chic's "Good Times." "Rapper's Delight" reached #36 on the Hot 100 in the fall of 1979, becoming the first rap hit.

KC and the Sunshine Band actually had the first new #1 hit of the eighties; their ballad "Please Don't Go" topped the Hot 100 in January 1980. But that was a last gasp. Richard Finch was already gone from the band by then, and Harry Wayne Casey dissolved the group soon afterward, trying for a solo career instead. Casey was partially paralyzed in a bad car accident in 1981, and he took years to recover. By then, pop music had moved on, and Casey and a reformed version of the Sunshine Band started touring the oldies circuit in the early nineties. Jerome Smith, the guitarist who played on "Rock Your Baby," died in 2000, at the age of forty-seven—crushed in a bulldozer accident while working a construction job in West Palm Beach. After a 2010 arrest in Ohio, Richard Finch served seven years in prison for sexually abusing teenage boys in his home recording studio.

As for George McCrae, he scored only a few more charting singles after the success of "Rock Your Baby." His wife, Gwen, topped the R&B chart and reached #9 on the Hot 100 with her sweaty 1975 soul single "Rockin' Chair." Gwen and George divorced in 1976, and they both continued to tour and record for years afterward, without any pop success. George McRae never made another big hit. He didn't stay famous, and he never got rich. But George still has the historic distinction of being the first disco hitmaker, and that makes him a crucial player in the history of pop music.

CHAPTER 8

Fleetwood Mac– "Dreams"

Released March 24, 1977
Hit #1 June 11, 1977
One-week reign

BY 1976, FLEETWOOD MAC WAS A CIRCUS. THE BAND'S TWO couples—Stevie Nicks and Lindsey Buckingham, Christine and John McVie—were both breaking up. Mick Fleetwood, the band's drummer and manager, was going through his own divorce. Everyone was fighting with everyone else. Everyone was writing songs about everyone else. Band members and associates were ingesting vast quantities of cocaine, marijuana, and alcohol.

In spite of all this chaos, though, Fleetwood Mac was a band of sonic perfectionists. The group put in long, expensive hours working on *Rumours*, its much-anticipated new album—playing songs over and over, then getting their producers to manually splice together tapes of their best parts. That left Stevie Nicks, the one nonperfectionist in the band, with nothing to do.

Nicks played piano, but she was the one member of Fleetwood Mac who didn't usually play an instrument on record. In his book *Making "Rumours,"* the album's coproducer Ken Caillat writes that Nicks "was foremost a singer-songwriter; she wasn't into the technical end of the music. So while all this experimentation was going on in the studio with the other members of the band, she was frustrated and pretty much bored out of her mind." Whenever Nicks could, she'd find a corner by herself. The studio, as it happened, had a pretty great corner, and that's where Stevie Nicks wrote "Dreams," Fleetwood Mac's sole #1 hit.

Fleetwood Mac spent the first few months of 1976 working on *Rumours* at the Record Plant, a sprawling compound in the Bay Area city of Sausalito. Using the Record Plant had a lot of perks: two limos on call, a speedboat, a staff of cooks who could whip up hash cookies whenever necessary. One of the office rooms had a floor made entirely out of waterbed. Another had been turned into the Pit.

Sly Stone, leader of Sly and the Family Stone, designed the Pit while recording the 1973 album *Fresh*. The Pit was a functional recording studio, but Stone had vibes in mind when he conceptualized it. The room's floors, walls, and ceilings were covered in red shag carpet. At the center of the room was a black-velvet four-poster bed; you had to climb through a giant pair of fuzzy lips to get into it. During the *Rumours* sessions, the Pit was a hangout spot; Mick Fleetwood later said that the room "was usually occupied by people we didn't know, tapping razors on mirrors." Sometimes, though, it was where Stevie Nicks went to get away from the rest of her band.

Fleetwood Mac's entire existence had been flux. By 1976, the band had already gone through seven different lead guitarists. Mick Fleetwood and bassist John McVie had teamed up with guitarist Peter Green to form Fleetwood Mac in 1967. All three musicians had been members of John Mayall & the Bluesbreakers, the British blues-purist institution that had also served as an early launching pad for musicians like Eric Clapton. Green, Clapton's replacement in the Bluesbreakers, was an eccentric guitar hero, and he named Fleetwood Mac after its rhythm section because he didn't want all the attention on him. The name proved prescient. Over the years, Fleetwood and McVie would be the band's only consistent members.

Early on, Fleetwood Mac was part of the same British psychedelic blues-rock scene as bands like the Yardbirds and Ten Years After. They had early success in the United Kingdom, hitting #1 with the 1968 instrumental "Albatross" and getting close with messily ruminative Peter Green songs like "Man of the World" and "The Green Manalishi (with the Two-Pronged Crown)." Along the way, the band added keyboardist and singer Christine Perfect, who married John McVie and joined Fleetwood Mac in 1970.

Fleetwood Mac idolized American bluesmen like Elmore James, but their early records simply didn't sell in the United States, despite steady touring. Until *Rumours*, the band was best known in America for recording the original 1968 version of "Black Magic Woman," a horny and mystical koan that Peter Green had written; two years later, Santana's cover of the song peaked at #4 on the Hot 100. Around the same time Santana's version of "Black Magic Woman" took off, Peter Green got heavily into Jesus and LSD, and he abruptly quit Fleetwood Mac midtour in 1970. Guitarist Jeremy Spencer, who took over frontman duties, left even more suddenly—walking off before a 1971 show in Los Angeles and never returning. When the band found him, he'd shaved his head and sworn allegiance to the cult known as the Children of God.

Fleetwood Mac found a new singer and guitarist in American musician Bob Welch, who convinced the band to relocate to Los Angeles. But Welch also left Fleetwood Mac for a solo career in 1974. Fleetwood Mac burned through more musicians, including one temporary frontman, Bob Weston, who got the boot after having an affair with Mick Fleetwood's wife. The band also got into a protracted court battle with a former manager who'd claimed that he owned the Fleetwood Mac name and sent a fake version of the band out on the road. All the while, the members of Fleetwood Mac partied hard; Mick Fleetwood once estimated that he'd snorted seven miles' worth of cocaine over the course of his career.

Even through all this pandemonium, Fleetwood Mac continued to function. In his 2015 memoir, *Play On*, Mick Fleetwood wrote, "We were an outfit that could be counted on consistently to move between 250,000 to 300,000 records whenever we put out an album, but that was about it. We never did better, we never did worse." One day, Mick Fleetwood went to check out the LA studio Sound City, and an engineer played him a tape of a duo called Buckingham Nicks, who'd been recording there. Fleetwood, once again in the market for a new frontman, was so impressed with the idiosyncratic fingerpicked guitar style of Lindsey Buckingham that he asked Buckingham to join the band. Buckingham would do it only if Stevie Nicks, his girlfriend and musical partner, was part of the deal. With Buckingham, Nicks, and Christine McVie, this new Fleetwood Mac had three members capable of writing songs and singing lead. After almost a decade of constant upheaval, Fleetwood Mac had found its lineup.

Before joining Fleetwood Mac, Buckingham and Nicks weren't selling any records on their own. The two had met as well-off teenagers at Menlo-Atherton High School in the Bay Area. (Nicks was born in Arizona, but she'd moved around a lot as a kid because her father was the CEO of the bus company Greyhound.) Buckingham and Nicks had started dating as teenagers in the late sixties, and they'd played together in a psychedelic folk-rock band called Fritz. That band hadn't worked out, and neither had the *Buckingham Nicks* album that Mick Fleetwood heard in the studio that day. Before taking the Fleetwood Mac job, Buckingham had been working the nostalgia circuit, playing guitar and singing backup for the Everly Brothers' Don Everly. Buckingham and Nicks turned out to be exactly what Fleetwood Mac needed. They brought a whole new personality and songwriting style to the group, and they jelled right away.

Fleetwood Mac's new style fitted perfectly with the sound of Los Angeles in the seventies. Three-fifths of Fleetwood Mac were British transplants, but most of the people on the LA music scene had also come from elsewhere. For years, pop musicians had been moving to Southern California, forming a tight community of hedonistic professionals. These musicians developed a shimmery, bucolic pop-rock sound that owed something to the idealistic folk-rock jangle of the Byrds and to the blissful harmonics of the Beach Boys. Many of them found huge pop success in the seventies.

Carole King, for one, moved to Los Angeles after her divorce from former songwriting partner Gerry Goffin. Her 1971 album, *Tapestry*, sold fourteen million copies, and she made a #1 single of her own with "It's Too Late." King's friends and collaborators James Taylor and Joni Mitchell also became huge stars in the seventies; Taylor landed his only #1 hit with his cover of King's "You've Got a Friend." After his time in the Byrds, David Crosby joined Buffalo Springfield's Stephen Stills and the Hollies' Graham Nash to form a harmony-singing supertrio. Neil Young, who often joined Crosby, Stills & Nash, had also recorded the country-flavored *Harvest*, the biggest-selling album of 1972. Other folk-rockers, like Eagles and Linda Ronstadt, were also playing around with country elements, adding them to their slick and harmony-heavy sound.

Most of these artists, based around LA's Laurel Canyon area, found their way to fame after the idealistic era of sixties protest art had died away. Their music generally did not have the searching, exploratory quality of "Mr. Tambourine Man" or "Good Vibrations." They weren't singing about imagining better worlds or different paths. Instead, they sang about bitterness and burnout—major themes for Eagles, whose 1977 chart-topper "Hotel California" is an allegory about how greed and hedonism had obliterated the dream of the sixties. The musicians got into complicated romantic entanglements with one another, and they wrote songs about those entanglements.

The music was warm and mellow, but its lyrics were often jarringly callous. As disco took over the Hot 100, the Laurel Canyon musicians' combination of bucolic reverie and erudite viciousness held sway over *Billboard*'s album chart.

Working with Stevie Nicks and Lindsey Buckingham, Fleetwood Mac tapped right into that sound on their tenth album, a self-titled affair that came out in July 1975. The band's new lineup immediately mastered a form of polished, harmonically rich pop music—soft rock that sometimes still rocked hard. Fleetwood Mac's self-titled LP was a slow burner, but the singles "Rhiannon" and "Say You Love Me" slowly rose on the charts, both peaking just outside the top 10. The album sold steadily, gaining steam over time and finally climbing to #1 more than a year after its release. At the end of 1976, *Billboard* named *Fleetwood Mac* the #2 album of the year, with only Peter Frampton's double-live monster *Frampton Comes Alive!* selling more copies.

But even as their album brought them entirely new levels of success, Fleetwood Mac were coming unglued. John and Christine McVie's marriage fell apart, with John drinking to excess and Christine enjoying a fling with the band's lighting director. Buckingham and Nicks also broke up, and Mick Fleetwood's wife left him for his best friend. Fleetwood and his wife would remarry while the band was still recording *Rumours*, and they'd divorce again a year after the album came out. The drama didn't end after that, either. Later, Mick Fleetwood would start an affair with Stevie Nicks, and then he'd leave her for her best friend.

Rumours was an album driven by this labyrinthine web of heartbreak and lust, and also by drink and drugs. Fleetwood Mac's whole soap opera played out in public, and it fueled the art, to the point that the band chose *Rumours* as the album title. The LP's creation took them a year, cost a million dollars, and it just about broke the band to pieces. The members of Fleetwood Mac fought bitterly. Christine and John McVie wouldn't speak to each other about anything but music, and even then, Christine had to tell John that her song "You Make Loving Fun" was about her dog, not the lighting director that she was having fun loving. But the work shows through. In its acrid bitterness, *Rumours* positively gleams.

Nothing gleams brighter than "Dreams," the song that Nicks wrote by herself on a Fender Rhodes keyboard in the Pit, Sly Stone's party-room studio. Talking to *Blender* in 2005, Nicks remembered, "I sat down on the bed with my keyboard in front of me. I found a drum pattern, switched on my little cassette player, and wrote 'Dreams' in about 10 minutes."

"Dreams" is a song aimed directly at Lindsey Buckingham, Nicks's bandmate and ex. The song doesn't sound bitter. It radiates a mystical serenity. "Rhiannon," Nicks's big hit from the *Fleetwood Mac* album, is about an ancient Welsh fertility goddess. With its talk of crystal visions and cleansing rains, "Dreams" creates a similar feeling, but the lyrics are unmistakably pointed. The opening line is a poison dart: "Now, here you go again. You say you want your freedom. Well, who am I to keep you down?" Elsewhere in the song, Nicks envisions Buckingham in the stillness of what he had and what he lost. It's a poetic fuck-you, but it's still a fuck-you.

Lindsey Buckingham had to play on "Dreams." Buckingham's guitar on the song finds a softly consoling tone, and its moaning, purring sound almost turns "Dreams" into a duet. Buckingham also sings backup. You can hear his voice singing the words that Nicks wrote about him. For his part, Buckingham was also writing songs about Nicks, and she was also singing backup on those songs. "Dreams" was the second single on *Rumours*. The first, the #10 hit "Go Your Own Way," is a Buckingham song where he sings that packing up and shacking up is all that Nicks wanted to do. Nicks has said that she "very much resented" having to sing on "Go Your Own Way." She still did it. That was the way things were in Fleetwood Mac. The turmoil drove the music, and everyone played their part, helping out on songs even when those songs directly targeted them.

"Dreams" is a simple song, built on just two chords. The song's arrangement is rich and subtle, and its pulse carries at least an echo of disco. Nicks wrote "Dreams" with a preset drum-machine beat— "a dance beat," as she later called it. Before "Dreams" had its title, the band referred to the track as "Spinners," since it reminded them of something the great Michigan orchestral soul group might've done. The drums on the final version of "Dreams" sound mechanistic because they are. Ken Caillat got Mick Fleetwood to play eight simple bars, and Caillat then edited those bars into a tape loop. This was just before the Bee Gees would do something similar with their own #1 hit "Stayin' Alive." By the mideighties, programmed drums would become a common pop-music trope. In the tape-loop groove of "Dreams," Fleetwood Mac were prescient.

That loop of Mick Fleetwood's drums isn't the same as a drum machine, though Stevie Nicks did use a preset beat when she was writing the song. Soon afterward, though, samplers would make it easy for producers to put together looped drum beats, and that new capability would drive rap and house and dance-pop. That simple, hypnotic pulse was a new thing for a blues-informed rock band like Fleetwood Mac, but Fleetwood Mac were, at the very least, interested in disco. On other tracks from the album, Lindsey Buckingham would coach Mick Fleetwood and John McVie to play with the same steady, basic beat that the Bee Gees had used on their disco breakthrough, "Jive Talkin'."

On "Dreams," the groove—those looped drums, the heavily treated moans of the guitar, the understated swagger of John McVie's bass line—conveys a numb sense of bliss. Stevie Nicks conveys something else. In her tone alone, Nicks radiates both fond regret and seething anger. Where Buckingham sounds raw and frustrated on "Go Your Own Way," Nicks comes off as a mystical being who's simply shaking her head at the small-minded pettiness of this man's actions. She sounds like she's above it and like she's both disappointed and lightly amused at the antics of mortal men. Even the voices behind

Nicks—including that of Buckingham, the song's mortal-man target—
add to the sense of luxuriant remove.

"Dreams" is full-immersion pop music. It's dense with meaning
and allusion, and it creates a strange, tingly out-of-time feeling. Fleetwood Mac's albums regularly sold better than their singles. Heard
on the radio, "Dreams" might not actively grab your attention in the
same way as something like KC and the Sunshine Band's "I'm Your
Boogie Man," the song that "Dreams" knocked out of the #1 spot. But
in its intricate expansiveness, "Dreams" creates its own uncanny sonic
environment. That's the quality that's helped "Dreams" linger in the
sonic imagination. In the summer of 2020, for instance, "Dreams"
returned to prominence after Idaho skateboarder Nathan "Doggface"
Apodaca posted a video of himself riding down a highway, swigging
from a bottle of Ocean Spray, and listening to "Dreams." That video
went megaviral for no real reason. It just had a vibe to it. That vibe
was "Dreams."

In the entire history of Fleetwood Mac—fifty-four years and counting, as I write this—the band has spent only one week atop the *Billboard*
Hot 100. Many of the various members and ex-members of Fleetwood
Mac have made hit singles, but none of those hits has topped the Hot
100. Even Stevie Nicks, who had a serious run as a solo star, has never
reached #1 without Fleetwood Mac unless you *really* stretch things
and count the sample from the 1982 single "Edge of Seventeen" that
drives Destiny's Child's 2001 smash "Bootylicious."

"Dreams," the song that Nicks spent ten minutes writing, was a
hit, but it wasn't exactly an earthshaker. When "Dreams" reached #1,
the shimmery California pop sound was near its peak. Eagles, friends
and contemporaries of Fleetwood Mac, had already scored two #1 hits
in 1977 alone. But "Dreams" belongs in this book because that song,
along with the rest of *Rumours*, recalibrated music-industry ideas about
how big an album could be. "Dreams" was the second single from the
LP. *Rumours* spun off a total of four singles, and all of them became
top-10 hits. That had never happened before.

In the sixties and seventies, pop artists were expected to crank out music at a furious clip, often releasing multiple albums per year. (The Beatles, for instance, made thirteen studio albums over a seven-year stretch.) Usually, those albums yielded only a couple of singles, and then the artist had to move on to the next thing. Fleetwood Mac released only three songs from their hugely successful 1975 self-titled album as singles; all of them made the top 20. Peter Frampton's *Frampton Comes Alive!*—the only album that outsold *Fleetwood Mac* in 1976—went through the same process: three singles, all hits, and then on to the next one. Four is only one more than three, but the difference mattered.

Five months before Fleetwood Mac released *Rumours*, Stevie Wonder came out with the massive double-album opus *Songs in the Key of Life*, the crowning achievement of a legendary years-long hot streak for Wonder. *Songs in the Key of Life*, instantly and rapturously received as a pop masterpiece, became only the third album ever to debut at #1 on the *Billboard* album charts, a near impossibility in the years before album sales were tallied electronically, and it went on to win Wonder his third consecutive Album of the Year Grammy. But even in an exceptional case like *Songs in the Key of Life*, Motown didn't see a lot of money in continuing to push the singles to radio. The first two hits from that album, "I Wish" and "Sir Duke," both topped the Hot 100. But the next two, "Another Star" and "As," reached only the bottom half of the top 40. Motown didn't even release seemingly surefire hits like "Isn't She Lovely" and "Ebony Eyes" as singles. It wasn't how things were done.

But *Rumours* was a perfect storm. When Warner Bros. released the album in February 1977, the label initially shipped eight hundred thousand copies, a tremendous number, gambling on the idea that people would want to hear the record right away. The gamble paid off. The timing of *Rumours* was perfect. Fleetwood Mac's self-titled album had been steadily selling all year, and it had reached #1 only the previous September. Fleetwood Mac themselves had become an object of public fascination, especially as all the romantic dynamics within the group became more widely known. The album itself was full of sounds piled on top of other sounds.

Rumours arrived just as *Fleetwood Mac* was fading, and it caught a wave of public interest. Americans could not resist this whole sordid farce or the songs that it inspired. Fleetwood Mac had taken a lot of time and spent a lot of money to make *Rumours*, but you could hear that time and money in the finished product. The band applied its sonic perfectionism to every song on the album, which wasn't common practice at the time. As a result, *Rumours* played like a ready-made greatest-hits album. Every song sounded like a potential single. Some of the best-known tracks from *Rumours*, like "The Chain" and "Gold Dust Woman," never became singles, but they remain in radio rotation to this day.

A couple of months before *Rumours* came out, Warner Bros. released "Go Your Own Way," a Buckingham song about Nicks, and it peaked at #10. "Dreams," with Nicks singing about Buckingham, went all the way to #1. People knew that these two were singing about each other and answering each other through song, and that drove interest. The next two singles were both Christie McVie songs: "Don't Stop," a #3 hit intended as a sort of nudge of encouragement to her bandmate and ex-husband, John, and "You Make Loving Fun," a #9 hit for the lighting director who had made loving fun.

All of those singles, "Dreams" included, were sparkling up-tempo pop songs. If you weren't invested in the Fleetwood Mac narrative, then you could simply hear them as sparkling up-tempo pop songs. (Bill Clinton, for instance, was presumably not thinking about John McVie's struggles with postdivorce alcoholism when he chose "Don't Stop" as the anthem for his 1992 presidential campaign.) But Fleetwood Mac also used their whole complicated saga to drive their celebrity, and Warner Bros. used their celebrity to drive their sales. The album's dominance itself became a selling point. *Rumours* was a conversation piece, a subject of cultural discussion. If you wanted to know what was going on, you needed to own a copy yourself.

Everything broke in the exact right way for *Rumours*, and the album became a phenomenon. *Rumours* topped the *Billboard* album chart for thirty-one weeks. In its first week, *Rumours* went gold. After a month, it was platinum. To date, *Rumours* has sold twenty million copies in the United States alone. *Rumours* established a new ceiling for how long an album cycle could last and how many songs could be sold as hits. The album stands as a musical equivalent to the groundbreaking blockbuster films of the seventies. Like *Jaws* or *Star Wars*, *Rumours* showed just how big a piece of art could become if it was good enough and if it was timed and marketed exactly right. Record labels learned from its example.

A year after *Rumours*, RSO released the Bee Gees–dominated soundtrack album for *Saturday Night Fever*. That soundtrack launched four #1 hits and almost immediately became, in its era, the biggest-selling album of all time. It also helped push the *Saturday Night Fever* movie to blockbuster status. The film was also an RSO product. The movie sold the album, and the album sold the movie. Back before "synergy" became a buzzword, *Saturday Night Fever* had it.

In the eighties, the marketing behind big albums came to rival that of big-budget Hollywood films. Labels used every tool at their disposal to push records like Michael Jackson's *Thriller*, Bruce Springsteen's *Born in the USA*, Whitney Houston's *Whitney*, and George Michael's *Faith*. Fleetwood Mac themselves never made anything else that reached the cultural level of *Rumours*. The band followed *Rumours* two years later with the relatively spiky and experimental *Tusk*. Lindsey Buckingham took control of the band's artistic direction, and under the influence of punk and new wave, he pushed Fleetwood Mac toward sparser and more challenging sounds. The album sold two million copies, and its title track reached #6, but these were paltry numbers compared with the lightning-in-a-bottle moment of *Rumours*.

In the early eighties, Stevie Nicks launched a hugely successful solo career. Her 1981 solo debut, *Bella Donna*, sold four million copies, and she finished the decade with a handful of platinum albums and top-10 hits. Nicks remained a member of Fleetwood Mac, and the band kept making hits into the late eighties. The internal soap opera also continued. Fleetwood Mac shed and regained members, and they broke up and reunited more than once. As recently as 2018, the rest of the band ousted Lindsey Buckingham from Fleetwood Mac. By the time you read this, he might be back in. The circus never stops.

CHAPTER 9

The Human League– "Don't You Want Me"

Released November 27, 1981
Hit #1 July 3, 1982
Three-week reign

W HEN MTV LAUNCHED IN AUGUST 1981, THE NEW CABLE network threw down a gauntlet. Famously, the first video that MTV ever played was the clip for "Video Killed the Radio Star," a 1979 song from a British synthpop group called the Buggles. This programming choice was sheer triumphal provocation: a new player announcing itself on the pop-culture stage. MTV didn't pick the Buggles' video because the song itself was popular. "Video Killed the Radio Star" had been a #1 hit in the United Kingdom, but in America, it hadn't gotten past #40. By 1981, the Buggles were already effectively done; bandleaders Trevor Horn and Geoff Downes had left to join the aging prog-rock group Yes. But "Video Killed the Radio Star" was the statement that MTV wanted to make. The fledgling network wanted to let the world know that the game had just changed.

If anything, though, MTV was getting ahead of itself with that statement. Cable TV was still a new phenomenon in 1981. Not many households had cable, and many cable providers didn't yet carry MTV.

(MTV was based in Manhattan, yet cable subscribers in Manhattan had no access to the network.) Also, in its early days, MTV mostly just played videos from radio stars.

MTV's programmers conceived the network as a cable-TV version of a rock radio station, and so the network's playlists reflected the state of early-eighties radio rock, which was not in a particularly healthy place. Over the course of the seventies, the radio format known as AOR, album-oriented rock, took over FM airwaves in America. It codified what counted as rock and what didn't. In 1975, Boston—the project of moonlighting guitar whiz Tom Scholz, a Massachusetts Institute of Technology grad who worked as an engineer at Polaroid—sold ten million copies of their self-titled debut. Boston's sound had a formula: nostalgic lyrics and Beatles-style melodies, hypercharged with big riffs and clean space-age studio techniques. That sound became a blueprint, and AOR radio soon became a stronghold for arena-rock bands with vague single-word names and albums with sci-fi cover art: Journey, Foreigner, Styx, Starship. The members of these bands mostly came from psychedelic and prog-rock backgrounds, but they figured out an almost scientific formula for making radio hits, and they stuck with it.

The highest-selling album of 1981, the year that MTV launched, was REO Speedwagon's sleek, crunching *Hi Infidelity*, which came out in November 1980. The first concert ever broadcast on MTV, a week into the channel's existence, was an REO Speedwagon show in Denver. In MTV's first hour on the air, Mark Goodman, one of the network's first VJs, explained the whole enterprise's concept over and over: "We'll be doing for TV what FM did for radio." In its early days, MTV largely stuck with FM-radio stars: Speedwagon, Styx, .38 Special. But these artists' videos were often hokey and awkward. The bands saw music videos as pain-in-the-ass record-label obligations, and their musicians had no idea how to play to the cameras. Plenty of those acts had only a few videos, and MTV, committed to staying on the air twenty-four hours a day, needed material. The station needed videos to play.

Rod Stewart had seen what was coming. Stewart, the rasping blues-rock star, had been making videos for years. When MTV started, it kept Stewart in constant rotation. (In its first hour, MTV played two different Rod Stewart videos.) But as a popular veteran rocker who knew how to present himself on camera, Rod Stewart was a rarity. As MTV developed, the station came to rely on the artists who adapted, the ones who embraced the flash and silliness and spectacle that the music-video format made possible. REO Speedwagon and Journey didn't really understand music videos. Others, like Pat Benatar or Daryl Hall and John Oates, had compelling screen presences, and they did well on MTV, but they hated the process of making videos. The artists who truly embraced the form and popped on MTV were the British art-school synth acts, the groups who made playing to the camera into an art form.

The United Kingdom never had AOR radio. Boston and Journey and REO Speedwagon barely made a ripple over there. Radio mattered in the UK, but pop music also had other avenues on the other side of the Atlantic. On the weekly prime-time music show *Top of the Pops*, hosts ran down the top 40 singles in the country, while artists lip-synched their songs in a studio that looked like the set of a sci-fi B-movie. Critical acclaim could also drive sales, thanks to the hyperactive churn of the nation's many snarky and omnivorous weekly music tabloids. The UK embraced disco in the seventies, but the smooth, blissed-out California act Eagles didn't translate. The *Rumours*-era lineup of Fleetwood Mac was 60 percent British, but that band did better in America than in its homeland. Instead, the acts who thrived in the United Kingdom were the ones with energy and attention-grabbing visual gimmickry working for them.

Over the course of the seventies, the young record buyers of the UK got into loud, cheeky new mutations like glam and punk rock. Neither of those genres resonated as pop music in America. Glam overlord David Bowie scored an American #1 with his 1975 single "Fame," but that was only after he left behind riffs and theatricality and embraced smooth American funk and soul sounds. Bubble-glam greats the Sweet had a few top-10 hits in the early seventies, and glam-adjacent teen sensations the Bay City Rollers made it to #1 in 1976 with their catchy chant-along "Saturday Night," but the United States didn't have a lot of use for Mud or Slade or Roxy Music or T. Rex or Gary Glitter. In the late seventies, British punk bands like the Sex Pistols, the Stranglers, and the Boomtown Rats became a constant presence in the UK top 10, but America didn't embrace any of them.

America didn't embrace its own punks, either. The bands who came out of New York clubs like CBGB and Max's Kansas City in the seventies attracted critical acclaim and culty devotion, but that rarely translated into actual pop stardom. The Ramones reached #66 with their 1977 single "Rockaway Beach," and then they never got higher. Television, the Dead Boys, Suicide, and Richard Hell & the Voidods never even charted. Patti Smith landed one big hit—"Because the Night," a 1978 single that she cowrote with Bruce Springsteen—but that was her only moment in the pop spotlight. The Talking Heads eventually did find mainstream stardom, but that took time. The band's twitchy art-pop had to get looser and funkier, and the pop mainstream had to move closer to their twitchy art-pop. Even with the convergence of those two forces, the Talking Heads only ever made one top-10 single: 1983's "Burning Down the House," which peaked at #9.

The only punk-identified American band who ascended to stardom in the pre-MTV era was Blondie, which made the leap with a series of distinctly unpunk singles. The year 1979's "Heart of Glass," Blondie's first #1 hit, was essentially a disco song, albeit a notably detached and distant one. In the years that followed, Blondie scored a remarkable run of chart-toppers by recognizing and toying around with new trends: synthetic Euro-disco on "Call Me," pop-reggae on "The Tide Is High," early hip-hop on "Rapture." Blondie should've been ideally suited for early-MTV stardom, but the band broke up in 1982, just as the network was getting going.

Instead, MTV turned out to be an ideal vehicle for a new crop of UK acts who had embraced glitter, makeup, and the art of the pose. These new groups were inspired by the theatricality of glam, the homespun spirit of punk, and the mechanistic sleekness of Giorgio Moroder's Euro-disco and Kraftwerk's synthetic art-rock. Electronic instruments were becoming cheaper and more widely available, so that was a factor, too. In the summer of 1979, London synthpop act the Tubeway Army made it to #1 in the United Kingdom with their single "Are 'Friends' Electric?" A few months later, Tubeway Army leader Gary Numan went solo and returned to #1 in the UK with "Cars." The Buggles' "Video Killed the Radio Star" was part of that wave, as was David Bowie's comeback smash "Ashes to Ashes." A Leeds duo called Soft Cell made it to #1 by turning Gloria Jones's obscure 1965 soul song "Tainted Love" into something detached and metronomic. And on Christmas 1981, the Human League's "Don't You Want Me" was the #1 single in the United Kingdom.

The Human League began in the depressed English steel town of Sheffield in the late seventies. Cofounders Martyn Ware and Ian Craig Marsh were young computer operators who'd both been in a performance-art collective called Musical Vomit. Both of them used their money to buy early synthesizers; Ware, in particular, turned to the keyboard because guitar strings made his fingers hurt. Together, the two of them started a group called the Future, which took inspiration from Kraftwerk and specialized in avant-garde electronic music. The Future took their early tracks to London and shopped them to record labels, but nobody was interested, so they decided that they needed a singer. Ware had been school friends with a young man named Philip Oakey, who was working as a hospital porter when Ware and Marsh contacted him by leaving a note on his front door. At the time, Oakey had no musical experience, but he was a presence on the Sheffield club scene. Oakey was a good-looking guy with expressive taste in clothes and a memorable haircut. He *looked* like a pop star, which remains a key qualification for actually *becoming* a pop star.

With Oakey on board, the Future changed their name to the Human League; Ware took the new moniker from a sci-fi board game called StarForce: Alpha Centauri. The Human League released their debut single, "Being Boiled," on a small independent label in 1978. The British press took note, and so did David Bowie, who caught an early performance and proclaimed the Human League "the future of pop music." The Human League signed to Richard Branson's Virgin label, but their early singles were abrasive, clanking art-pop, and they made no impression on the UK charts. A rift developed within the group. Martyn Ware and Ian Craig Marsh wanted to make adventurous, experimental music. Oakey wanted to make pop. In 1980, Ware and Marsh left the group that they'd started, and they formed a new group called Heaven 17. (Heaven 17 never made a significant American hit, but the duo later played a key role in resurrecting Tina Turner's career in the early eighties. They produced her dance-pop covers of the Temptations' "Ball of Confusion" and Al Green's "Let's Stay Together," which became comeback hits and helped usher in Turner's dominant mideighties run. Ware also coproduced Terence Trent D'Arby's 1988 chart-topper "Wishing Well.")

When Ware and Marsh left the Human League, Philip Oakey kept the group's name, and he also kept its obligations. The Human League had a tour of the UK and Europe coming up, and Oakey had to put together a whole new band. Oakey lined up a couple of keyboard players, and he also met two teenage best friends, Susan Ann Sulley and Joanne Catherall, at Sheffield's Crazy Daisy nightclub. Sulley and Catherall looked cool and danced well, and Oakey invited them to join the band as backup singers and dancers even though neither had any musical experience whatsoever. The two girls were already Human League fans, and they had tickets to see the group on their coming tour. Convincing them to join wasn't hard.

The tour went badly. Without much time to rehearse or jell, the performances were reportedly rushed and sloppy. Audiences were upset to learn that the group was no longer the one they'd paid to see. But

Oakey quickly developed a new style for the Human League, largely based around the visual dynamic of himself with Sulley and Catherall. Together, the three of them—all androgynous, all wearing tons of makeup—looked dramatic and glamorous. In 1981, "The Sound of the Crowd," the first single that the Human League recorded with Sulley and Catherall, became their first real UK hit, reaching #12. Their next two singles, "Love Action (I Believe in Love)" and "Open Your Heart," both made the top 10.

After those three singles, the Human League released their album *Dare*. They recorded it with producer Martin Rushent, who'd worked with melodic punk bands like the Buzzcocks and the Stranglers and also had experience programming synths. At the time, Sulley and Catherall were still in school, and they had to take the bus from Sheffield to London on weekends to record their parts for the LP. The musicians who made *Dare* were green and amateurish, but they made that work for them. *Dare* is a boundlessly confident album with a cold, mechanistic sheen and a forceful, provocative energy. Oakey doesn't *sing* in any traditional sense; instead, he delivers his lines in a hard, declamatory monotone. Sulley and Catherall's voices sweeten the sound, and their raw enthusiasm more than makes up for any lack of technical skill. The album also bursts with commercial ambition. The Human League were writing for mass audiences, and their hooks had a giddy urgency.

"Don't You Want Me" is the last track on *Dare*. Philip Oakey wrote the song with Human League instrumentalists Jo Callis and Philip Adrian Wright, and his lyrics were inspired by the 1976 movie *A Star Is Born* and by a photo essay in a magazine for teenage girls. Oakey conceived "Don't You Want Me" as a duet between an older man and a younger woman, and Susan Ann Sulley, who'd previously sung only backup, shared lead vocals with Oakey. The song's narrative has layers. Oakey's character found Sulley's character when she was working as a waitress in a cocktail bar. She's spent five years with him, and she's moved on and become successful. She's eclipsed him. He's hurt and angry, and he lashes out, snarling that he made her and that he can unmake her. On the chorus, his desperation comes out: "Don't you want me, baby? Don't you want me? *Aaaoow!*"

Sulley tries to let Oakey down easy. She tells him that she still loves him. Their five years together have been "such good times," but she needs to move on. She says all the right things, but she sounds bored and resentful—a possible by-product of the chilly synthetic backing track and the relative stiffness of the two singers. There's no romance in "Don't You Want Me," just resentment and despair. Oakey himself has acknowledged that "Don't You Want Me" is "a nasty song about sexual power politics." It has no resolution. When Sulley puts Oakey down, all he can do is sing the chorus, again and again, the bitterness and futility growing with each repetition.

"Don't You Want Me" is a song about turbulent emotion, yet Oakey and Catherall sound wry and detached. Underneath them, the music tics and twinkles with robotic restraint. Like so many of the synthpop songs of its era, "Don't You Want Me" succeeds as pop music, but it also sounds like a distant commentary on pop music. That self-conscious quality affected everything the Human League did. In videos, Oakey, Sulley, and Catherall would stare into the middle distance, their expressions unchanging, pale as mannequins. The *Dare* album cover imitated an issue of *Vogue*. Theatrical irony was built into the Human League's persona. Rather than attempting to hide the artificiality of all-synth music, the Human League put that artificiality front and center. These were amateur outsiders, not veteran musicians, and that's what made them new and fresh and glamorous.

That whole approach isn't necessarily conducive to actual pop-chart success, and the Human League sometimes got in their own way. When the group first recorded "Don't You Want Me," it was an icy, austere song, but producer Martin Rushent heard the pop potential in it. He recorded the track with Linn's new LM-1 drum machine, which sampled real drum sounds rather than electronic ones. (Prince would embrace the contraption in the years to come.) Rushent also remixed "Don't You Want Me," layering the song's synth hooks over top of each other and making the track warmer and breezier. Oakey hated the remixed version of "Don't You Want Me" and considered it to be pure filler material. Virgin exec Simon Draper saw things differently. After three Human League hits, Draper insisted that the group release "Don't You Want Me" as a single. Oakey fought bitterly against it, but Draper won. "Don't You Want Me" exploded, topping the UK charts for five weeks and landing the coveted Christmas #1 spot.

Virgin gave the Human League a serious budget to make a video for "Don't You Want Me," and they enlisted Steve Barron, an Irish director who'd worked with new-wave stars like the Jam and Adam and the Ants. Barron has said that "Don't You Want Me" is the first music video ever shot on 35mm film. Barron created a classic cinematic look for the video—trench coats, klieg lights, revolvers, long zooms. He was inspired by the movie-within-a-movie concept of Truffaut's 1973 art film *Day for Night*. The "Don't You Want Me" clip has a fairly incomprehensible narrative, but few early music videos had stories that made much sense. The "Don't You Want Me" video had a sense of mystery, and that helped it stand out. MTV started playing the video before the Human League even had an American record deal.

That video became the first calling card for Steve Barron. Because of the "Don't You Want Me" video, Quincy Jones recruited Barron to direct Michael Jackson's "Beat It" video a year later. In the years ahead, Barron made videos that helped define the form, like a-ha's "Take on Me" and Dire Straits' "Money for Nothing." Both of those songs became #1 hits largely on the strength of Barron's videos. Later, Barron directed the 1990 *Teenage Mutant Ninja Turtles* movie, which, for nearly a decade, was the highest-grossing independent film in history.

When the "Don't You Want Me" video went into heavy MTV rotation, Virgin came to an agreement with the American label A&M. *Dare* came out in America in February 1982, and "Don't You Want Me" finally topped the Hot 100 in July, nine months after its UK release. Other songs had capitalized on MTV success before "Don't

You Want Me." Partly on the strength of its winky music video, Olivia Newton-John's frisky dance-pop single "Physical" topped the charts for an astonishing ten-week run between 1981 and 1982. But Newton-John was an established star by then, and "Physical" was also driven by radio, by club play, and by the emerging aerobics trend. The success of "Don't You Want Me," on the other hand, was pure MTV.

American audiences had shown some interest in arty British synth-pop before "Don't You Want Me." "Pop Muzik," a sticky and disco-adjacent single from an artist known only as M, had reached #1 in 1979, and it had employed an early version of the detached monotone vocal that Oakey used on "Don't You Want Me." A year later, Gary Numan's #1 UK hit "Cars" reached a peak of #9 on the Hot 100. "Pop Muzik" and "Cars" both succeeded in the pre-MTV era, presumably because of some combination of club play and novelty. But "Don't You Want Me" marked the moment that American audiences truly embraced this new form of arch, ironic, British art-school techno-pop.

On the last week that "Don't You Want Me" topped the Hot 100, Soft Cell's similarly stark "Tainted Love" reached its #8 peak on the Hot 100. In the months ahead, more and more striking, provocative British acts rode MTV play to the top of the Hot 100: Eurythmics, Culture Club, Tears for Fears, Pet Shop Boys. Duran Duran, a group of Birmingham club kids, reached #1 twice and became one of the iconic groups of the early MTV era.

In a vaguely alarmist 1983 article called "Anglomania: The Second British Invasion," *Rolling Stone* editor Parke Puterbaugh pointed out that English acts had come to utterly dominate the American pop charts. One week that summer, eighteen of the top forty songs in America had come from the United Kingdom. Even in the peak British Invasion days of 1965, English artists hadn't taken up that much chart real estate. That week, the Police's stalker ballad "Every Breath You Take" held the #1 spot, and it went on to become the year's biggest hit.

In the article, Puterbaugh identified "Don't You Want Me" as the "breakthrough song" of this second British Invasion: "This was a very different New Wave record: it was apolitical, there were no guitars, and it was poppish, up-tempo, and danceable—so much so that it could fit in nicely at the stateside discos frequented by all the John Travolta white-suit types. And do so without mortally offending the musical sensibilities of those who hated such places. Obviously, some sort of bridge was being built here." Once the Human League crossed that bridge, more acts followed. After "Don't You Want Me," MTV became a breeding ground for British synthpop hits. ABC, Kajagoogoo, Spandau Ballet, Depeche Mode, a Flock of Seagulls, the Thompson Twins, and many others scored American hits. American artists like Prince took note, adapting the spiky sonic minimalism of British new wave.

More conventional British pop stars also benefited. The fresh-faced young duo Wham! used videos to highlight their bright-white smiles and floofy hair. Later, after the group's breakup, Wham! member George Michael became one of the biggest stars of the late eighties. Sheffield hard rockers Def Leppard used elaborate production and cartoonish videos to capture American imaginations; they had a #1 hit of their own by the end of the eighties. Phil Collins, who'd started out as the drummer of the seventies prog band Genesis before becoming the group's frontman, went solo with an album of stark, synthy laments about the end of his marriage. In the early years of MTV, Collins cultivated an image as an affable middle-aged everyman, and he took it to the bank. By the end of the eighties, Collins had seven #1 hits as a solo artist, plus one more with Genesis.

Ultimately, video did not kill the radio star. The elaborately made-up UK bands eventually inspired an American backlash. The seventies radio-rock titans returned. In the mideighties, Boston, Foreigner, REO Speedwagon, and Heart all enjoyed resurgences, and all of them landed #1 hits in the United States. American bands developed their own flashy and theatrical forms of pop music. Glam metal, which was somehow both macho and androgynous, colonized MTV, effectively replacing synthpop. With the blockbuster success of stars like Michael Jackson and Bruce Springsteen, pop production became slick and loud and maximalist, and sounds like the arch synthpop of the Human League fell out of favor.

The Human League themselves struggled to follow "Don't You Want Me." After that song reached #1, *Dare* went platinum. "(Keep Feeling) Fascination," a follow-up single added to the album's American version, reached #8. But the group spent three years recording *Hysteria*, their follow-up album. On that record, the Human League tried adding rock guitars, a sound they'd always belittled as "archaic" in interviews, and attempted to sincerely address political issues. The album tanked badly, and lead single "The Lebanon" peaked at a pitiful #64. The Human League eventually returned to #1 in America, but they had to become a completely different beast to do it.

By 1986, the Human League's membership had become a revolving door, and the band couldn't settle on a sound for their next album. A&M exec John McClain hit on the idea of teaming the Human League up with the songwriting and production team of Jimmy Jam and Terry Lewis. Jam and Lewis were both former members of the Time, the Prince-allied Minneapolis funk band, and their style was a funked-up take on the dance-pop of the moment. Earlier in 1986, McClain had paired Jam and Lewis up with Michael Jackson's younger sister, Janet, whose career hadn't yet taken off. Jam and Lewis had worked with Janet Jackson on her album *Control*, and that album had become a blockbuster, one of the year's biggest sellers. In the winter of 1987, then, the Human League went out to Minneapolis to work with Jimmy Jam and Terry Lewis.

Jam and Lewis essentially seized control of the Human League while working on the album *Crash*. Jam and Lewis tossed out many of the songs that the group had written, subbed in their own tracks, and used their own session musicians. The producers wrote the lead single, "Human," which is its own tale of sexual power politics. On "Human," Philip Oakey plays half of a broken-up couple. He begs to get back together and admits that he's cheated: "I'm only human / Of flesh and blood I'm made." Joanne Catherall eventually admits that she's cheated, too. The track sounds nothing like the Human League of five years earlier, but apparently that's what the group needed. "Human" reached #1 in November 1986. The Human League never had another significant hit after that. In the nineties, the Human League found their way to the nostalgia circuit.

The synthpop era that the Human League kicked off with "Don't You Want Me" didn't last long. The synths remained, but within a few years, the pop charts had become the domain of bigger, slicker, more demonstrative music. Still, the success of "Don't You Want Me" heralded a decisive break in the pop-music lineage. MTV was a whole new form of music-based communication, a new way for artists to grab the imaginations of record buyers. With the rise of MTV, the pop charts became brighter, more playful, and more adventurous. Once MTV stopped thinking of itself as a visual equivalent of rock radio, things changed again. It took a shamefully long time for MTV to start playing Black artists. Once that finally happened, though, one pop star reached whole new levels of blockbuster success that nobody had ever even considered possible.

CHAPTER 10

Michael Jackson—
"Billie Jean"

Released January 2, 1983
Hit #1 March 5, 1983
Seven-week reign

"THOSE WERE GOOD SONGS," SAYS MICHAEL JACKSON, flashing a smile at the camera. Then his eyes go down. He's breathing heavily, looking wistful for the moment that has just happened, his long-awaited onstage reunion with his brothers. "I like those songs a lot. But especially . . . I like . . . the new songs." With those pauses, Jackson's body language changes. He's not reminiscing anymore. He's seizing his moment. Jackson looks up, finds the camera with his eyes again. His eyebrows arch. The crowd buzzes louder and louder with each pause. They know what's coming. Before Jackson is even done with the sentence, someone yells, "Billie Jean!" When he finishes talking, the crowd screams.

Jackson bends down and picks up a black fedora. He spins around, his body forming an angular geometric puzzle of a silhouette before the drums even kick in. The crowd is on its feet before the bass line arrives. Then, a few minutes later, the crowd screams again, but it's a different kind of scream. It's not the scream of an audience watching a beloved performer launching into a hit song. It's a sound of rising disbelief, of delight that borders on terror. It's the sound of people who are seeing something they've never seen before.

On the wordless bridge of his song "Billie Jean"—the passage where the only vocals are *hee!s* and *hoo!s*—Jackson's body moves into a series of shifting poses. Then he glides backward across the stage, seemingly moving in multiple directions at once. That's where the audience loses its mind. Jackson comes out of that glide by spinning around three times, then by dipping into a crouch, his body balanced on his toes. After the performance, Jackson was reportedly upset. He wanted to hold that frozen *en pointe* moment for longer. He thought he'd failed. Nobody else thought that. Everybody else was just reeling from the sensation of seeing Jackson slide across that stage like a magician.

That backward-glide move was not new. Before Michael Jackson, the move was known as the backslide. Cab Calloway may have been doing some variation on that move as early as the thirties. Versions of that move appear in Hollywood musicals, executed by stars like Judy Garland, Bill Bailey, and Dick Van Dyke. In the 1974 film *The Little Prince*, choreographer Bob Fosse did his own version of the backslide, and everything about Jackson's "Billie Jean" performance, from the tight black suit to the liquid slinkiness of the poses, echoed Fosse's performance of "A Snake in the Grass." James Brown, another clear Michael Jackson influence, had done the backslide; so had the Temptations' David Ruffin. A dance group called the Electric Boogaloos backslid to the Michael Jackson song "Workin' Day and Night" on *Soul Train* in 1979. Three years later, Jeffrey Daniel, a member of the dance-funk group Shalamar, did the backslide on the United Kingdom's *Top of the Pops*.

Years later, both Jeffrey Daniel and the Electric Boogaloos' Cooley Jaxson claimed that they'd shown Michael Jackson how to do the backslide. Daniel said, "Michael was fascinated with the backslide, as was everyone, because it's not so much a dance step as an illusion, and people couldn't figure out how it was done. They thought I had wheels on my shoes or a rope pulling me across the floor. [Jackson] got in touch and wanted me to show him how to do it." When Michael Jackson did the backslide, though, he transformed it into something even more dramatic and hypnotic. Jackson had a new name for it, too: the Moonwalk.

The night Michael Jackson did the Moonwalk, his single "Billie Jean" had been the #1 song in America for two weeks. Motown, Jackson's former record label, had thrown itself a big party at the Pasadena Civic Auditorium. Many of the label's former stars, figures like Diana Ross and Marvin Gaye, returned for a grand concert to celebrate Motown's twenty-fifth anniversary. On the show, Jackson signed on to reunite with his brothers, bringing back the original Jackson 5 lineup for the first time in eight years. (When the Jackson brothers left Motown for CBS Records in 1975, Jermaine Jackson, who'd married Berry Gordy's daughter Hazel, remained at Motown as a solo artist. Since Motown owned the Jackson 5 name, the brothers recorded as the Jacksons, with youngest brother Randy replacing Jermaine.) Michael agreed to the performance, but only if he could sing his own new single, as well. Berry Gordy enthusiastically agreed.

At the Pasadena Civic Auditorium, the Jackson 5 sang a beautiful, electric medley of their seventies hits—songs that they'd all performed together as children. They all embraced together before ceding the stage to Michael. Michael Jackson wore clothes covered in sequins and sparkles, including a single rhinestoned white glove. Since Motown wasn't certain whether its live band could adequately replicate the "Billie Jean" groove, Michael Jackson lip-synched his own record. That night, "Billie Jean" was the only non-Motown record performed at Motown's big celebration.

Two months later, NBC aired the concert as a TV special. By that time, "Billie Jean" had fallen from #1, and another Michael Jackson single, "Beat It," had taken that top spot. But that "Billie Jean" performance still came to define Michael Jackson in the popular imagination. Jackson seemed like a mystical figure—a young man with intense eyes who moved like a mirage, hovering and sparkling. When NBC aired *Motown 25: Yesterday, Today, Forever* in May 1983, thirty-four million people tuned in to watch. The next day, an eighty-four-year-old Fred Astaire called Michael Jackson to congratulate him for what he'd just done: "You're a hell of a mover. Man, you really put them on their asses last night."

Astaire's validation meant the world to Michael Jackson because Jackson saw himself as something akin to Fred Astaire. Jackson was a pure entertainer, a figure whose sheer physical presence could trigger rapture in mass audiences. He had started to envision his music videos as versions of the old Hollywood musical numbers that he loved. With his *Thriller* album, Jackson moved pop music to the center of popular culture, occupying a space in the American dream life that only film stars like Fred Astaire had ever known.

When "Billie Jean" reached #1, and when that Motown special aired, Jackson was twenty-five years old, and he'd been performing for most of his life. Jackson was the eighth of ten children born into a working-class family in Gary, Indiana. His father, Joe, worked as a crane operator at a steel mill and played guitar in an R&B group on the weekends. One day, Joe found out that his son Tito had been messing with his guitar, and Joe demanded to see what Tito could do with it. Impressed, Joe bought Tito a guitar, and then he organized five of his sons into a singing group. Joe drilled his sons relentlessly, beating and berating them until they achieved perfect precision. His abuse landed especially hard on five-year-old Michael, the youngest member of the group. (Joe would call Michael "big nose"; Michael would later go through multiple rounds of cosmetic surgery until he'd more or less removed his nose entirely.) Joe booked the Jackson 5 at Black venues like the Apollo in New York and the Regal in Chicago. The Jackson brothers released a single on a local Gary label in 1967, and they auditioned for Motown more than once before Berry Gordy agreed that they were ready.

By 1969, when Gordy finally signed the Jackson 5 to Motown, Michael was a young hurricane of charisma. He sang in a squeaking, overjoyed yelp, and he danced like a tiny version of James Brown and Jackie Wilson, R&B's greatest showmen. Gordy put all of Motown's muscle behind the Jackson 5, and the label devised the fictional backstory that Diana Ross had discovered the group. Gordy himself cowrote many of the Jackson 5's early singles, forming a new crew of songwriters, nicknamed the Corporation, to come up with their tracks. The Jackson 5's first Motown single, the incandescent and ebullient "I Want You Back," reached #1 early in 1970. At the time, Michael Jackson was eleven. To this day, he remains the youngest person ever to sing lead on a #1 hit. (Born in the summer of 1958, Jackson is also the first Hot 100 chart-topper who wasn't yet alive at the beginning of the Hot 100 era.)

The Jackson 5's first four singles all reached #1—a record that stood unsurpassed for two more decades. Michael sang lead on all of those singles, and he also landed a #1 hit of his own in 1972. "Ben," Michael's first solo chart-topper, was the theme from the film of the same name. The movie, the sequel to 1971's *Willard*, is a horror story about a boy who befriends rats and uses them to murder his tormenters. With "Ben," the fourteen-year-old Michael Jackson had to sing a tender platonic love song to a rat. Young Michael delivered the song with tremulous sincerity, never acknowledging the absurdity of the enterprise, and he wound up with a song that probably became more popular than the film it soundtracked.

The Jackson 5 eventually drifted down the charts, and Joe Jackson, believing that Motown wasn't prioritizing his boys anymore, took them to the CBS imprint Epic in 1975. Over the next few years, Michael wrote more and more of the Jacksons' singles, sometimes in collaboration with his younger brother, Randy. In 1978, Michael also took his first and only role in a Hollywood film, playing the Scarecrow in Sidney Lumet's version of *The Wiz*—*The Wizard of Oz* reimagined as a musical with an all-Black cast. (Michael's former labelmate Diana Ross played Dorothy.) Working on the movie, Michael moved to New York, where he frequented clubs like Studio 54 and immersed himself in the sound of disco. Michael also got to know Quincy Jones, the producer of the film's soundtrack, and he asked Jones to produce his next solo album.

Quincy Jones had started out as a jazz musician in the fifties, and he'd quickly worked his way up the record-industry ladder to become a composer, arranger, and producer. In the early sixties, working with the young white singer Lesley Gore, Jones became one of the first Black producers to achieve mainstream pop success; Gore's Jones-produced "It's My Party" topped the Hot 100 in 1963. Quincy Jones also became one of the first Black composers to score a major motion picture when Sidney Lumet hired him for 1964's *The Pawnbroker*. In the sixties and seventies, Jones worked with pre–rock 'n' roll greats like Frank Sinatra, Ella Fitzgerald, Dizzy Gillespie, and Count Basie, and he also learned how to adapt his layered, symphonic sounds to an evolving pop landscape.

Working together on the 1979 album *Off the Wall*, Michael Jackson and Quincy Jones came up with a sleek, sophisticated new sound. The Jackson 5's early hits had been up-tempo R&B, so adapting to the disco era wasn't a huge leap. But on *Off the Wall*, Jackson and Jones moved beyond disco, into a lush and overpowering new zone of soaring, expansive pop music. Jones hooked Jackson up with a team of ace session musicians and songwriters, and Jackson also wrote some of the album's songs himself. All the assembled talents helped Jackson reach a different level as a musician, as Jackson's fragile, giddy tenor ascended to new realms of expressive power.

In 1979, Michael Jackson fired Joe Jackson as his manager. With *Off the Wall*, Michael effectively separated himself from his family and found his own voice. Michael released *Off the Wall* a few weeks before he turned twenty. The album's first single, "Don't Stop 'til You Get Enough," reached #1. Jackson wrote that one, and his delivery on the song was somewhere between an ecstatic sigh and a disbelieving whoop. He sounded like a baby superhero, just beginning to unlock the possibilities of what he could do.

Off the Wall sold seven million copies, and it sent another single, the tingling ballad "Rock with You," to #1. Two more singles, "Off the Wall" and "She's Out of My Life," also reached the top 10. In the 1980 calendar year, only Pink Floyd's *The Wall* and Eagles' *The Long Run* sold more copies than *Off the Wall*. But Jackson was disappointed when his album won only one Grammy in 1980. He thought he could sell more, that he could do better. He was right.

Michael Jackson and Quincy Jones specifically conceived *Thriller* as something that could become the biggest album in the world. For a Black artist in 1982, this was an audacious goal. In the years after disco fell out of favor, the pop music world grew more and more segregated. Radio stations, driven by consumer research, adapted segmented, targeted formats, and white stations rarely played Black artists. MTV did the same; the only Black artists on the station were occasional novelties like the British kiddie-reggae group Musical Youth, whose 1982 single "Pass the Dutchie" reached #10.

In 1982, the year that Michael Jackson released *Thriller*, only two Black singers, Lionel Richie and Stevie Wonder, notched #1 hits. Richie, the former Commodores leader, got there with the adult-contemporary ballad "Truly." Wonder's big success was "Ebony and Ivory," a racial-harmony duet with former Beatle Paul McCartney. McCartney wrote that song, and its utopian view of race relations seemed naive even at the time. R&B and soul songs still regularly topped the Hot 100 in the early eighties, but the people making those songs, by and large, were white. Daryl Hall and John Oates, two white guys who had come up on the Philadelphia soul scene, had become hugely popular in the early eighties by making twitchy, synthy versions of R&B. MTV didn't play Black artists, but it did play Hall and Oates.

With *Thriller*, Michael Jackson and Quincy Jones were determined not to make an album that could be dismissed as simply R&B.
Thriller would be pop music, and it would leave out no potential audiences. The LP was built on the shivery, exuberant postdisco sound of
Off the Wall, but different songs drew on influences from across the
musical map. Jones used the members of Toto, the white rock group
that reached #1 with the 1983 single "Africa," as studio musicians, and
Toto member Steve Lukather cowrote the ballad "Human Nature."
Jones also told Jackson to write a rock song, something like the Knack's
1979 hit "My Sharona," and Jackson responded with "Beat It," a stomping and riff-driven dance-metal track. Lukather helped arrange "Beat
It," and he played the song's central guitar riff. As a favor to Quincy
Jones, Eddie Van Halen, the flamboyant virtuoso from the band who
bore his name, played the song's pyrotechnic guitar solo, asking for no
payment in return.

Epic rolled out *Thriller* with the same precision as a blockbuster
film or a presidential campaign. The album's first single was "The Girl
Is Mine," a knowingly silly duet with Paul McCartney. "The Girl Is
Mine" might be the worst, most insubstantial song on *Thriller*, but it
was transparently not an R&B song. Instead, "The Girl Is Mine" was
a playful and approachable bid for white radio. McCartney's presence
was a statement. With the Beatles, McCartney had arrived in America
nearly two decades earlier, playing music that drew heavily on Black
American R&B; his bass playing was especially influenced by that of
Motown house musician James Jamerson. After the Beatles' breakup,
McCartney was still a star. McCartney remained a pop force through
the seventies, topping the charts as a solo artist and with his band
Wings. McCartney had written "Girlfriend," one of the songs from
Off the Wall, and he'd just had a huge success with his Stevie Won-
der duet. More important, McCartney was a living reminder of the last
time a pop act had achieved true world-dominating success. Jackson
had his sights set on Beatles-level omnipresence. With "The Girl Is
Mine," he made the connection explicit.

Jackson followed "The Girl Is Mine" with the sheer pop master-piece "Billie Jean," and that became the first *Thriller* single to reach #1. "Billie Jean" draws its power from its tension and its anger. Jackson later said that the character of Billie Jean is a composite figure, not based on any one person. In his memoir, *Moonwalk*, Jackson claimed that he'd seen versions of the "Billie Jean" story as a child, in the group-ies who would approach the Jackson 5: "There were a lot of Billie Jeans out there. Every girl claimed that their son was related to one of my brothers." Michael found this both fascinating and repellent.

Michael himself had stalkers. One woman reportedly wrote let-ters to Michael, claiming that he was the father of one of her sons and threatening to kill both herself and the child. Another jumped the fence of Michael's house and sat patiently waiting for him in his kitchen. Michael wrote "Billie Jean" in 1981, the same year that dis-turbed, obsessive young men had shot two of the most famous people in the world. Mark David Chapman had murdered John Lennon, and John Hinckley had shot Ronald Reagan, the newly elected president, because of his fixation on Michael's fellow child star Jodie Foster. But Michael didn't write "Billie Jean" about a young man with a gun. He wrote it about a girl.

In the song, Billie Jean tells Michael's narrator that he's the father of her son. Jackson sounds anxious, paranoid, furious. The lyrics never make it clear whether Jackson's character really is the father. On the chorus, the narrator denies all of Billie Jean's claims. He protests that Billie Jean is not his lover and that the kid is not his son. But that same narrator also admits that the boy's eyes look like his, that the law is on her side. The narrator's mother tells him that "the lie becomes the truth," and that leaves open the question of who's lying. Jackson sounds like he's trapped in a horror-movie scenario, questioning his own truth and uncertain about what's real and what's not. For a pop song, "Billie Jean" paints a strikingly layered psychological portrait.

Jackson sings "Billie Jean" without the sheer, effortless joy that he'd brought to *Off the Wall* singles like "Don't Stop 'til You Get Enough."

Instead, the Jackson of "Billie Jean" sounds cold and intense. His voice is an anguished yelp. He's lost and scared and vulnerable, and he uses rhythmic ad-libs like armor. His delivery is full of Tourettic tics, grunting and yipping and gasping. The beat throbs mercilessly, and Jackson pushes his voice against it, like a prisoner helplessly thrashing at the bars of his cell.

When he wrote "Billie Jean," Jackson came up with the groove first. The source of that groove is a matter of some debate. Daryl Hall once said that the "Billie Jean" bass line came from Hall and Oates's 1982 chart-topper "I Can't Go for That (No Can Do)." Hall claimed that Jackson approached him when the two of them were working on the 1985 all-star charity song "We Are the World" and that Jackson said, "I hope you don't mind, but I stole 'Billie Jean' from you." (Hall's response: "It's all right, man, I just ripped the bass line off, so can you!")

Quincy Jones, meanwhile, once said, "Michael stole a lot of stuff, man. He stole a lot of songs. 'State of Independence' and 'Billie Jean.' The notes don't lie, man. He was as Machiavellian as they come." "State of Independence" was a 1981 song from Yes singer Jon Anderson and Greek keyboard auteur Vangelis. In 1982, Quincy Jones produced Donna Summer's cover of "State of Independence," and Michael Jackson added backing vocals. The "Billie Jean" bass line sounds a bit like the "I Can't Go for That (No Can Do)" bass line, and it also sounds a bit like the "State of Independence" bass line. But neither of those possible inspirations has anything like the sheer dramatic impact of "Billie Jean."

In his autobiography, Jackson claimed that he knew "Billie Jean" was a hit as he was writing it. Jackson would walk around with the song in his head, obsessing over it to the point where he didn't notice what was happening in the world around him. At one point, Jackson was so "absorbed" in thinking about the song, he wrote, that he didn't realize that his car was burning: "We were getting off the freeway when a kid on a motorcycle pulls up to us and says, 'Your car's on fire.' Suddenly, we noticed the smoke and pulled over, and the whole bottom of the Rolls Royce was on fire. That kid probably saved our lives."

Michael Jackson recorded the original demo for "Billie Jean" at home, singing over a programmed drum machine. On the demo, Greg Phillinganes, a session musician who played on many of Jackson's songs, played the bass line on a mini-Moog keyboard. The demo is rough and muffled. The full song structure isn't there yet, and Jackson simply hums a few melodies that don't yet have lyrics, but that bass line is fully formed. Jackson and Quincy Jones then went to work on the demo.

Jackson and Jones are both listed as the producers of "Billie Jean," and both of them tweaked the song extensively, working to make sure they got exactly the sound they wanted. Jones persuaded Jackson to sing some of his vocal overdubs, for instance, through a six-foot cardboard tube. Jackson asked bassist Louis Johnson, from psychedelic soul group the Brothers Johnson, to play the bass line on every instrument he owned, finally deciding that a Yamaha bass had the right tone. Johnson overdubbed that bass line three times to give it the right level of thickness.

For the drums, Quincy Jones kept Michael Jackson's drum-machine beat, but he also recruited jazz drummer Ndugu Chancler to play along on his wooden kit. Engineer Bruce Swedien custom-built a wooden drum platform and a special bass-drum cover just to get the right sonic personality from those drums. When the song was almost finished, Jones also brought in Tom Scott, a saxophonist who'd played on many of that era's hits, to add some notes on a Lyricon, a strange wind-powered synth instrument built by a company that had already gone bankrupt. The Lyricon on "Billie Jean" is the kind of thing you might not even consciously notice while hearing the song, but it was important to Jones. "It was a last-minute overdub thing," Scott later said. "Quincy calls it 'ear candy.' It's just a subliminal element that works well."

With all those subliminal elements in place, "Billie Jean" is a marvel of engineering. The song's groove is cold and merciless, and it doesn't seem to belong to any particular genre of music. In "Billie Jean," you can hear the lockstep groove of disco, the icy textures of synthpop, and the rich melodic layers of pure pop music. Jackson has some of the breathless intensity of a soul yowler like James Brown, but his voice is soft and feathery, not rough and commanding. There's funk in the guitar upstrokes. The string arrangement is full of emotional punctuation marks, like a film score. The song works as a sonic character study, as the internal monologue of a frantic mind. It also works as dance music.

In less assured hands, all these different elements might be messy and contradictory. On "Billie Jean," all of it makes sense. With its anxious pulse and its tortured melodies, "Billie Jean" sustains a mood. It has presence. In the "Billie Jean" video, Jackson translates that presence into movement. Where Jackson's videos for his *Off the Wall* singles had been low-budget and perfunctory, Jackson wanted the "Billie Jean" video to be something special.

Steve Barron, fresh from his work on the Human League's "Don't You Want Me" video, films Jackson on a set made to look like a trash-strewn alleyway. Jackson plays a mysterious, magical figure. As he walks down the street, the slabs of concrete light up under his feet. As he flips a coin into a homeless man's cup, the man's raggedly clothes are transformed into a spotless white suit. A paparazzo stalks Jackson, trying to sneak a photo of him, but the film won't capture his image. Jackson dances down the street, staring angrily into the camera.

At the end of the video, Jackson climbs a fire escape and into a window, then climbs into bed with an unseen partner. When the paparazzo tries to get another picture, Jackson vanishes into thin air, and police show up late to arrest the photographer for peeping. The video's story doesn't reflect the lyrics, and it's crude and primitive when compared with the cinematic visions that Jackson and his collaborators would later conjure. But the clip still reflects the eerie intensity of the song, and it showcases Michael Jackson as a figure defiantly determined to keep a sense of mystery around himself.

At first, MTV rejected the "Billie Jean" video. The reasoning was that MTV was a rock station, and "Billie Jean" was not a rock song. Furious CBS executives threatened to pull all the videos from CBS artists if MTV wouldn't play "Billie Jean." Walter Yetnikoff, head of the label, later claimed that he'd threatened to go to the press about MTV's racism. Finally, MTV caved. The early MTV executives have claimed that the whole story of the "Billie Jean" video is overblown, that the station was happy to play Michael Jackson. But by the time MTV added "Billie Jean" to light rotation, the song was already the #1 single in America, and *Thriller* was already the #1 album. Michael Jackson wasn't the first Black artist to appear on MTV, but the addition of "Billie Jean" opened the network up and transformed it into something other than a rock station.

On MTV, "Billie Jean" resonated, as did Jackson's elaborate musical-number video for "Beat It." "Beat It" reached #1 soon after "Billie Jean," and Jackson's two videos were more vivid and ambitious than just about anything else on MTV at the time. By the end of the year, Jackson had the idea to create a big-budget mini-movie for "Thriller," and he recruited film director John Landis to turn the song into a sort of horror mini-epic. In an era when music videos usually cost around $50,000, the "Thriller" video had a $1 million budget. By that time, Jackson was so important to MTV that the network helped to pay for the video.

In the wake of those Michael Jackson videos, MTV's ratings surged, and other artists made their own videos more elaborate and cinematic. The early faces of MTV were the British new-wave and synthpop artists who used videos to show off the playful, glamorous images that they'd created for themselves. Jackson went further, using videos to transform himself into a movie star. Others followed.

The blockbuster pop artists of the eighties—Madonna, Prince, Bruce Springsteen, Phil Collins, George Michael, even Michael's baby sister, Janet—followed Michael Jackson's blueprint. None of these figures became as big as Jackson, but all of them worked from his playbook. After what Jackson did with *Thriller*, it was rare to see a hit song that didn't have a sharp, creative music video. Jackson helped MTV move from the cultural fringes to the center of the American imagination. More than any other artist of his generation, he understood that imagery was just as important as music. Jackson was already a huge pop star before *Thriller*. With the combination of the "Billie Jean" video and the *Motown 25* performance, Jackson became something else: a figure of wonder.

Before Michael Jackson, most pop stars were either transgressive outré figures, products of various countercultures, or they were hokey variety-show types like Tony Orlando or Donny Osmond. Michael Jackson was neither. To kids in the eighties, Michael Jackson was a figure as recognizable and fantastical as Mickey Mouse. (Jackson even became a Disney World attraction himself in 1986. For years, Disney parks were the only places where you could watch Jackson in the Francis Ford Coppola–directed 3-D sci-fi mini-musical *Captain EO*, a truly strange time-capsule artifact.)

In the wake of *Thriller*, Michael Jackson, pressured by his parents, reunited with his brothers and headed out on the Victory Tour, a Pepsi-sponsored stadium spectacle with tickets so expensive that they triggered a massive backlash. Attending the show's opening night in Kansas City, critic and Michael Jackson biographer Nelson George compared the experience to the Ice Capades: "No dangerous adolescent lust or unbridled urban anger rippled through the crowd that beautiful still evening in the heartland. Instead, we had kids spending much of the time looking at a huge TV screen to ascertain whether the doll-like stick figure wiggling in the distance was indeed Michael. . . . They were looking for family entertainment; a little sentiment, a little fantasy, a little dancing, a little nostalgia, a lot of glitter."

Jackson was a true eccentric, and the press had a field day with quirks like his collection of exotic animals, his friendships with faded Hollywood icons, and his soft and childlike speaking voice. But there was nothing outwardly subversive about the way that Michael Jackson presented himself. Instead, Jackson's fame was transcendent and self-sustaining—larger than pop music itself. Later, that cultural dominance would take on a sinister edge. Families accused Jackson of sexually abusing kids, and the ensuing scandals overwhelmed Jackson's career, in part because it was clear how easily Jackson could've taken advantage of his power over kids' imaginations. Jackson had been a victim of horrific child abuse, and that was public knowledge by the time the allegations against Jackson came to light. Jackson had always seemed childlike, almost asexual. A song like "Billie Jean" drew some of its charge from Jackson's horror at the mere idea of sexuality. Jackson seemed afraid that this woman was pursuing him, that he might be at the mercy of his own weaknesses. The abuse allegations put the entire narrative of Jackson's career in a terrible new light.

In the *Thriller* era, though, Michael Jackson's strangeness only added to his power. He seemed to float above the rest of the world—a figure untouched by sex or violence or racism or poverty. This was all projection, and Jackson's life was harder and sadder than the public knew. At the time, though, Jackson seemed to glide through popular culture as effortlessly as he glided across the *Motown 25* stage.

Thriller sold in overwhelming, baffling numbers—numbers that would've seemed impossible a few years before. At its peak, *Thriller* moved a million copies a week. Jackson released seven of the nine tracks on *Thriller* as singles, and all seven made the top 10. *Thriller* had a global reach; it topped charts in Asia and Africa and anywhere else where American pop music was commercially available. In the USSR, where Jackson's music was officially banned, bootleg cassette copies of *Thriller* were reportedly hot items on the black market. By the end of 1983, *Thriller* had sold thirty-two million copies around the world. *Billboard* named *Thriller* as the best-selling album of both 1983 and 1984. At the 1984 Grammys, Michael Jackson won eight awards—at that point, the most ever won by an artist in a single night. As Jackson accepted the Album of the Year gramophone trophy, CBS boss Walter Yetnikoff joined him onstage to announce *Thriller* as "the biggest-selling album in the history of music." Decades later, *Thriller* still holds that record.

Thriller was good for the entire industry. Starting in 1979, as disco fell from popular favor, the record business went into a profound slump that lasted for years. *Thriller* ended that slump almost single-handedly. The sound of *Thriller*—huge, glossy, lively, not beholden to any particular genre—became the new sound of pop music. Other artists adjusted. Bruce Springsteen injected his hoary, dramatic, introspective arena rock with bright keyboards and dance textures on his 1984 album *Born in the USA*, and the LP approached *Thriller*-level success, spinning off seven top-10 singles of its own. New York postdisco singer Madonna followed a promising self-titled 1983 debut with *Like a Virgin*, the bright and slick blockbuster that she recorded with Chic leader and super-producer Nile Rodgers. Jackson's fellow soul veterans Lionel Richie and Tina Turner messed around with dance-pop and arena rock, and they became stadium-level global stars in the process.

None of these artists could equal the success of *Thriller*. Even for Michael Jackson, that wasn't a realistic goal. The period after *Thriller* was a complicated time for Jackson. On the Victory Tour, Michael and his brothers performed for upwards of two million fans, but many of those fans were angry over the high ticket prices, and the tour itself was planned so badly that it still lost money. (Promoter Chuck Sullivan, then the owner of the New England Patriots, had to sell both his football team and his stadium to cover those losses.) Michael didn't want to do the tour in the first place, and as it ended, he announced that it would be the last time he would head out on the road with his brothers. Michael stuck to his word there, and he didn't perform even a one-off with the other Jacksons again until a 2001 TV special.

After *Thriller*, Michael became increasingly isolated from both his family and his faith. The leaders of the Jehovah's Witnesses, Jackson's church, demanded that Jackson apologize for the horror-movie imagery in the "Thriller" video. Michael went along with it, but he distanced himself from the church afterward. Michael also signed an expensive endorsement deal with Pepsi. At a commercial shoot, an errant firework set Michael's hair on fire. In the aftermath, Michael developed a dependence on painkillers that eventually led to his death at age fifty.

Finally, five years after *Thriller*, Jackson released his album *Bad*. Working once again with Quincy Jones, Jackson tried to sound tougher, adapting the jagged and percussive sounds of the various kinds of electronic dance music that had come along in the years after *Thriller*. *Bad* was a huge success, and five of its singles reached #1, a number that no album has ever exceeded. But *Bad* sold only about ten million copies in the United States. For any other artist, that would've been a career-vindication number. For a post-*Thriller* Michael Jackson, it was a disappointment.

Jackson's later years would be defined by confusion and scandal. Jackson would go back and forth between total reclusion and tone-deaf attempts to return to public life. In 2003, Jackson told journalist Martin Bashir that he didn't molest kids but that he routinely had kids over at his house to spend the night with him: "It's not sexual. We're going to sleep." Jackson released his final #1 hit—"You Are Not Alone," written by future pariah R. Kelly—in 1995. He barely released any music in the years that followed. When Jackson died of an accidental drug overdose in 2009, he was preparing for a run of comeback concerts in London. He hadn't released an album in eight years.

Ultimately, Michael Jackson is a tragic and troubling figure, but he's also a pivotal one. With "Billie Jean" and *Thriller*, Jackson changed the size and scope of pop music. He moved things away from segregated radio formats and toward a pan-racial, pan-genre music-video future. He left behind music that's too deeply embedded in our shared cultural memory to ever disappear. Every time there's another round of stories about Jackson's alleged sexual abuses, I wonder if those songs will finally slip from circulation—if I'll stop hearing those songs at parties and weddings and over supermarket speakers. It never happens. Jackson's music is as present today as it was when he lip-synched "Billie Jean" on that Pasadena stage in 1983.

CHAPTER 11

Prince–
"When Doves Cry"

Released May 16, 1984
Hit #1 July 7, 1984
Five-week reign

PRINCE HAD NO BUSINESS BECOMING A MOVIE STAR. LONG before Prince, plenty of pop stars had turned to film, and plenty had been successful. Frank Sinatra won an Oscar as an actor. Elvis Presley was a mini-movie industry unto himself, starring in dozens of cheap and low-stakes programmers between 1956 and 1970. The Beatles made only a few films, but *A Hard Day's Night*, their 1964 onscreen debut, remains the purest and most entertaining document of Beatlemania at its height. In 1983, though, Prince Rogers Nelson was nowhere near the level of those past stars. At that point, Prince had only one hit album to his name. Still, Prince was determined to make Hollywood his. He tried, and he succeeded.

If Michael Jackson understood the value of image, Prince took it further. Prince knew mythmaking. Even as a teenage funk prodigy coming out of the relative hinterlands of Minneapolis, Prince cultivated a sexed-up and elusive mystique. He was not a woman. He was not a man. He was something that we would never understand. Prince played with genre and gender with equal aplomb, and he turned himself into an enigmatic genius figure, an unknowable fuck-sphinx who could move mountains with a sneer or a squeak. At his peak, Prince was a complement and counterbalance to Michael Jackson—a transcendent eighties pop figure who built his empire on sex and mystery rather than flash and movement.

Prince worked as an oppositional force to Michael Jackson in part because the two men had so much in common. Like Jackson before him, Prince was a Black prodigy from the Upper Midwest, born in the summer of 1958. (Prince was a few months older than Jackson.) Like Jackson, Prince came from a family of musicians; Prince's father, a jazz pianist, had once used Prince Rogers as a stage name, and he later cowrote a few of his son's songs. Unlike Michael Jackson, though, Prince actively sought the spotlight; his family didn't thrust him into it. Prince arrived almost a decade after Jackson, but he did it on his own terms.

Prince started writing songs on piano when he was seven years old. In high school, he had a tumultuous family life, shuttling between the houses of parents and friends, but he still played three sports and studied dance. He also learned how to play guitar, bass, drums, and keyboards. At nineteen, Prince recorded a demo at a local studio, and three different major labels tried to sign him. The young artist was very deliberate about his choices. He made demands.

Warner Bros. offered Prince a three-album deal with near-complete creative control. At Prince's insistence, the label signed him as a pop act, promoting him to more than just Black radio stations. Like Michael Jackson, Prince wasn't interested in playing to a particular audience. He wanted everyone. Maurice White, frontman of the sophisticated pop-funk group Earth, Wind & Fire, offered to produce Prince's 1978 debut album, *For You*, but Prince turned him down, preferring to produce himself. He recorded the album at Sausalito's Record Plant, the same studio where Fleetwood Mac had made *Rumours*, and he played every instrument on the LP himself.

Prince's early records were sharp, funky dance-pop that fitted loosely within the late-seventies disco zeitgeist. His biggest early hit, 1979's "I Wanna Be Your Lover," was essentially a disco song, and it just missed the top 10, reaching #11 on the Hot 100. But by the time he made the 1980 album *Dirty Mind*, Prince was playing around with both sound and sexuality. On the *Dirty Mind* cover, Prince posed in a trench coat and a pair of bikini briefs. He sang enigmatically about incest and group sex. He protected his elusive, slippery public image, refusing to give interviews and making sure he looked stage ready any-time he was out in public. He also experimented musically. Prince absorbed the beats of UK synthpop early, and the sparse precision of those records crept into his own. He was also a masterful guitar shred-der, and he wasn't shy about showing off.

Like Sly Stone before him, Prince recruited a backing band with Black and white members and with men and women. Lisa Coleman, keyboardist for the Revolution, later said, "The band was such an important media tool for him. . . . His dream was that we would be Fleetwood Mac mixed with Sly and the Family Stone." On the *Dirty Mind* anthem "Uptown," Prince imagined his Minneapolis hometown as a border-free musical utopia: "Black, white, Puerto Rican, every-body just a-freakin'." But in the racially stratified early-eighties radio landscape, Prince had trouble fitting in anywhere. He toured as the opening act for funk star Rick James, who accused Prince of ripping off stage moves and actually stole some of Prince's programmed key-boards. A pair of dates with the Rolling Stones in 1980 proved disas-trous. The predominantly white Los Angeles audience booed Prince as soon as he stepped onstage. After that, Prince never played another show where he wasn't the headliner. Rather than attaching himself to the stars of Black or white radio, Prince simply became an institution unto himself.

Prince's first four albums sold respectably and got good reviews, and the artist developed a reputation as an incendiary live act, but he didn't become a pop star until he came out with the double album *1999* in 1982. Released a month before Michael Jackson's *Thriller*, *1999* benefited from a new landscape where radio no longer shied away from genre-fluid, dance-heavy pop music from Black artists. The slinky, horny video for "Little Red Corvette" broke through on MTV after "Billie Jean" and "Beat It," and it became Prince's first top-10 pop hit, peaking at #6. Soon after, "Delirious" made it to #8, and rising star Eddie Murphy took its title for his 1983 stand-up comedy special.

Prince used MTV, just as Michael Jackson had done, but he was never a music-video artist like Jackson. Prince didn't put himself at the center of Hollywood-style musical extravaganzas. Instead, videos for Prince hits like "Little Red Corvette" were mostly just minimally produced depictions of the Prince live show. They made for bewitching television simply because Prince himself was bewitching. He could *move*, strutting and preening and spinning across stages. He never broke character.

Jackson had captured America's heart as an evolutionary song-and-dance man, a family entertainer for the whole world. There was sex in Jackson's music, but it was an undercurrent. With Prince, sex couldn't be more overt. Jackson's success had opened things up for an artist like Prince to finally take mainstream pop by storm, but even as a star, Prince remained slippery and mysterious. Where Jackson aimed for the dead center of mainstream fame, befriending veteran movie stars and appearing with Ronald Reagan at the White House, Prince presented himself as something stranger and more rebellious. His act probably worked, at least in part, because it stood in such stark contrast to what Jackson was doing at the same time.

After the success of *1999*, Prince set his sights on film stardom. The artist gave his managers an ultimatum: they would find him a movie deal, or he would take his business elsewhere. The music and film departments at Warner Bros. hadn't fully bought into the idea of corporate synergy, and the movie studio's last pop-star vehicle, Paul

Simon's 1980 vanity project *One Trick Pony*, had flopped. Prince himself wasn't yet an established star, and he'd never acted before. The studio was understandably skeptical about investing too much money in this young pop star's vision. But new things were happening in film, and the people at Warner knew that they needed to keep up.

MTV was just starting to change movies. In 1983, *Flashdance*, a low-budget triumphant-underdog story about a steelworker trying to get into a prestigious dance school, had adapted MTV-style quick-cut editing, bringing its own sense of neon cocaine delirium to the cinema. *Flashdance* became one of the year's biggest hits, and its soundtrack album sold millions. As with *Saturday Night Fever* six years earlier, the album sold the movie, and the movie sold the album.

After *Purple Rain* went into production, something similar happened with *Footloose*. There were no pop stars in the *Footloose* cast, but the entire thing was the brainchild of Dean Pitchford, a hitmaking songwriter and first-time screenwriter. The movie had tons of scenes that looked and moved like music videos. Pitchford cowrote all the songs on the soundtrack, including #1 hits from Kenny Loggins and Deniece Williams. The *Footloose* movie and album were both smashes. People were going to the movies to watch things that felt a whole lot like MTV. In the years ahead, that whole style would help drive blockbusters like *Beverly Hills Cop* and *Top Gun*, both of which came from Jerry Bruckheimer and Don Simpson, the *Flashdance* producers who understood the allure of MTV. As an MTV star in this climate, Prince was in a good position.

Still, *Purple Rain* was not a priority for Warner Bros. The film had a small budget and almost no professional actors in the cast. Apollonia Kotero, Prince's *Purple Rain* love interest, was a last-minute replacement for Prince's departing protégé Vanity, who had left Prince's orbit to sign with Motown and later starred in the Berry Gordy–produced kung fu cult classic *The Last Dragon*. Kotero had been in a TV movie called *The Mystic Warrior*, a very Prince title, but she wasn't exactly a screen veteran. Clarence Williams III, the actor who played Prince's character's father, had been one of the stars of the late-sixties TV series *The Mod Squad*, and he was easily the most experienced actor on set.

Virtually the entire *Purple Rain* cast was made up of people from the Minneapolis music scene, all playing lightly fictionalized versions of their own personae. Even director Albert Magnoli was a newcomer, a recent film-school graduate who was working as a film editor and who'd only ever directed a college-project short film. This unlikely group shot *Purple Rain* during a freezing Minneapolis winter. Against odds, they made a movie that captured the popular imagination.

Purple Rain is essentially Prince's version of his own myth. It's the story of a Minneapolis kid—literally known simply as the Kid—whose music reaches another artistic level when he digs deeper into his own traumas. As a movie, *Purple Rain* is formulaic in a pleasant, satisfying way. As a piece of persona craftsmanship, it's a masterpiece. Prince manages to tell some version of his own story without revealing anything much about himself *or* his character, and he does it with an incredible blitz of musical performances that, in terms of sheer presence, made him the closest thing that Michael Jackson ever had to a peer or a competitor.

Prince exists at the center of *Purple Rain* as a quiet, pulsating presence. Piloting his gleaming motorcycle through Minneapolis, Minnesota, Prince is a beautiful, shimmering blank. Onstage at his Minneapolis home base, First Avenue, he's a sexual-expressionist dervish. In the film, he surrounds himself with similarly colorful characters; Morris Day, leader of the villainous rival group the Time, pops especially hard as an outsize comic presence. In real life, Day was a Prince protégé. Prince had assembled the Time from the membership of the local funk group Flyte Tyme. Prince and Day had gone to high school together, and Day had once been a drummer in the Prince-led band Grand Central. Prince installed Day as the leader of the Time. Prince also wrote all the songs and played all the instruments on the Time's records; the entire point of the band was for Prince to give himself some competition. With the Time and with his various other protégés and side projects and offshoots, Prince essentially remade the Minneapolis music scene in his own image, and that scene is on full glorious display in *Purple Rain*. The film makes the icy midwestern city look like the coolest place in the world.

But that larger music scene doesn't appear on the *Purple Rain* soundtrack. The Time give a handful of wildly entertaining performances in the movie, and other Prince-associated acts like Apollonia 6 and the Modernaires also make appearances. The soundtrack album, however, is all Prince's show. For the LP, Prince distilled all his pop savvy and disparate influences into a tight, flashy nine-song package. Every song on *Purple Rain* crackles with electricity, and every one goes in a different musical direction. Opening track "Let's Go Crazy" is Prince's hypercharged, euphoric take on a party-starting sixties rock 'n' roll rave-up. Meanwhile, Prince recorded the closing track "Purple Rain" live at First Avenue, and it's his glorious version of the sort of power ballad that rock acts like Bob Seger and Journey were using to fill early-eighties arenas. In between we get shimmering psychedelic pop on "Take Me with U," gently pleading new-age soul on "The Beautiful Ones," strutting synth-funk showmanship on "Baby I'm a Star."

"When Doves Cry" was the last track that Prince recorded for his *Purple Rain* soundtrack. Albert Magnoli, the movie's young director, told Prince that the film needed one more song—something that would directly touch on the film's themes, something that could play in the background during a montage where Prince rode a motorcycle around while looking pensive. Prince disappeared into his studio and returned two days later with "When Doves Cry." Where most of the *Purple Rain* soundtrack is credited to Prince and the Revolution, "When Doves Cry" is all Prince. Prince wrote, produced, and arranged the song, and he played every instrument on it.

"When Doves Cry," like "Billie Jean" before it, has no genre. But "When Doves Cry" is even more aggressive in its rootlessness. There's plenty of funk in "When Doves Cry," especially in the way Prince

translates James Brown grunts into sex-frenzy panting. But unlike practically any funk song in history, "When Doves Cry" has no bass line.
Prince recorded one, but he decided that the song sounded better without it. Even the members of the Revolution were shocked at Prince's
decision to release the song—or any song—without a bass line, but
that decision helped the song stand out. That absence at the center of
the track gives "When Doves Cry" a spartan minimalism. The mechanistic thump of its stark, brittle drum-machine beat ties the track in
with the synthpop of its era; in clubs, "When Doves Cry" could play
straight into a song like Duran Duran's "The Reflex," the new-wave
dance track that Prince's song knocked out of the #1 spot.

On the "When Doves Cry" intro, Prince shreds like Eddie Van
Halen, showing off his guitar skills and drawing connections between
himself and soaring, arena-conquering heavy metal. Michael Jackson
had done something similar on "Beat It," but Jackson had brought
in Steve Lukather and Eddie Van Halen to add guitar pyrotechnics.
Prince had supplied his own. Prince's guitar heroics weren't new, but
"When Doves Cry" foregrounds them and makes them impossible
to ignore or dismiss. Elsewhere, Prince also plays bombastic neoclas-
sic keyboard riffs. Embellishments like that could sink a song, but in
Prince's hands, they don't come off as indulgent. They simply add new
shades.

Prince's "When Doves Cry" lyrics do tie in specifically, if briefly,
with the themes of *Purple Rain*, with the struggles between Prince's
character and his parents. In the film, "When Doves Cry" plays when
Apollonia has just left Prince to join Morris Day's girl group, when
Prince's character needs to consider his own failings and goals. But
"When Doves Cry" is not utilitarian plot music. Instead, it's an elliptical swirl of sex and chemistry and attraction. Prince sings of oceans of
violets in bloom, of a heat between people so powerful that it makes
animals strike curious poses. He imagines himself covered in someone
else's sweat. He makes the phrase "maybe you're just like my mother"
sound seductive, a feat that no other human being could accomplish.

The out-front sexuality of "When Doves Cry" is a huge part of what makes the track so striking. Sex and pop music had been deeply intertwined before Prince was even born, but Prince weaponized sex in ways that few others had done before him. He presented himself as an androgynous enigma, someone whose hunger couldn't be contained by societal norms. The "When Doves Cry" video is the first Prince clip that didn't center around his live-performance powers. Instead, the video shows Prince slowly rising, naked, from a steaming bathtub, staring deep into the camera's eye. He stretches his hand toward us, a messianic beckon. He crawls slowly across a bathroom floor. Most of the video is simply clips from *Purple Rain*, but those few seconds of bathroom footage were so captivating and definitional that Prince used the bathtub as a stage prop during his Purple Rain tour.

Purple Rain was scheduled to hit theaters in July 1984, and test screenings had drawn such rapturous responses that Warner Bros. was worried that Prince's team was manipulating the numbers, secretly filling the theaters with the musician's fans. With the prospect of a hit on their hands, the Warner team scheduled the soundtrack's release with careful precision. First, the "When Doves Cry" single came out in May. The full album followed in June. By the time *Purple Rain* arrived in theaters, both the single and the album were hits. When you've got a movie coming out, it helps if you've already released a masterful, massively popular album to promote that movie. When the film arrived, it earned nearly $8 million in its first weekend, earning back its entire production budget and knocking *Ghostbusters* out of the top box-office spot. That week, Prince became the first person ever to have the #1 single, album, and movie in America.

"When Doves Cry," Prince's first #1 single, held down the top spot for five weeks. "Let's Go Crazy" also hit #1, while "Purple Rain" reached #2 and "I Would Die 4 U" made it as high as #8. *Billboard* later named "When Doves Cry" the biggest single of 1984, a year full of big pop singles. One of those big pop singles was Bruce Springsteen's catchy, muscular synth-rocker "Dancing in the Dark," which represented the peak of Springsteen's commercial aspirations and ended up stuck at #2 behind "When Doves Cry." "Dancing in the Dark" remains Springsteen's highest-charting single of all time, and that means that Prince is the reason that he never climbed to the top spot.

Springsteen's *Born in the USA* album came out three weeks before *Purple Rain*, and the two albums became twin blockbusters. *Purple Rain* knocked *Born in the USA* out of the #1 spot on the albums chart, and Prince's album held that spot from August until January—an uninterrupted twenty-four-week run. When *Purple Rain* finally fell from #1, *Born in the USA* replaced it, eventually becoming the biggest seller of 1985.

Springsteen was never bitter about "When Doves Cry" blocking "Dancing in the Dark" from the #1 spot, and he and Prince, both famous for putting on marathon stadium shows, spoke admiringly of one another. (Springsteen eventually joined Prince onstage during one of Prince's 1985 shows.) Springsteen and Prince may have competed for the American record-buying ear, but they saw each other as kindred spirits, and the arrival of those two albums represents a pinnacle moment for pop music: two records of supreme artistic and commercial ambition coming out and hitting at the exact same time in the post-*Thriller* moment when a great pop album could occupy the center of popular culture.

But Prince, being a restless spirit, wasn't nearly as comfortable holding that center for long. In January 1985, dozens of pop stars, including Springsteen, converged on A&M Recording Studios in Los Angeles to sing on "We Are the World," the all-star charity single that Michael Jackson and Lionel Richie had written. Producer Quincy Jones wanted Prince to sing on the song, even imagining a Prince-Jackson back-and-forth moment, but Prince wasn't interested. He offered to play guitar on the song, rather than singing, but Jones didn't want that. (*Purple Rain* producer and Prince manager Bob Cavallo says that Jones yelled at him about the offer: "I don't need [Prince] to fucking play guitar!") Instead, Prince went out partying in LA clubs after the award show was over, and he earned a ton of bad press when one of his bodyguards manhandled a fan. Prince soon became the target of a *Saturday Night Live* sketch for refusing to participate in the song's recording, even though he contributed a song of his own to the *We Are the World* album.

Prince's tour behind *Purple Rain* was a full-on stadium spectacular, the biggest of his career. But Prince quickly tired of the tour and eventually canceled its European leg. In between tour dates, he worked on his album *Around the World in a Day*, which came out nine months after *Purple Rain*, when the singles from that album were still charting. *Around the World* was full of flowery late-Beatles psychedelic experimentation, a sharp left turn from *Purple Rain*. *Around the World* still had hits, and the glowing single "Raspberry Beret" reached #2, but the album sold a fraction of what *Purple Rain* had moved. Prince remained a consistent presence in the top 10 into the early nineties, and he notched three more #1 singles. But his music grew increasingly insular and idiosyncratic, and he never had another completely dominant moment like *Purple Rain*.

Prince's pop run effectively ended shortly after his 1993 dispute with Warner Bros., when he changed his name to an unpronounceable glyph and started writing the word "slave" on his cheek. For years, Prince experimented with releasing his own albums directly to fans on the Internet or with signing short-term licensing agreements with major labels. By the early 2000s, Prince had become a beloved legacy pop figure who continued to tour relentlessly and release relatively low-stakes new music to his diehard fans. That's the cultural position that Prince occupied in 2016, when he died of an accidental fentanyl overdose at the age of fifty-seven. The public outpouring of grief in the months afterward was intense. Fans put together makeshift memorials outside First Avenue, and both "Purple Rain" and "When Doves Cry" returned to the top 10.

The *Purple Rain* era loomed large in Prince's iconography not just because of its commercial success but also because of the sense of possibility that it reflected. After *Thriller*, Black and white versions of pop music were closer to one another than they'd been since the early rock 'n' roll era. White British new-wave acts openly idolized Black American R&B. Wham! and Culture Club riffed on Smokey Robinson's soft soul. Duran Duran fixated on disco greats Chic and landed their first American #1 hit, the one that would be unseated by "When Doves Cry," when they brought in Chic's Nile Rodgers to remix their dance-pop single "The Reflex." The appreciation went both ways. Black stars like Lionel Richie and Tina Turner drew on the sparkle of new wave, while Billy Ocean, a journeyman British Trinidadian singer, followed his breakout hit "Caribbean Queen (No More Love on the Run)" with "Loverman," a revved-up rocker cowritten with Mutt Lange, the arena-rock mastermind who had helped turn AC/DC and Def Leppard into stars.

Many of the blockbuster albums of 1984 were collisions of genres. Veteran stars like Tina Turner and ZZ Top opened themselves up to bright, wiggly dance-pop and became bigger than they'd ever been. Van Halen, America's reigning purveyors of howling party-time hard rock, played around with bright, clubby keyboard sounds on their single "Jump," which built on the success of Eddie Van Halen's "Beat It" guitar solo and gave the band its only #1 hit. Big-voiced thrift-shop cartoon character Cyndi Lauper emerged out of the new-wave club scene with a form of centrist pop that was sillier and more colorful than anything else on the charts; she covered Prince's "When You Were Mine" on her massively successful debut, *She's So Unusual*. At the end of the year, New York dance-pop singer Madonna emerged with her Nile Rodgers–produced smash *Like a Virgin*, an album that took Prince's theatrical sexuality as a starting point. With her own blend of Hollywood-style image manipulation, omnivorous pop craftsmanship, and sexual provocation, Madonna soon became a peer to both Michael Jackson and Prince—the third part of the Holy Trinity of eighties pop. In retrospect, 1984 was a utopian pop moment, and Prince was at the center of it all.

Prince was everywhere on the charts in 1984, and not just because of *Purple Rain*. The previous year, Stevie Nicks had made it up to #5 with "Stand Back," a song that she wrote while humming along to "Little Red Corvette." The song was so close to Prince's original that Nicks offered Prince a songwriting credit, and a flattered Prince came to the studio to play keyboards on the track. In 1984, Prince wrote hits for protégés like the Time and virtuoso drummer Sheila E., while the funk belter Chaka Khan took a deeply funky cover of Prince's "I Feel for You" to #3.

In the years ahead, Prince wrote hits for artists like the Bangles and Sheena Easton. In 1990, Irish singer Sinéad O'Connor reached #1 with her raw, devastating take on "Nothing Compares 2 U," a song that Prince had written in 1985 for a band of protégés called the Family. In the latter half of the eighties, the songs that Prince wrote for his peers did almost as well as the ones that he wrote for himself—especially once you consider that Prince originally wrote "Kiss," his biggest post–*Purple Rain* hit, for Mazarati, a band led by the Revolution bassist Brown Mark.

Prince's songs became culturally influential in ways that Prince himself never could've anticipated. In 1985, Tipper Gore, wife of Tennessee senator and future vice president Al, was shocked to find her eleven-year-old daughter, Karenna, listening to "Darling Nikki," a *Purple Rain* song with a lyric about a girl masturbating with a magazine in a hotel lobby. In flabbergasted response, Gore cofounded the Parents Music Resource Center, a lobbying group dedicated to pressuring the music industry to curb the outwardly sexual content of pop songs. The industry, scrambling to appease Gore and her acolytes, eventually adapted the Parental Advisory sticker as a compromise. That sticker actually became a marketing point, and sales of explicit rock and rap skyrocketed in the late eighties and early nineties. In a way, then, the rise of unapologetically profane rap may have been, at least in part, a ripple effect of Prince's freakiness.

In more obvious ways, though, Prince remained a massively influential pop-music figure for years. The Jets, the Tongan American Mormon family band who scored five top-10 hits in the late eighties, came from Minneapolis; they weren't associated with Prince, but that Minneapolis mystique was crucial to their success. Other R&B groups came out of the Midwest in the years after, patterning themselves after different aspects of Prince's sound, and some, like Flint's Ready for the World and Grand Rapids's DeBarge, became significant stars. In the years immediately after *Purple Rain*, house music emerged from the gay Black clubs of Detroit and Chicago, and the genre's earliest anthems sounded like minimalist takes on Prince's squelching Minneapolis funk.

Established pop stars tried to capture some of Prince's mojo, too. Phil Collins built his 1985 chart-topper "Sussudio" on the keyboard groove that Prince had used for "1999" less than three years earlier. Songwriters Tom Kelly and Billy Steinberg attempted to replicate Prince's magic on "So Emotional," the 1987 hit that they wrote for Whitney Houston. Michael Jackson wrote "Bad," the title track from his *Thriller* follow-up, as a possible duet with Prince. (Prince declined.) George Michael, who wrote and produced nearly everything from his 1987 blockbuster, *Faith*, was a clear Prince acolyte. By the late eighties, artists like Paula Abdul, Jody Watley, and Fine Young Cannibals were flocking to Minneapolis, recording with producers who had any kind of Prince connection.

The story of Prince's influence is clearest in the rise of Jimmy Jam and Terry Lewis, the hitmaking songwriting and production team who started out as, respectively, the keyboardist and bassist in the Minneapolis funk band Flyte Tyme. When Prince turned Flyte Time into the Time, Jam and Lewis stayed in the band, but they also started producing records for acts like the SOS Band and Cherrelle. One night, as Jam and Lewis worked on an SOS Band session, a blizzard made them late for one of their shows with the Time. Prince fired both of them from the band immediately.

After their dismissal, Jam and Lewis thrived. Their signature style—a clattering, electronic take on Prince's sound—was in demand. A&M Records exec John McClain paired them with Michael Jackson's younger sister, Janet, who'd made a pair of unsuccessful pop albums on her own. Over the objections of father Joe, Janet went to Minneapolis to record with Jam and Lewis. The duo cowrote and produced Janet Jackson's 1986 smash *Control*, which generated five top-10 hits and sounded a whole lot more like Prince than like Michael Jackson. In the wake of *Control*, Janet Jackson became an A-list pop star; by the early nineties, she was arguably bigger than her older brother. As behind-the-scenes hitmakers, Jam and Lewis eventually came to eclipse Prince. The duo ultimately produced sixteen #1 hits—for Janet Jackson and also for artists like the Human League, George Michael, Boyz II Men, and Usher.

Control helped inspire the rise of new jack swing, the hybrid of R&B, dance-pop, and rap music that took over the R&B charts in the late eighties. Prince struggled to catch up with new jack swing and with the rap music that began to take over in its wake. But Prince's influence lingered on in hip-hop and R&B for years. In the twenty-first century, artists like Usher, OutKast, D'Angelo, Miguel, and Frank Ocean developed their own miasmic, shape-shifter versions of funk and soul, and all of them paid tribute to the master of the form. Meanwhile, Prince's experiments rippled across the rest of the pop landscape, sometimes in unexpected places. Take, for example, Prince's flamboyant guitar theatrics, and turn them up to eleven.

CHAPTER 12

Bon Jovi–
"You Give Love a Bad Name"

Released July 23, 1986
Hit #1 November 29, 1986
One-week reign

EVER SINCE THE LATE SIXTIES, HARD-ROCK BANDS HAVE BEEN using distortion-drenched guitar riffs and strangulated vocals to pack stadiums and sell millions of records. Until the mideighties, though, those bands only rarely made a dent in the pop charts. Heavy metal pioneers like Vanilla Fudge, Deep Purple, and Led Zeppelin all had top-10 hits in the late sixties and early seventies, when their swampy, bluesy riff-rock wasn't terribly far removed from the psychedelic mainstream. Vanilla Fudge, for instance, got to #6 with their 1968 cover of the Supremes' "You Keep Me Hangin' On," a twist on a song that would've been familiar to radio listeners. But none of those groups ever reached #1. Led Zeppelin were one of the most popular bands in the world for a solid decade, but they only ever hit the top 10 once, when their early classic "Whole Lotta Love" climbed as high as #4 in 1970.

As heavy metal developed into its own genre, it moved away from the Hot 100. Acts like Black Sabbath and Ted Nugent could draw tens of thousands of fans in any American city, but they barely ever charted. The problem was the radio. Top-40 radio programmers, shooting for the widest-possible audiences, worried that power chords would chase away listeners. There was a huge audience for metal, but that audience, at least according to conventional wisdom, was overwhelmingly male and working class. Even on the fast-exploding album-oriented rock format, programmers leaned on relatively anonymous and inoffensive studio-rock acts like Boston and Kansas rather than heavier fare like Thin Lizzy or Blue Oyster Cult, neither of whom ever reached the top 10.

A few hard-rock singles reached #1 in the seventies, but those success stories were outliers. Michigan's Grand Funk Railroad were already stadium-conquering commercial behemoths by the time they cleaned up their sound, hired producer Todd Rundgren, and landed a couple of chart-toppers with the 1973 party anthem "We're an American Band" and with their 1974 cover of "The Loco-Motion," the "Twist"-adjacent dance song that Carole King and Gerry Goffin had written for their babysitter a decade earlier. Canadian bands the Guess Who and Bachman-Turner Overdrive, neither of whom were ever especially heavy, made it to #1 with, respectively, 1970's "American Woman" and 1974's "You Ain't Seen Nothing Yet," two exceedingly catchy and horny tunes. In 1973, the Edgar Winter Group scored a freak chart-topper with their heavy blues-rock instrumental "Frankenstein." These were the exceptions. Most of the seventies ragers that remain in classic-rock radio rotation today simply couldn't get airplay when they were new. Since *Billboard* uses radio plays, as well as sales, to tabulate the Hot 100, the hesher heroes of the world were at a distinct disadvantage.

Even the most commercial hard-rock bands of the seventies and early eighties couldn't crack the radio code. Aerosmith, shameless showmen who sold an Americanized version of Rolling Stones boogie-rock, had a couple of top-10 hits in their early career, and a handful of them after the band was resuscitated in the second half of the eighties, but they didn't reach #1 until 1998, when they finally got there with the sappy soundtrack ballad "I Don't Want to Miss a Thing." Kiss used costumes and face paint to stand out, pioneering a version of metal that was so theatrical that it practically crossed over into pantomime, and they captured millions of imaginations and turned themselves into iconic figures in seventies pop culture. But the band's only top-10 hit came when they put aside the pyrotechnics and got sensitive; "Beth," a softhearted love ballad, took the band to #7 in 1976. Working with maximalist producer Mutt Lange, Australian band AC/DC streamlined their sound to a mechanized crunch, and their 1980 album *Back in Black* remains one of the highest-selling LPs of all time. Yet that album's irresistible single "You Shook Me All Night Long" couldn't get past #35.

MTV changed things for metal, just as it changed things for pretty much every genre in the eighties. From the very beginning, metal was part of the mix at MTV; the station played an Iron Maiden video in its first hour on the air. For the most part, though, the denim-and-boots aesthetics of early-eighties hard rock didn't make for the most compelling visuals, and most heavy bands didn't arrive with visual presentations as arresting as those of the British new-wave bands who became the first MTV stars. But one metal band figured out how to pop onscreen, and they spawned legions of imitators.

By the time they became MTV fixtures, Van Halen were already one of the biggest rock bands in America. The Pasadena group came up through the Los Angeles club circuit, and they were a huge draw by the time they signed with Warner and released their self-titled debut album. That LP came out at the beginning of 1978, and it was platinum by the end of the year. Over the next two decades, the album sold more than ten million copies. It was a game changer, and its pyrotechnic guitar work and cartoonish party-time personality proved vastly influential. Within a few years, a whole glam-metal scene developed around the nightclubs of Hollywood's Sunset Strip, with every band trying to capture some of Van Halen's magic. Still, the biggest single from Van Halen's debut album, a cover of the Kinks' "You Really Got Me," peaked at #36. Van Halen were rock stars long before they were pop stars.

But Van Halen were made for MTV. The band had two showboats in its ranks, the high-kicking flamboyant frontman David Lee Roth and the squeedling guitar virtuoso Eddie Van Halen. In videos, the band leaned into Roth's hamminess, and he held the screen by mugging frantically. Eddie Van Halen, meanwhile, pushed the group's sound in a more pop-friendly direction. After raising the band's profile by playing the famous guitar solo on Michael Jackson's smash "Beat It," Eddie used a bright, anthemic dance-pop synth riff to drive the 1983 Van Halen single "Jump." Roth objected strenuously to the sonic makeover, but "Jump" turned out to be the right song at the right time. Early in 1984, "Jump" rose to #1, and it held the spot for five weeks. But the internal fractures within the band turned out to be too much, and Roth was gone from Van Halen by the end of the year. In the years ahead, Roth would score multiple top-10 hits as a solo artist with a goofy, outsize persona. Van Halen, who'd replaced Roth with Sammy Hagar (much less of a persona), would do the same. But neither would ever return to #1.

The glam-metal bands who sprang up in Van Halen's wake got heavy MTV play, but they struggled to turn that into radio success. With their outlandish looks and slapstick-heavy videos, groups like Ratt and Twisted Sister made for great TV, but neither band ever cracked the top 10. Mötley Crüe, the biggest and most infamous of the Sunset Strip acts, wouldn't reach the top 10 until 1989, when "Dr. Feelgood," their biggest hit, got as high as #6. The Crüe's 1985 power ballad "Home Sweet Home," inescapable on MTV, reached only #89 on the Hot 100. The British band Def Leppard, working with AC/DC producer Mutt Lange, landed on a shimmering, expansive, synth-dominated sound, and that style proved hugely successful. Def Lep's 1983 album, *Pyromania*, sold six million copies in two years, peaking at #2 on the album charts. (Only the ongoing dominance of *Thriller* kept it out of the top spot.) *Pyromania* made Def Leppard one of the biggest acts on the planet. Even then, though, none of the album's singles made the top 10. ("Photograph," the biggest of them, came close, peaking at #12. Their more significant chart success was yet to come.)

The group who best exemplified metal's move toward pop in the early eighties was a Sunset Strip band who wholeheartedly endorsed the term "metal." Quiet Riot's sound was more simplistic and anthemic than that of Van Halen, and they were less showy about their virtuosity. (Quiet Riot took off only after guitarist Randy Rhoads, widely considered the second-best metal guitarist in Los Angeles behind only Eddie Van Halen himself, left to join Ozzy Osbourne's band. Rhoads died in a 1982 plane crash after playing with Osbourne for two years.)

Quiet Riot's stomping sing-along cover of "Cum on Feel the Noize," a decade-old glam-rock song from the UK band Slade, reached #5 on the Hot 100. The band's 1983 album, *Metal Health*, went platinum six times over. For a single week in November of that year, *Metal Health* knocked the Police's *Synchronicity* off the top of the *Billboard* album charts. In the process, Quiet Riot became the first heavy metal band with a #1 album. But the band rushed their 1984 follow-up, *Critical Condition*, and it tanked. Quiet Riot's success was one more indication that heavy metal *could* break through to pop audiences, but it would take another couple of years before another band showed just how big it could be.

The group who truly turned metal into pop music came from New Jersey and didn't even consider themselves a metal band. John Bongiovi grew up working class in Perth Amboy. His father was a barber, and his mother a florist; both had served as Marines. A teenage Bongiovi had dreamed of pop stardom, despite his limited singing range, and he'd led a few bar bands on the Jersey club circuit. Those dreams seemed attainable because Bongiovi had an in.

In 1977, John's cousin Tony Bongiovi was one of two people who bought a Con Edison power plant in midtown Manhattan and converted it into a recording studio called the Power Station. Disco acts like Chic recorded at the Power Station, and Tony produced records from punk and new-wave bands like the Ramones and the Talking Heads. Tony also coproduced a #1 hit: a 1977 disco version of John Williams's instrumental *Star Wars* theme, credited to a session musician who went by the name Meco. Meco kept making *Star Wars*–themed pop records for years, including a 1980 holiday LP, on which a sixteen-year-old John Bongiovi made his recorded debut on a song titled "R2-D2, We Wish You a Merry Christmas."

John got a gofer job at the Power Station, and his cousin let him record demos of the songs he'd written in his off-hours. In 1982, Bongiovi worked with a group of session musicians, including E Street Band keyboardist Roy Bittan, on a demo of a song called "Runaway." Labels turned down Bongiovi's demo, but Bongiovi used it to join a local-band songwriting contest that the Long Island radio station WAPP was holding. "Runaway" won the contest, and WAPP put the song into rotation and included it on a compilation of local songs. Soon, other stations in the region started playing the song, and Bongiovi signed to Mercury. He changed his name to the anglicized Jon Bon Jovi, and he rounded up a group of local musicians to serve as his band. On the advice of someone at Mercury, Bon Jovi named his band after himself, just as Eddie and Alex Van Halen had done years earlier. "Runaway," released under the Mercury banner, eventually peaked at #39.

Jon Bon Jovi saw Bon Jovi as a mainstream rock act, not a metal band. But the group signed on with Doc McGhee, an ex-drug smuggler who'd become Mötley Crüe's manager. McGhee's strategy was to book Bon Jovi to play as many shows as possible, especially as an opening act on arena tours. Jon Bon Jovi wanted to tour with Bryan

Adams or the Cars, but McGhee, understanding the loyalty of metal fans, booked them with bands like the Scorpions and Kiss. Bon Jovi leaned into the image, adapting the same teased-hair look and energetic, strutting stage presence as their contemporaries. Partly because Jon Bon Jovi was a positively beautiful young man, the pose worked.

Bon Jovi's first two albums, released in 1984 and 1985, sold respectably, but not well enough to get the band out of the opening-act slot. In 1984, Bon Jovi toured Europe with Kiss, and Kiss coleader Paul Stanley suggested that Bon Jovi try writing some songs with an outside songwriter. He had someone in mind: Desmond Child, a one-time disco artist who'd worked with acts like Cher and Billy Squier. In 1979, Kiss reached #11 with "I Was Made for Lovin' You," a disco-influenced song that Child cowrote. Stanley connected Child with Bon Jovi. When the band got back from tour, Child flew to New Jersey to write some songs with Jon Bon Jovi and guitarist Richie Sambora. They all got together in the basement of Sambora's mother's house, where Sambora was still living at the time.

While working on "You Give Love a Bad Name," the song that would become Bon Jovi's debut single, Child ripped himself off. Child had written "If You Were a Woman (and I Was a Man)," a single that the Welsh howler Bonnie Tyler released in 1986. Three years earlier, Tyler had reached #1 with "Total Eclipse of the Heart," an overwhelming, blood-pounding, larger-than-life sing-along. "If You Were a Woman" was a song built to be as vast as that one, but it petered out at #77, and Child reused the exact same chorus melody for "You Give Love a Bad Name." Bon Jovi, meanwhile, reused the phrase "shot through the heart," which they'd used as a song title on their debut album.

Really, nothing about "You Give Love a Bad Name" was original. The song—a howl of frustration from a guy who's been left behind— drew on ancient stereotypes about man-eating jezebels, a particular lyrical fixation for just about every glam-metal band in America. On the song, Jon Bon Jovi wails about a woman with a painted smile on her lips and blood-red nails on her fingertips. Her very first kiss was her first kiss good-bye, and now Bon Jovi's passion is a prison; he can't break free. It's an absolute cliché, but Bon Jovi delivers the song without anything resembling venom or anguish. Instead, the song works as a pumping, energetic rocker with an absolute steamroller of a chorus. The three songwriters open the song with that chorus, turning it into a massive a cappella sing-along before the guitars even kick in. The band repeats that hook again and again. Anyone who heard "You Give Love a Bad Name" once could sing along by the end.

On paper, "You Give Love a Bad Name" is a spiteful song. On record, though, it's all pomp and energy—mane-shaking riffs, thud-shimmy drums, irrepressible *whoa-oh-ohs*. Richie Sambora pulls growling, squealing Van Halen moves with his guitar solo. To record the song and the rest of their third album, *Slippery When Wet*, Bon Jovi went to Vancouver to work with Bruce Fairbairn, a producer who'd helped bands like Loverboy achieve crunch-rock grandeur. Fairbairn added gloss and heft to Bon Jovi's sound. Bon Jovi had never been as flashy as they were on "Bad Name."

For the "Bad Name" video, Bon Jovi worked with Wayne Isham, Mötley Crüe's preferred director. Rather than translating the lyrics into a narrative, Isham simply filmed Bon Jovi playing in front of a crowd. Jon Bon Jovi preens and twirls and hair-tosses his way across an arena stage, flashing constant billion-dollar grins at Isham's camera. He doesn't just hold the screen; he eats it up. With a video like that, Bon Jovi didn't seem like a band for dirtbag rocker dudes. Girls started to notice.

Unlike some of their peers, Bon Jovi didn't need to make a simpering ballad to reach a mainstream pop audience. Instead, they got there with an energetic rocker that emphasized their bulldozer melodies and the shimmering brightness of their sound. There was nothing remotely rebellious or forbidding about "You Give Love a Bad Name." Plenty of people were *annoyed* by the song, but it didn't *scare* anybody. Instead, with its sheer simplistic pop-music ebullience, the song recalled the bubblegum pop of decades past. Plenty of metal fans rejected the shiny, happy hooks of Bon Jovi and their peers, but that only drove another kind of success as those fans turned to bands like Metallica and Slayer. The explosive popularity of the thrash underground was a word-of-mouth sensation that emerged around the same time. But from a pop perspective, Bon Jovi were undeniable.

"You Give Love a Bad Name" happened to reach #1 at a time when pop music had gotten particularly sedate and complacent. The biggest single of 1986 was "That's What Friends Are For," a calm and reassuring number from sixties pop queen Dionne Warwick. That song, an all-star fund-raiser like the previous year's "We Are the World," reunited Warwick with her oldest collaborator, songwriter Burt Bacharach, and it featured the voices of fellow pop-star veterans Stevie Wonder, Gladys Knight, and Elton John. Bacharach and his then-wife, Carole Bayer Sager, also wrote another 1986 pop smash, the Patti LaBelle–Michael McDonald duet "On My Own." Peter Cetera, the former Chicago singer and bassist, landed two #1 hits that year, both tinny and treacly love ballads. Rock-establishment types like Genesis and Steve Winwood claimed their first #1 hits that year. The highest-selling album of 1986 was the self-titled debut from Whitney Houston, the young vocal prodigy whom Arista Records boss Clive Davis had shaped into a middle-of-the-road smooth-pop juggernaut. In a landscape like that, Bon Jovi stood out.

"You Give Love a Bad Name" was not a fluke. A couple of months after Bon Jovi's pop breakthrough topped the Hot 100, the band returned to that spot with "Livin' on a Prayer," a beautifully shameless attempt at the kind of working-class anthem that Bon Jovi's home-state hero Bruce Springsteen had been making for years. "Livin' on a Prayer" held the #1 spot for a full month. Another *Slippery When Wet* single, the lovably ludicrous rock-star-as-cowboy fist-pumper "Wanted Dead or Alive," reached #7. In 1987, *Slippery When Wet* outsold smashes from acts like Paul Simon and the Beastie Boys to become the #1 album of the year.

More important, Bon Jovi opened up a mainstream-pop lane for other hard rock bands with big dreams and bigger hair. Later in 1987, veteran British band Whitesnake topped the Hot 100 with "Here I Go Again," a version of an older song that they'd rerecorded to better fit the glam-metal zeitgeist. Billy Idol, a former punk singer whose club-friendly sound flirted with both hard rock and new wave, charged up to #1 with a fired-up live cover of Tommy James and the Shondells' garage-rock oldie "Mony Mony." Heart, seventies hard-rock veterans who'd embraced big-hair hooks after a long fallow period, experienced a true commercial resurgence, and their howling ballad "Alone" became their second #1 hit.

By the end of the eighties, a handful of other metal giants would all land #1 hits, though most of them would pull off those chart triumphs with sad-eyed and tenderhearted love songs that dialed back their hell-raiser images. That trick made chart-toppers out of Guns N' Roses ("Sweet Child o' Mine"), Def Leppard ("Love Bites"), and Poison ("Every Rose Has Its Thorn"). Sunset Strip contemporaries like Warrant, Lita Ford, and Great White never reached #1, but all of them sold millions and scored top-10 hits. White Lion, a New York band with a Sunset Strip sound, reached the top 10 a couple of times. Bon Jovi helped mentor East Coast glam-metal bands like Philadelphia's Cinderella and New Jersey's Skid Row, and those bands had huge late-eighties and early-nineties runs, as well.

Pretty soon, mainstream pop artists started getting in on the action. Michael Jackson wrote "Dirty Diana," a hybrid dance-pop/glam-metal freak-out about an aggressive groupie, and he brought in Billy Idol guitarist Steve Stevens to shred all over the song. "Dirty Diana" wasn't quite as big as "Beat It," Jackson's previous hard-rock experiment, but it still became the fifth #1 hit from *Bad*, Jackson's 1987 album. Even soft-rock stars like Richard Marx adapted glam-metal aesthetics, feathering their hair and lacing their singles with triumphant guitar solos.

Bon Jovi themselves continued to thrive. The band followed *Slippery When Wet* with *New Jersey*, a 1988 album that generated two #1 hits and three more top-10 singles. When Bon Jovi took a break after touring behind *New Jersey*, Jon Bon Jovi doubled down on the whole cowboy thing, recording an entire solo album "inspired by" the 1990 western *Young Guns II*. The wailing, theatrical single "Blaze of Glory" gave Jon Bon Jovi yet another #1 hit.

Conventional wisdom says that the arrival of Nirvana and the attendant early-nineties Seattle grunge explosion doomed the glam-metal boom. The grunge bands' shambling sloppiness definitely worked as a kind of rebuke against the streamlined sonics and flirty preening of the glam-rock stars. When Guns N' Roses tried to recruit Nirvana as an opening act, Nirvana refused, citing Guns N' Roses' homophobic lyrics; eventually, Axl Rose and Kurt Cobain got into a famous shoving match backstage at MTV's Video Music Awards in 1992. In the moment, it was easy to look at bands like Bon Jovi and Guns N' Roses as dinosaurs.

But grunge never dominated the Hot 100 the way glam metal had done. Nirvana's biggest hit, the totemic 1991 anthem "Smells Like Teen Spirit," got only as high as #6 on the charts. Other alternative-rock bands came from the same scenes and had plenty of influences in common with the glam-metal bands. Soundgarden, for instance, really *did* tour with Gun N' Roses, while the Red Hot Chili Peppers, who climbed as high as #2 with their own power ballad "Under the Bridge," played shows with Sunset Strip bands in their early days. When early-nineties alternative rock had its surge in popularity, it represented a break from hair-metal style, but all those bands were part of the same hard-rock continuum. The change was big, but it wasn't radical.

But if glam metal had taken off, at least in part, as a reaction against the gloopy soft rock that dominated the mideighties charts, it eventually became gloopy soft rock itself. In the early nineties, bands like Extreme, Mr. Big, and Nelson—the duo of Matthew and Gunnar Nelson, twin sons of original Hot 100 hitmaker Ricky—were all marketed as metal, and all of them had #1 hits. But those #1 hits were sappy low-energy ballads without a trace of energy. There was nothing new or exciting about what those bands were making.

Bon Jovi suffered, as well. Four years after releasing *New Jersey*, the band returned in 1992 with their album *Keep the Faith*, and they learned that the world had changed. *Keep the Faith* struggled to reach platinum status, and the most successful of its singles, the histrionic power ballad "Bed of Roses," topped out at #10 on the Hot 100. Power ballads turned out to be Bon Jovi's most durable weapons. As late as 1994, long after most of their glam-metal peers had faded away, Bon Jovi were able to score a #4 hit with "Always." Unlike most of those other glam-metal bands, Bon Jovi found a way to successfully rebrand themselves as a mainstream rock act—which, after all, was how Jon Bon Jovi originally envisioned the band.

The initial burst of excitement that Bon Jovi brought to the charts in 1986 couldn't last, but the band's battering-ram bubblegum hooks became influential in other ways. Swedish pop mastermind Max Martin, now one of the most successful songwriters and producers in pop history, was once a hair-band guy. In the eighties and nineties, Martin led an unsuccessful Swedish glam-metal band called It's Alive. Martin clearly picked up some tricks from Bon Jovi. Writer and podcaster Chris Molanphy once pointed out that one of Martin's go-to moves in the boy-band era was to start a song with a brute-force a cappella chorus, just as Bon Jovi had done on "You Give Love a Bad Name."

If Max Martin learned how to achieve pop supremacy by studying Bon Jovi, then he found a way to repay the favor. In 2000, when his teen-pop productions were taking over the planet, Martin cowrote Bon Jovi's comeback single, "It's My Life." That song peaked at #33 on the Hot 100, but it became a worldwide smash, and it helped usher Bon Jovi into elder-statesman status. In the past two decades, Bon Jovi haven't once touched the Hot 100, but they've become a legacy-touring behemoth, selling out arenas around the planet. Their hits helped kick off a ridiculous, exciting era that plenty of rock fans do not remember fondly. But the songs also survived that era, aging more gracefully than those of most of their peers.

After the glam-metal boom, hard rock mostly disappeared from the pop charts. It only really returned for a moment in the early 2000s, when postgrunge yarlers like Creed and Nickelback were at their apex. Soon enough, Bon Jovi's brand of glam metal would become a nostalgic exercise, and the pop charts would have to look elsewhere for excitement.

CHAPTER 13

Mariah Carey–
"Vision of Love"

Released May 15, 1990
Hit #1 August 4, 1990
Four-week reign

THE FIRST WORD ON "VISION OF LOVE," MARIAH CAREY'S debut single, isn't a word at all. Instead, it's a sound, or maybe a series of sounds. After an ominous keyboard clang, the type of tone that might herald the arrival of a killer robot in an eighties sci-fi movie, Carey lets loose with something that's part sigh, part ululation. If you were to type out that opening nonword word, it might look something like this: "Haaaaoweeaahwuuuah-weah-mmmwueeeah." This isn't language, exactly. Instead, it's a signal. Before the song even properly begins, Carey puts on a display, giving a slight indication of the things that her voice can do.

All throughout her career, critics like me have discussed Mariah Carey less as an artist and more as an athlete. Early on, profile writers dwelled on Carey's seven-octave vocal range in the same way that a sportscaster might fixate on a high school basketball prospect's wingspan. As Carey aged, the terms of discussion around her voice changed. Commentators wondered whether she was still capable of the same vocal feats. When Carey introduced simple, whispery singsong melodies on her late-career hits, it came off almost like Michael Jordan developing his fadeaway jumpshot, leaning on that instead of his explosive dunks.

Mariah Carey isn't an athlete. She's a pop-music innovator, a creature of the studio whose perfectionism quickly became the stuff of show-business legend. Starting with "Vision of Love," Carey took nineteen singles to #1—more than any other solo artist in history, and just one shy of the Beatles' all-time record. (By the time you read this, there's a decent chance that she will have caught up.) Carey wrote or cowrote all but one of her chart-toppers, and she had a hand in producing more than half of them. She's broken a whole array of chart records, and she's also spent decades traversing a changing pop-music landscape, anticipating new mutations in the mainstream and sometimes helping those mutations along herself, all with her share of occasional ignominy. But her voice is so dazzling that it tends to dim all else.

From the very beginning, Carey understood that her voice was what set her apart. "Vision of Love," Carey's debut single, is a vehicle for that voice, a means by which she could present that voice to the world. "Vision of Love" is also a sleek piece of pop craftsmanship, a canny showcase for a fully formed persona, and a moving account of personal triumph. But it all starts with the voice.

Mariah Carey was still a teenager when she recorded "Vision of Love." She'd grown up on Long Island, the daughter of a Black man and a white woman. Carey's father was an aeronautical engineer who was mostly out of the picture during her childhood, and her mother was a former opera singer who'd become a vocal coach. Carey has long described her childhood as a traumatic one. She moved constantly, to different parts of Long Island, and rarely had time to forge lasting friendships. She learned about pop music by listening to her older siblings' soul records, but those same older siblings were chaotic influences; in her memoir, Carey writes that she was twelve years old when her sister tried to sell her out to a pimp. Carey has also spoken of how her mixed-race heritage made her feel like an outcast, even within her own family. From childhood, though, Carey understood that she wanted to become a singer, and she organized her entire life around making that happen.

At sixteen, Carey recorded her first demo in New York. Through friends of her brother, Carey had met Gavin Christopher, a songwriter and producer who'd once been in the seventies soul-funk band Rufus and just recorded the minor 1986 dance-pop hit "One Step Closer to You." At seventeen, Carey moved out of her mother's house, crashing with Christopher's girlfriend, Clarissa Dane, in Manhattan. At a recording session with Christopher, Carey met a drummer named Ben Margulies, who had a small studio in the back of his father's cabinet factory in Chelsea. While Carey held down short-term jobs in bars and restaurants, she and Margulies worked on songs, some of which would eventually end up on Carey's debut album. Margulies is credited as cowriter on seven of the songs from Carey's debut album, including "Vision of Love," though Carey later insisted that his contributions were minimal. After that album, she never worked with him again.

Carey eventually found work as a backup singer for Brenda K. Starr, a dance-pop artist whose biggest hit, the 1988 ballad "I Still Believe," peaked at #13. Starr became both a friend and a mentor to Carey. (A decade later, Carey covered "I Still Believe" as a tribute to Starr, and she took the song to #4.) One night, Carey was Starr's guest at a music-business party, and that's where she met Tommy Mottola, the former manager of Daryl Hall and John Oates who'd recently become the chief executive at Sony Music. Carey gave Mottola her demo tape, and he listened to it in his limo on the way home from the party. When he heard Carey's voice, Mottola made his driver take him back to that party to find Carey, but she'd already left. He finally tracked her down a few days later and signed her to Columbia, the biggest of the labels under the Sony umbrella.

In the early years of Carey's career, before she married and divorced Tommy Mottola, the press would treat that story as a kind of fairy tale.

Carey was around nineteen when she met Mottola—she's always been a bit cagey about her actual age—and he was at least twenty years older. He started making romantic overtures almost immediately. Later, Carey would speak of Mottola as a repressive, controlling force. She now describes the mansion that she and Mottola shared as a jail. But Carey has also written that Mottola felt like a protective presence and that he "ruthlessly" believed in her talent.

Right away, Columbia made Mariah Carey into a priority. In rolling out Carey's self-titled debut, the label followed an established playbook. Five years earlier, Clive Davis and his Arista label had given a similar full-court press to another self-titled debut album from another beautiful young R&B prodigy. Like Carey, Whitney Houston was nineteen when she signed her first major-label deal. At that point, Houston was a seasoned performer. Houston had grown up singing in church, and she was around pop stars constantly as a kid. Dionne Warwick was Houston's cousin, and Aretha Franklin was a close family friend. Cissy Houston, Whitney's mother, was a prolific backup singer. Whitney herself had emerged under her mother's tutelage as a young gospel powerhouse. But when Clive Davis signed her, he made her over as a middle-of-the-road adult-contemporary singer.

Houston still sang R&B ballads, and she topped the *Billboard* R&B chart before scoring her first #1 on the Hot 100, but Davis was careful to present Houston as a crossover star. According to former Arista executive Kenneth Reynolds, when Houston was working on her debut album, "anything that was too 'Black-sounding' was sent back to the studio." Houston's voice was a volcanic force, but Davis took care to present that voice only in very specific ways. On her first few albums, Houston mostly sang schmaltzy Broadway-style ballads and ebullient dance-pop tracks. Davis's instincts proved sharp. Houston's debut album, released in early 1985, was a slow burner on the chart, but became 1986's biggest seller, and her second was the first album from a female artist ever to top the album chart in its first week in late June 1987—a feat that was even more meaningful in the era before *Billboard* used electronic data to tabulate that chart. By the time Mariah Carey released "Vision of Love," Whitney Houston already had seven #1 hits.

Carey took a more active role in planning out her early career than Whitney Houston did. Carey wrote her own songs, and she soon started to produce, too. Carey hadn't grown up singing in church, as Houston had. Instead, Carey discovered gospel music only by checking out the influences of the artists she loved. She was a student of pop music, and she experienced gospel as part of that mix. Houston had been one of the first pop stars to truly weaponize the melisma—the gospel technique with which a singer stretches one syllable over multiple notes. Carey took Houston's melisma even further, turning it into something more like a cutting-edge special effect. Carey quickly became the Eddie Van Halen of melisma—a singular artist whose theatrical displays inspired entire generations of imitators.

Tommy Mottola wanted to present Mariah Carey as a down-the-middle pop artist, just as Clive Davis had done with Whitney Houston. To that end, Mottola recruited many of Houston's closest collaborators. Narada Michael Walden, the producer who helmed Houston's biggest dance-pop hits, worked on many of the tracks from Carey's debut album. Walden coproduced "Vision of Love" with veteran studio musician Rhett Lawrence. Walter Afanasieff, who'd done arrangements on Houston's albums, produced Carey's second #1 single, "Love Takes Time," and he kept working with her through the nineties.

Until Carey and Houston recorded the 1998 duet "When You Believe" together, the press usually portrayed the two singers as adversaries. Both of them made vaguely icy comments about one another at various points, and their various collaborators were happy to speak to their similarities and differences. In 1991, Afanasieff told the *New York Times*, "Whitney has a beautiful voice, but Mariah has infinitely more control." Walden said that he was "honored to work with both of them," but he commented on Carey's level of perfectionism: "Mariah is very astute in the studio, very picky. . . . She knows she wants to hear herself sound a certain way."

Carey wrote "Vision of Love" about a week after signing her Columbia contract. On paper, it's a love song with serious shades of gospel. Carey could be singing to a lover or to God: "It took so long, still I believed / Somehow the one that I needed would find me eventually." But the "love" is a misdirect; it's the "vision" part that truly resonates. Carey wrote the song as a howl of triumph after making it through her chaotic, uncertain early years. She had to be strong, so she believed, and she succeeded in finding the place she conceived. She's singing to herself, about herself. It's a song about perseverance.

Carey recorded the first "Vision of Love" demo with Ben Margulies. When Mottola and the other label bosses heard the song, they thought it sounded like a hit, but it needed work. They flew Carey to Los Angeles to rerecord the song with Narada Michael Walden and Rhett Lawrence. In the process, the three of them changed the structure and the key of the song. In its final form, "Vision of Love" sounds almost chintzy. The song self-consciously evokes classic soul, with keyboards playing a loping, bluesy chord progression. But the instrumentation is the same kind of twinkly, artificial late-eighties synthpop that previous teen sensations like Debbie Gibson and Tiffany were using around the same time. None of that holds Carey back. Instead, the full focus of the song is Carey's voice, which does things that remain dumbfounding.

At the beginning of "Vision of Love," Carey sings without too many embellishments. As the song unfurls, though, she shows off more and more of what her voice can do. She never loses the melody or the emotional focus of the song. Instead, she builds it toward a climax, pushing toward gospel-style transcendence. As she gets closer and closer to her grand-showoff moments, Carey gets wilder and fiercer in the way she uses that voice. She holds grand, loud notes for long stretches, like a Broadway singer. She lets her voice fly all over the scale in the space of a single syllable, giving displays of melisma that not even Whitney Houston had attempted. In the song's grand finale, Carey flies up into the whistle register, the highest-pitched sound that a human voice can make.

"Vision of Love" wasn't the first chart-topping pop song to feature the whistle register. Minnie Riperton had shown that ability on "Lovin' You," a ballad that she'd taken to #1 in 1975. But Carey deploys that note as just one weapon in her arsenal, one flourish in a song that's practically nothing but flourishes. Even today, "Vision of Love" remains a wild highlight reel of a song. It's not just Carey's technique. It's the way she unveils that technique, one piece at a time. Carey knew that her vocal feats would astound people, so she built them up, adding one new piece at a time. That's showmanship.

With "Vision of Love," Columbia didn't just have a hit song on its hands. It had a perfect introduction for a new superstar, a track that worked as a display of firepower and a statement of intent. "Vision of Love" is a song rooted in soul and gospel, but its instrumentation is pure plastic circa-1990 pop, and the label presented Carey as a middle-of-the-road pop star rather than an R&B singer. (According to Carey, Tommy Mottola insisted that she be styled to look Italian rather than Black.) The label filmed an expensive video for the song, and when that one didn't turn out well, they shot another one with director Andy Morahan, who'd been George Michael's prime music-video collaborator since his Wham! days. The final "Vision of Love" video looks mythic and dreamlike, with dramatically backlit Carey singing in a giant window frame while sun shines on her in impossible, unnatural colors. She looks like a near-psychedelic vision herself.

Around the same time that Carey debuted with "Vision of Love," a lip-synching scandal was shaking the music business. The two supremely telegenic members of Milli Vanilli, a German-based dance-pop duo, had not sung a single note on their massive-selling debut album, *Girl, You Know It's True*, and their producer, Frank Farian, would finally admit to the ruse a few months later. Rumors were already circling Milli Vanilli before the big revelation; a malfunctioning

backing tape at a live performance in Connecticut had fed a growing backlash against the group. Other dance-pop acts, like Technotronic and Black Box, had used session singers to belt out huge, soulful
vocals, and then they'd used models to lip-synch those vocals in their
videos, but when Farian finally admitted that Milli Vanilli was a falsi-
fied studio creation, the backlash was immense and immediate. Fans
launched a class-action lawsuit against Arista, Milli Vanilli's label, and
the Recording Academy revoked the duo's Grammy—the only time
that's ever happened.

Columbia took care in presenting Carey as someone who looked
like a model but who really *could* sing those impossible notes. Carey
wasn't an experienced live performer, but Columbia booked her to
sing "Vision of Love" on shows like *Arsenio Hall* and *Good Morning
America*, and she was able to re-create those showboaty vocal runs flu-
idly and flawlessly. A few months after the Milli Vanilli revelation,
Carey won the Grammy for Best New Artist, the award that had gone
to Milli Vanilli the previous year. In the wake of the Milli Vanilli affair,
it wasn't just Columbia that needed a new face like Mariah Carey. It
was the music business as a whole.

Carey's arrival changed the commercial trajectory of R&B. Before
Carey showed up on the scene, many of the biggest chart stars were
white acts, like New Kids on the Block or Taylor Dayne, who sang sanitized forms of Black music. Carey's whole presentation was more pres-
tige driven than those artists, but her music slotted in next to theirs on
radio playlists where you could hear the difference immediately.

"Vision of Love" hit like a bomb. The song, released three weeks
before Carey's debut album, topped *Billboard*'s R&B and adult-
contemporary charts at the same time as it took over the Hot 100.
The album spun off three more singles after "Vision of Love," and all
three of them—"Love Takes Time," "Someday," and "I Don't Wanna
Cry"—reached #1. In the process, Carey became the second artist
ever to top the Hot 100 with her first four singles. Before Carey, only
the Jackson 5 had pulled that off.

Carey's self-titled debut album didn't reach #1 on the album charts for months; two phenomenally successful pop-rap albums, MC Hammer's *Please Hammer Don't Hurt 'Em* and Vanilla Ice's *To the Extreme*, held that spot for the entire second half of 1990. In February 1991, though, *Mariah Carey* finally knocked *To the Extreme* down from the #1 spot, and it held that spot for eleven weeks. Carey's album went on to become the biggest seller of 1991. A year after its release, *Mariah Carey* had sold nearly six million copies.

Mariah Carey launched an arms race. The singers who emerged after Mariah Carey all had to contend with her sheer ability. In the years after "Vision of Love," melisma-heavy R&B became the center of pop music. Whitney Houston moved away from middle-of-the-road pop toward hard-belting soul, and she remained a towering figure on the charts well into the decade. Singers like R. Kelly and Toni Braxton had #1 hits built around showy, theatrically wobbly vocals, as did groups like Boyz II Men and SWV.

Younger generations also heard what Carey had done on "Vision of Love" and built entire styles on that song. A young Beyoncé Knowles started singing vocal runs after hearing "Vision of Love," and other future chart-toppers like Christina Aguilera and Kelly Clarkson have said that Carey's debut single was a eureka moment for them. Knowles, Aguilera, and Clarkson were all children when "Vision of Love" came out. For them, the song was foundational. Carey's approach to singing—the melisma, the showmanship—eventually became the dominant vocal style on the singing-competition reality show *American Idol*, the highest-rated TV series in America through most of the 2000s. Most of the singers who competed on *Idol* were the children of Mariah Carey in general and "Vision of Love" in particular.

R&B changed in the nineties, and Mariah Carey changed with it. When her debut album tore up the charts, Carey decided not to tour. Instead, she went straight to work on *Emotions*, her second album, releasing it barely a year after her first. Carey coproduced all of *Emotions*, and she recorded much of it with Robert Clivillés and David

Cole, the two dance-pop producers whose project C+C Music Factory had a #1 hit of their own in 1991 with "Gonna Make You Sweat (Everybody Dance Now)." Working with Clivillés and Cole, Carey pushed her music in more club-friendly directions. Soon afterward, Carey worked with house DJ David Morales on clubby remixes. For songs like the 1993 chart-topper "Dreamlover," Carey recorded entirely new vocals for the Morales remixes, making sure that her pop tracks could still play in the club.

When the title track of *Emotions* reached #1, Carey set a new chart record. She'd gotten to #1 with her first five straight singles—one more than the Jackson 5 had managed decades earlier. Carey's record still stands; no other artist has ever arrived with such an immediate and sustained pop-chart hot streak. And it's fun to speculate how much longer it could have lasted, if, for example, Carey's sixth single, "Can't Let Go," could have risen past #2, or the single after that, "Make It Happen," past #5. In 1992, with her eighth single, Carey paid tribute to the Jackson 5, covering their song "I'll Be There" on her *MTV Unplugged* special. Her live cover of that song became her sixth #1 hit, the only Mariah Carey chart-topper that she didn't have a hand in writing. It was followed by her third proper album, *Music Box*, containing two more #1 hits in "Dreamlover" and "Hero" and a #3 hit in "Without You." The final single off of *Music Box*, "Anytime You Need a Friend," was a real dud at #12. It's extraordinary.

As a fan of pop music, Carey was drawn to newer sounds—not just to the dance-pop of "Emotions," but also to rap, which broke through on the Hot 100 around the same time that she arrived. On early singles like "Vision of Love," it's possible to hear loose connections between Carey's vocals and the linguistic twistiness of early-nineties rap. In her cadences, Carey would sometimes twist her voice around tracks like a rapper, and she'd cram in more words than some of her peers. Back then, the connection between Carey and rap was mostly implicit. Carey emerged at a time when rap and R&B were starting to fuse.

Mariah Carey released her debut album during the heyday of new jack swing, a strain of R&B that fused up-tempo soul with clattering club beats and hip-hop swagger. New jack swing was a short-lived phenomenon, and Mariah Carey wasn't a part of it; Columbia presented her as something much frothier and less dangerous. Over the years, though, Carey made stronger and stronger connections with rap, often over the objections of then husband Tommy Mottola. In 1995, Carey started inviting rappers to appear on remixes with her. That year, Carey and Mary J. Blige producer Dave Hill built Carey's song "Fantasy" around a sample of "Genius of Love," a 1981 club hit from Tom Tom Club, a Talking Heads side project, that had been popular among early break-dancers. Carey recruited Sean "Puff Daddy" Combs to remix the track, and she brought in Wu-Tang Clan member Ol' Dirty Bastard for a giddy, wild-eyed guest verse. There was nothing obvious about the alchemy of Mariah Carey and Ol' Dirty Bastard over a Tom Tom Club sample noodled with by Puff Daddy. But "Fantasy" became a sensation, topping the charts for eight weeks before Whitney Houston's "Exhale (Shoop Shoop)" finally knocked it out of the top spot. After a one-week-and-done reign from Houston's song, Carey returned to #1.

Carey intended her Boyz II Men collaboration "One Sweet Day," the song that kicked "Exhale (Shoop Shoop)" out of the #1 spot, to be an elegy for C+C Music Factory's David Cole. Carey's former collaborator had died earlier that year from complications of AIDS. "One Sweet Day" held the #1 spot for sixteen straight weeks—at the time, the longest that any song had ever been at #1. Carey and Boyz II Men held that record for twenty-four years, before Lil Nas X and Billy Ray Cyrus's "Old Town Road" exceeded the "One Sweet Day" streak with a nineteen-week run at the top.

"One Sweet Day" was a grand weeper of a ballad, but the key to Carey's sustained appeal turned out to be clubby, rap-inflected songs like "Fantasy." In the midnineties, groups like TLC and Jodeci found huge success by putting on Mariah Carey–style vocal displays over hip-hop beats. Carey worked more and more often with rap producers like Jermaine Dupri, Puff Daddy, and Q-Tip. By 1997, when Carey separated from Tommy Mottola, she'd gracefully transitioned to a rap-dominant era, sharing chart space with stylistic descendants like Usher, Brandy, and Monica. The first time Jay-Z ever reached #1, it was with a guest verse on Carey's 1999 hit "Heartbreaker."

Carey had a series of public setbacks in the 2000s. She played the lead in the 2001 movie *Glitter*, an unqualified bomb. She went about five years without a #1 hit, and she changed record labels a couple of times. In 2001, Carey was hospitalized for exhaustion after a strange, awkward appearance on MTV's *Total Request Live* and after she left notes on her website questioning whether she still wanted to keep making music. But in 2005, Carey surged back with her album *The Emancipation of Mimi*, which became the biggest seller of that year. The single "We Belong Together" spent fourteen weeks at #1; *Billboard* eventually named it the #1 single of the decade.

In 2008, Carey's single "Touch My Body" became her eighteenth chart-topper—giving her an eighteen-year span of dominant hits and putting her in shouting distance of the Beatles' all-time record. Carey slowly faded from pop supremacy after that. She did Vegas shows, became a mother, and made music that was mostly pitched toward her large and devoted cult. If that had been the end of Carey's time as a hit-maker, she would've still had a historic run. But Carey wasn't yet done with the #1 spot, or maybe the #1 spot wasn't done with her. Carey finally made it back to #1 with a twenty-five-year-old song.

In 1994, Carey had released a hugely successful holiday album called *Merry Christmas*, and "All I Want for Christmas Is You," a song she'd cowritten and coproduced with Walter Afanasieff, had gone on to become a seasonal perennial. Carey never released "All I Want for Christmas Is You" as a single, so the song didn't crack the Hot 100 until it had been out for years. But *Billboard* kept making changes to its chart tabulation, and "All I Want for Christmas Is You" first appeared on the chart in 2008 on the strength of iTunes downloads. For years, the song regularly reappeared on the charts around Christmastime, climbing a little higher each year. In 2019, its twenty-fifth year of existence, "All I Want for Christmas Is You" became the #1 song in America. It returned to #1 the next year. It'll probably be back at #1 again every year for the foreseeable future. With apologies to Pentatonix, "All I Want for Christmas" might be the very last nearly universally recognized holiday classic of its kind.

When "Vision of Love" topped the Hot 100, it would've been impossible to predict three decades of pop-chart ripple effects. But even if none of those other eighteen Mariah Carey singles reached #1, then "Vision of Love" would've still been a game changer—the song that established melisma-heavy R&B as a powerful commercial force. That style would dominate for years, but it wasn't the only vocal style that took over the pop charts in the nineties. Shortly after "Vision of Love," rap music finally arrived at #1.

CHAPTER 14

Vanilla Ice—"Ice Ice Baby"

Released August 22, 1990
Hit #1 November 3, 1990
One-week reign

RAP MUSIC FIRST TOUCHED THE *BILLBOARD* CHARTS IN OCTOber 1979. Before that, rap had been a purely underground phenomenon—a mutant strain of party music that emerged in the South Bronx and spread to the rest of New York City, starting in the midseventies. Competing DJs would build sound systems and would set off neighborhood parties by cutting between the best parts of funk singles. Rappers would hype crowds up by talking about the DJs. Out of this, a whole underground culture emerged, but nobody thought of turning it into pop music until Sylvia Robinson, an R&B singer and songwriter who'd made her first hit in 1957, had the idea to put out a rap record.

Robinson and her husband, a former Harlem numbers runner named Joe, had founded a small funk label called Sugar Hill Records, and they approached some of the Bronx rap groups about making a record. Those groups weren't interested, so Robinson put together her own group, auditioning young rappers in Englewood, New Jersey, and assembling a trio that she called the Sugarhill Gang. At Robinson's

behest, those three rappers spent fifteen minutes chattering and brag-
ging and telling absurdist stories over an instrumental version of Chic's
"Good Times," a disco hit that had gone to #1 in August. Robinson
hired a group of local funk musicians to play the "Good Times" backbeat as closely as possible. The Sugarhill Gang's rappers famously took
a good chunk of their lyrics from Grandmaster Caz, the leader of the
Bronx crew known as the Cold Crush Brothers, who got no credit.
Neither, for that matter, did Chic, at least until "Good Times" songwriters Nile Rodgers and Bernard Edwards threatened to sue and were
given songwriting credit.

The Sugarhill Gang's delightfully goofy single "Rapper's Delight"
came out on Sugar Hill Records in September 1979, and it first
reached the Hot 100 a month later. In January 1980, "Rapper's
Delight" climbed to #36, its Hot 100 peak. Around the world, "Rapper's Delight" did even better, making the top 10 in the United
Kingdom and France and West Germany and even reaching #1 in
Canada, Spain, and the Netherlands. But it would be more than a
decade before a rap song would finally reach #1 in the country where
the music was invented.

Over the course of the eighties, rap evolved at dizzying speeds,
from the bubbly and disco-adjacent "Rapper's Delight" to an international underground scene full of different regional sounds and subgenres. By the mideighties, the Queens trio Run-DMC, rap's first true
crossover stars, were selling millions of albums. In 1986, at the behest
of producer Rick Rubin, Run-DMC got together with Steven Tyler
and Joe Perry, the two leaders of the washed-up Boston hard-rock act
Aerosmith, to record a new version of Aerosmith's 1975 hit "Walk This
Way." Run-DMC's take on "Walk This Way" became rap's first top-10
hit, peaking at #4—six spots higher than Aerosmith's original version of
"Walk This Way" had charted. The "Walk This Way" remake helped
spur a commercial renaissance for Aerosmith, who experienced a
whole new wave of popularity that would impact the charts for another

fifteen years. More important, the single proved that rap, in the right circumstances, could become pop music.

That point should've been obvious. Even before "Walk This Way," Run-DMC were racking up gold and platinum albums and touring arenas. The same year that Run-DMC and Aerosmith recorded "Walk This Way," Run-DMC's tourmates the Beastie Boys, a trio of white ex-punks from Brooklyn and Manhattan, released *Licensed to Ill*, their snottily swaggering goof of a debut album. Early in 1987, *Licensed to Ill* became the first rap album to reach #1 on the albums chart, and it spent seven weeks there. By the end of the year, *Licensed to Ill* was quadruple platinum, and *Billboard* named it the #3 album of 1987, behind only Bon Jovi's *Slippery When Wet* and Paul Simon's *Graceland*. But even with all those albums sold, the Beastie Boys never became much of a factor on the Hot 100. Only one of their singles reached the top 10, and that song wasn't even really rap. The beautifully stupid "(You Gotta) Fight for Your Right (to Party)" was a shouty frat-rock novelty, and it peaked at #7.

Both "Walk This Way" and "Fight for Your Right" were explicit attempts to reach beyond rap's Black fan base, to appeal to white suburban rock fans. Rick Rubin, producer of both singles, was a white suburban rock fan himself, and his crossover instincts proved sharp. (It's no coincidence that the Beastie Boys, the first white rap group to reach any level of prominence, were also the first to become mainstream stars.) Even after Run-DMC and the Beastie Boys, though, rap still faced a big barrier on the Hot 100. With the chart determined by both singles sales and radio play, rap songs would have to cross over into multiple radio formats to get far on the Hot 100. In the eighties, radio programmers generally feared that this stark, confrontational music would persuade listeners to switch stations. Even R&B stations were reluctant to add rap to heavy rotation. The #1 hits that did feature something that vaguely resembled rap—like Blondie's 1981 experiment "Rapture" or Falco's German-language 1985 smash

"Rock Me Amadeus"—used the genre as a kind of knowingly ridiculous flavoring, and they came from artists outside the rap community.

In the late eighties, the barrier separating rap from mainstream pop slowly eroded. In 1989, the gruffly charismatic LA rapper Tone Loc made it to #2 with "Wild Thing," a comically horny story-song built around a Van Halen sample. Soon afterward, Tone repeated that success, reaching #3 with the similarly frustrated "Funky Cold Medina," which took its guitar riff from an old Foreigner hit. That same year, Young MC and Biz Markie had top-10 hits with dance-rap songs that flirted with comedy. At the time, the biggest names in rap were hard, unapologetic firebrands, like the self-styled revolutionaries in Public Enemy and the profane nihilists in N.W.A. But radio mostly stayed away from Public Enemy and N.W.A, so they never had a chance on the pop charts. The tracks that did reach the top 10 were the ones that made a point to be relatively fluffy and approachable. A whole lot of rappers and fans were deeply skeptical of those hits and of the groups— Digital Underground, Kid 'n Play, DJ Jazzy Jeff & the Fresh Prince— who indulged in that kind of frothiness.

Bobby Brown never had to deal with that kind of skepticism, possibly because he wasn't a rapper. Instead, Brown was simply a singer who sometimes rapped. Brown, a former member of the pioneering boy band New Edition, fashioned himself into the face of new jack swing, a new genre that fused rap's ferocious swagger with R&B melodies and clattering dance-pop tempos. New jack swing was the creation of Teddy Riley, a Harlem producer and songwriter who produced tracks for rappers like Kool Moe Dee and Big Daddy Kane and formed the singing group Guy. In 1988, Riley produced and cowrote Bobby Brown's sneering, defiant new jack swing "My Prerogative," which reached #1 in January 1989.

Bobby Brown was a true showman, an expressive singer and dancer, but he carried himself with the hardened posture of a rapper. In some ways, "My Prerogative," a song that's explicitly about Bobby Brown refusing to apologize for anything, is the first real rap song to top the Hot 100, with the crucial caveat that there's really no rapping on the song. Still, Bobby Brown helped rap music break through on pop radio. In 1990, he even rapped a guest verse on "She Ain't Worth It," a wan attempt at new jack swing from white singer Glenn Medeiros, and that song topped the Hot 100 right before Mariah Carey's "Vision of Love." Bobby Brown might not have been a rapper, but he was still the first person ever to rap a guest verse on a #1 hit.

Another high-stepping showman became a huge crossover figure in 1990. That's when Oakland's athletic MC Hammer released "U Can't Touch This," an irrepressible pop-rap anthem built on a barely altered chunk of Rick James's 1981 funk hit "Super Freak." Hammer was colorful and physical and anodyne, and "U Can't Touch This" caught on immediately. It probably would've been rap's first #1 hit, if not for one fateful decision. Capitol, Hammer's label, opted not to release the "U Can't Touch This" single on cassette, the dominant format of the day. Instead, the "U Can't Touch This" single was available only on twelve-inch vinyl, a format used by DJs and basically nobody else. The more expensive compact disc was starting to change record-label profit margins, and Capitol didn't want people to pay a dollar for a cassingle when they could charge sixteen dollars for a full-length MC Hammer CD. The ploy worked. While "U Can't Touch This" stalled out at #8 on the Hot 100, Hammer's album *Please Hammer Don't Hurt 'Em* sold ten million copies and spent eighteen weeks at #1.

Instead, the first rapper to reach #1 was a young white guy who took off running with MC Hammer's ingratiating, dance-floor-centric approach. Robert Van Winkle, who was thirteen when "Rapper's Delight" took off, grew up in the suburbs of Dallas and Miami. Van Winkle's father wasn't around. His mother taught music at a small college, and his stepfather, an Ecuadorian immigrant, worked at a car dealership. As a kid, Van Winkle fell in love with hip-hop when he saw the bright, goofy 1984 movie *Breakin'*, which was, to some degree, part of the wave of eighties underdog dance movies that produced top albums and hits. The young Van Winkle formed a break-dancing crew, and he danced and rapped for tips at Dallas malls. His friends, high-lighting the fact that Van Winkle was the only white guy in the crew, nicknamed him MC Vanilla.

A twenty-year-old MC Vanilla started to frequent the hip-hop nights at the Dallas nightclub City Lights. One night, on a dare, he joined a talent contest and won the crowd over. City Lights manager John Bush caught Vanilla's routine and recommended him to club owner Tommy Quon, who hired Vanilla as the house act at City Lights and also became Vanilla's manager. At City Lights, Vanilla was a nightly spectacle, and he opened shows for national touring acts like Paula Abdul, 2 Live Crew, Public Enemy, and MC Hammer. Eventually, Quon changed MC Vanilla's name to Vanilla Ice and paired him with DJ Earthquake, City Lights' in-house record spinner. Vanilla and Earthquake started making tracks together.

Vanilla Ice's hit was supposed to be "Play That Funky Music," a clumsy rap built from a sample of Wild Cherry's 1976 disco hit. Quon convinced the Atlanta indie label Ichiban, home to underground rappers like Willie D and MC Breed, to release "Play That Funky Music" as a single, and he tirelessly promoted that single to Black radio DJs throughout the South. Those DJs weren't especially interested in "Play That Funky Music," but a few of them were impressed when they flipped the single over and listened to the B-side, an itchy and propulsive dance-rap song called "Ice Ice Baby."

Vanilla Ice has said that he wrote "Ice Ice Baby" when he was sixteen, which would mean that he came up with the song in 1984 and that he had it sitting around for years before releasing it. Other people have told other stories. Earthquake has said that he came up with the beat, a whispery, synthy track built around the nervous bass line of Queen and David Bowie's 1981 hit "Under Pressure." Earthquake also takes credit for the hook, a chant that the Black fraternity Alpha Phi Alpha had been using for years and that can be heard in Spike Lee's 1988 movie *School Daze*. Earthquake claims that he and Vanilla fought over the track, with Vanilla wanting an instrumental version to play in his car and Earthquake refusing to give him one. According to Earthquake, he didn't give Vanilla permission to use the beat, and he didn't know Vanilla had recorded over it until he heard "Ice Ice Baby" on the radio. When "Ice Ice Baby" came out nationally, Vanilla Ice was credited as the producer and Earthquake as a cowriter.

"Ice Ice Baby" is a truly silly song. The groove is spartan and muscular and slightly menacing. Vanilla Ice himself is not. On "Ice Ice Baby," Vanilla raps without subtlety or nuance. He touts his own microphone supremacy in puzzling terms: He flows like a harpoon daily and nightly? His style's like a chemical spill? There's also an extended narrative about an attempted carjacking in Miami. Ice talks about gunshots ringing out and shells falling on the concrete, but he escapes unscathed. Cops show up to arrest the jackers, and they don't bother Vanilla, even though he's holding his gun. Vanilla presents this as a happy ending: "Police on the scene, you know what I mean? / They passed me up, confronted all the dope fiends." The first rap song ever to reach #1 on the Hot 100 works as an unintentional lesson on the power of white privilege.

It's easy to make fun of "Ice Ice Baby," and people have been doing that for decades. But the track also has a strange magnetism. A good deal of that credit goes to that bass line, a sparse and efficient riff that had already powered a theatrical rock classic. (The origins of that bass line are a little mysterious; Queen bassist Roger Deacon says that David Bowie came up with it, while Bowie always credited Deacon.) But Vanilla Ice's presence also drives the track. As a technical rapper, Vanilla is graceless and ungainly, but there's no denying his confidence. He believes that he's cool, even if he can't fully justify it. Vanilla has the self-assurance to sell an utterly nonsensical opening line— "All right, stop, collaborate, and listen"—and to make it stick in the brain of anyone who hears it once. To the elementary school kids of 1990, the simplicity of "Ice Ice Baby" was a selling point. This was a rap song that you could *very easily* memorize and then repeat to your friends. Vanilla's lines stuck in your head, and they became weird little mantras.

When "Ice Ice Baby" started to gain steam regionally, Tommy Quon put up $8,000 of his own money to film a video. The clip is crude and sloppy, and it's mostly just Vanilla Ice and his friends dancing in front of the Dallas skyline. But Vanilla himself is almost cartoonishly handsome, with diamond-sharp cheekbones. Also, Vanilla, like MC Hammer before him, could dance. The video got a lot of play on the request-driven cable channel the Box, and "Ice Ice Baby" became the centerpiece of Vanilla's album *Hooked*, which came out on Ichiban late in 1989. Vanilla went out on tour, opening for Public Enemy and N.W.A.

With "Ice Ice Baby" bubbling, major labels came calling. Vanilla Ice got offers from Def Jam and Atlantic. Vanilla says that Public Enemy's Chuck D tried to help him get a deal at Def Jam and that he was about to sign that contract before SBK Records came through with a bigger offer. SBK, a subsidiary of EMI, had just started in 1989, and it had already released pop hits from Wilson Phillips and Technotronic. The label didn't really have any rap artists, but a DJ played "Ice Ice Baby" over the phone for CEO Charles Koppelman, and Koppelman immediately figured out that he could market Vanilla Ice as a crossover pop artist. He was right.

In August 1990, SBK gave "Ice Ice Baby" a proper major-label release. The next month, the label released Vanilla's album *To the Extreme*, a repackaged version of the indie LP *Hooked*, and sent Vanilla out on tour with kindred spirit MC Hammer, whose album held the #1 spot through that summer and fall. Hammer had primed the world for Ice's brand of catchy surface-level pop-rap, and Ice, being a good-looking white guy, became an immediate sensation. As "Ice Ice Baby" gained steam, SBK stopped manufacturing the single. Following the MC Hammer model, the label wanted people to pay more to buy *To the Extreme* in full, preferably on CD. Major labels would keep this practice up with many of their biggest hits for the remainder of the decade. Smashes like No Doubt's "Don't Speak," the Cardigans' "Lovefool," and the Fugees' version of "Killing Me Softly" were never officially released as singles. Since *Billboard* tracked only proper singles on the Hot 100, those songs never charted, which means the charts gave a terribly distorted image of the pop landscape in the nineties. SBK stopped making "Ice Ice Baby" singles just before the track reached #1, which presumably explains why "Ice Ice Baby" had only a one-week run at the top of the charts.

Once again, the plan worked. A week after "Ice Ice Baby" hit #1, *To the Extreme* knocked *Please Hammer Don't Hurt 'Em* out of the #1 spot on the album chart, and it stayed there for four months. Soon afterward, SBK released "Play That Funky Music" as a single, and that one, which had died when it first came out on Ichiban a year earlier, made it to #4. *To the Extreme* went platinum in November, and it kept moving units. At its peak, the album was selling a hundred thousand copies a day. By the end of January, seven million Americans had bought *To the Extreme*, which made it, to that point, the fastest-selling rap album in history. Vanilla Ice dropped off the MC Hammer tour and started headlining arenas himself. He filmed a cameo in the hit movie *Teenage Mutant Ninja Turtles II: The Secret of the Ooze* and starred in his own low-budget cinematic vehicle, *Cool as Ice*. Within a few months, Vanilla Ice had risen to levels of mainstream stardom that few rappers had ever touched. Naturally, consequences followed.

For one thing, Vanilla Ice had never cleared that sample of David Bowie and Queen's "Under Pressure." At the time, this was standard operating procedure in rap music. Producers would take shards of old records, often split-second drum breaks from semiobscure funk singles, and build entire tracks from them. But the "Under Pressure" bass line is not a breakbeat; it's an indelible seven-note refrain that's instantly recognizable to anyone who's spent enough time listening to the radio. When ultraobvious samples started turning up on hit songs like "Ice Ice Baby" and "U Can't Touch This," it made sampling a much more difficult process.

Lawyers for Queen and Bowie threatened Vanilla Ice with lawsuits shortly after "Ice Ice Baby" hit #1, and the parties settled out of court.

In a radio interview decades later, Ice claimed that he paid $4 million to just buy the publishing rights for "Under Pressure" outright, though this story is impossible to substantiate. David Bowie and the four members of Queen were also given songwriting credits for "Ice Ice Baby." During that whole legal kerfuffle, Vanilla, grinning widely, tried to argue in an interview that the "Under Pressure" bass line and the "Ice Ice Baby" bass line were different things, and that only fed a growing backlash.

Within rap music, people had problems with Vanilla Ice. This white guy had invaded a predominantly Black art form, made a goofy song, and ridden it straight to the top. In the ascendant rap magazine the *Source*, columnists cautioned that Vanilla Ice could become an Elvis figure for hip-hop. SBK Records had put out a bio claiming that Ice had been a national motocross champion and that he'd gone to the same Miami high school as 2 Live Crew's Luther Campbell. This was all wrong; Ice had distinguished himself in local motocross races in Dallas, and he'd never been to that Miami high school. When the news came out that Ice was really from suburban Dallas, the press had a field day. In a combative interview on *The Arsenio Hall Show*, Ice was in the unenviable position of arguing that he was not a fake. He seemed surprised and defensive at Hall's line of questioning, and he did not make a convincing case for himself.

Vanilla Ice became an irresistible target. On the surging sketch comedy show *In Living Color*, a rubber-limbed young Jim Carrey uncorked a devastating Ice impression on a parody song called "White White Baby": "I'm living large, and my bank is stupid / Because I just listen to real rap and dupe it." The band 3rd Bass, a white group from New York with stronger rap-world connections, clowned Ice on their minor hit "Pop Goes the Weasel": "You stole somebody's record, and you looped it, you looped it." In the video, the group beats up Vanilla Ice, who is played, inexplicably, by Henry Rollins. On "Scenario (Remix)," A Tribe Called Quest's Phife Dawg simply sniffed, "Vanilla Ice platinum? That shit's ridiculous."

Some of Ice's problems went beyond the courts of law and public opinion. One of those problems took the form of Marion "Suge" Knight, a former NFL prospect who'd worked as a bodyguard for Bobby Brown and for LA rapper the D.O.C. Knight had formed his own management company, and one of his clients was Mario "Chocolate" Johnson, a Dallas rapper with connections to "Ice Ice Baby" producer Earthquake. Johnson claimed that he'd written "Ice Ice Baby" and some of Vanilla's other songs and that he'd never been paid for his work. While Ice was eating at the Palm, a steakhouse in Los Angeles, Knight walked in with a group of large men, pushed Ice's security aside, and sat down to demand a percentage of the "Ice Ice Baby" publishing rights. Later, on the same night that Ice was on *The Arsenio Hall Show*, Knight and his associates appeared at Ice's suite at the Bel Age Hotel in Beverly Hills.

The story of Suge Knight dangling Vanilla Ice off his hotel-room balcony is almost certainly overblown urban-legend stuff; Ice and Knight have both said that it didn't happen like that. Instead, Ice says that Knight merely *threatened* to throw him off his balcony. Ice also claims that Knight's people pulled guns and beat up his bodyguard. In any case, Ice agreed to sign away part of the "Ice Ice Baby" royalties—a slice of the pie that Ice later claimed was worth millions. That transaction gave Suge Knight some important seed money. In 1992, along with former N.W.A member Dr. Dre, Knight formed a new label called Death Row Records, and that label almost immediately reshaped rap music.

Death Row's first LP, Dr. Dre's 1992 solo debut, *The Chronic*, presented a slick blockbuster vision of the bleak, misanthropic street rap that Dre had been making with N.W.A. Dre assembled a vivid cast of supporting characters, including a debuting Snoop Doggy Dogg, and gave musical heft and grandeur to stories about killing and robbing. The popularity of *The Chronic* can probably, at least in part, be considered a reaction against the flossy pop-rap of MC Hammer and Vanilla Ice, whose careers never recovered. Ironically, the biggest single from

The Chronic, "Nuthin' but a 'G' Thang," peaked at #2. The song that kept it from the top spot was "Informer," from the white Canadian dancehall reggae toaster Snow—a figure more than a little reminiscent of Vanilla Ice.

In signing away his royalties, a decision motivated by self-preservation, Ice helped fund the movement that would replace his style of rap music. In the years ahead, Death Row released landmark albums from Snoop, Tha Dogg Pound, and 2Pac. In a *Rolling Stone* interview years later, Ice acknowledged how strange that was: "I gave millions away, which was the start of Death Row. That's how [Knight] got the money to start Death Row Records, and then you got Snoop Dogg, and then you got Dr. Dre and 2Pac, and that's the whole saga. It started off with me, I guess. But it's a roundabout thing. It's weird." (For his part, MC Hammer briefly signed with Death Row and recorded with 2Pac, but Death Row shelved the album that Hammer recorded for the label.)

Still, in the immediate aftermath of "Ice Ice Baby," pop-rap prevailed. As it happens, the second rap single to hit #1 also came from a white rapper: future movie star Mark Wahlberg, then known as Marky Mark. In 1991, Marky Mark and his Funky Bunch reached #1 with the hip-house track "Good Vibrations," which was produced by Mark's older brother Donnie, of the hugely popular boy band New Kids on the Block. (The New Kids, incidentally, were assembled by New Edition's former manager, and they sometimes threw their own hokey rap verses into their singles, though they can't really be considered rappers.) For years after that, the only rap singles that topped the Hot 100 were essentially novelties.

After 1991, Vanilla Ice never appeared on the Hot 100 again. In the years ahead, he dealt with drug problems and depression. He overdosed on heroin and attempted suicide. He grew dreadlocks and attempted to present himself as a hardcore rapper on his 1994 album *Mind Blowin'*, a resounding flop. Later, Ice joined the late-nineties rap-rock wave, forming a band and releasing a metal version of "Ice

Ice Baby." Eventually, he recorded a series of independent albums, built up a nostalgic fan base, and became a fixture on reality TV. He also started buying and flipping houses, which led to a long-running gig hosting the DIY Network home-improvement series *The Vanilla Ice Project*.

It's tempting to look at Vanilla Ice's brief, bright-burning pop career as an anomaly, a strange blip in history. But it's more than that. Vanilla Ice will always be the first rapper with a #1 single. That mere distinction makes him a pivotal historical figure and "Ice Ice Baby" a pivotal historical moment, since rap eventually became the dominant form of pop music, first in America and then in the rest of the world. He was a sign of changes that were already underway, and his presence also helped push those changes forward.

"Ice Ice Baby" had other consequences. In the baldness of its "Under Pressure" sample, the song changed the creative process for rap music. When the genre grew in popularity, more and more artists and publishers started filing lawsuits over samples. Queen and David Bowie were not the first to threaten legal action over samples, but they were the first to truly realize how lucrative that legal action might be.

After Queen and David Bowie came for Vanilla Ice's royalties, rap producers had to change the way they approached sampling. They could either pick obscure scraps of music and hope that nobody noticed or pay exorbitant sums for recognizable pieces of music. The giddy collage style of late-eighties albums like De La Soul's *3 Feet High and Rising* or the Beastie Boys' *Paul's Boutique* was no longer possible. In that way, "Ice Ice Baby" helped change the game.

And of course, however unintentionally, "Ice Ice Baby" also helped fund the rise of Death Row Records and a new form of brash and violent and unapologetic rap music. It would take years for that stuff to conquer the pop charts, but it would happen. When this form of rap finally did take over, it had become big and bright and shiny and fully dependent on obvious pieces of eighties pop songs. It had become something not entirely unlike "Ice Ice Baby."

CHAPTER 15

Puff Daddy–
"Can't Nobody Hold Me Down"
(Featuring Mase)

Released February 11, 1997
Hit #1 March 22, 1997
Six-week reign

"YOU NAME IT, I COULD CLAIM IT. YOUNG, BLACK, AND famous, with money hanging out the anus." That's how twenty-seven-year-old label boss Sean "Puff Daddy" Combs described himself on "Can't Nobody Hold Me Down," his debut single as lead artist. "Can't Nobody Hold Me Down" is a song-length boast, with both Puffy and his twenty-one-year-old teddy-bear protégé Mason "Mase" Betha describing a fantastical life of overwhelming finery: "We spend cheese in the West Indies, then come home to plenty cream Bentleys."

These were not idle boasts. Long before releasing his first single under his own name, Sean Combs had built an empire by turning rap's living-large pretensions into a foundational aesthetic. Bad Boy Records, the label that Puff founded, scored its first crossover #1 hit with Puff's first single, and that label would go on to dominate the Hot 100 for the next year. In the process, Puff Daddy established a version of blockbuster-level hip-hop flash that would serve as a blueprint for a whole generation of rappers, moving rap itself to the absolute center of the pop universe.

When Vanilla Ice's "Ice Ice Baby" topped the Hot 100 in 1990, rap music did not immediately replace everything else atop the pop charts. That took time. In the six years after "Ice Ice Baby," most of the rap crossovers that reached #1 were, in one way or another, gimmicks and novelties. In 1991, P.M. Dawn, a Jersey City duo who depicted themselves as astrally minded flower-child types, topped the chart with their unapologetically soft "Set Adrift on Memory Bliss." In 1992, Kris Kross, a duo of baby-face Atlanta teenagers who famously wore their clothes backward, ascended the chart with "Jump," a song seemingly built for middle school dance floors, while Seattle's Sir Mix-A-Lot followed them to the top with "Baby Got Back," a big-butt anthem laser-targeted at middle school locker rooms.

Outside of the pop spotlight, though, rap music went through its own momentous shifts and internal schisms. By the early nineties, there were multiple different factions on the rap landscape: crossover-minded dance acts, Afro-centric political thinkers, hard street storytellers. Some of those rappers came close to conquering the Hot 100. Dr. Dre and his protégé Snoop Doggy Dogg had a series of top-10 hits between 1993 and 1994, and they reached #2 with their collaboration "Nuthin' but a 'G' Thang." Dre and Snoop's style was rough enough to capture teenage imaginations but smooth enough to play on pop radio, and it turned Death Row into an album-sales behemoth. But profane nihilism was the Death Row house style, and that gave them an uphill battle on the pop charts. Dre didn't reach #1 until 1996, when he rapped a guest verse on "No Diggity," a sleek and lascivious song from the R&B group Blackstreet.

Blackstreet was the creation of Teddy Riley, the Harlem producer who had invented new jack swing in the late eighties. "No Diggity" was a comeback hit for Riley. Early on, Riley had recognized the commercial possibilities of combining rap swagger with R&B melodies. By the time of "No Diggity," that combination had made a lot of people rich. One of those people was record-label executive Andre Harrell, an ex-rapper who founded the label Uptown Records in 1986 and understood Riley's vision early on.

Harrell had been half of a hitless mideighties rap duo called Dr. Jeckyll and Mr. Hyde. After he started Uptown, Harrell signed Riley's group Guy, and he also gave deals to slick and melody-friendly rappers like Heavy D and Father MC. In 1990, on Heavy D's recommendation, Harrell met with an ambitious young Howard University student named Sean "Puffy" Combs. Combs, born in Harlem and raised mostly in the Westchester County suburb of Mount Vernon, was a working-class striver who'd lost family to crime. His father, a numbers runner and drug dealer, was shot dead in his Mercedes in Central Park when Combs was two years old.

A young Sean Combs fell in love with hip-hop and frequented clubs, where he developed a reputation as a sharp dresser and dancer. (As a child, Combs was nicknamed "Puff"; he claimed it was because of the way he'd huff and puff when he lost his temper.) While still in high school, Combs danced in music videos for artists like Diana Ross, Babyface, and the Fine Young Cannibals. In his freshman year at Howard, Combs promoted parties that drew hundreds of people, then thousands. At the first of those parties, Combs booked a lineup of celebrity guests that included fellow Mount Vernon native Heavy D and Riley's group Guy. Heavy persuaded Andre Harrell to take the meeting with Combs, and Combs persuaded Harrell to take him on as an intern.

In his sophomore year at Howard, Combs would take the Amtrak from DC up to the Uptown Records offices in New York twice a week, sometimes hiding from the conductor in the bathroom to avoid paying for a ticket. Combs impressed Harrell with his frantic work ethic, and when Combs dropped out of college, Harrell hired him as an A&R director and even invited him to live in his New Jersey house.

Combs started working with the North Carolina R&B group Jodeci, and he hit on the idea of dressing the group in baggy jeans and baseball jerseys rather than the square suits that most R&B singers wore in that era. Combs essentially had the singers in Jodeci dressing and carrying themselves like rappers. Changes to the music followed. Combs remixed Jodeci's 1991 single "Come and Talk to Me," adding the drums from EPMD's rap hit "You're a Customer." "Come and Talk to Me" reached #1 on the R&B chart and #11 on the Hot 100, proving Combs's instincts right.

But not all of Combs's instincts were right, and he made some deadly mistakes in 1991. At the end of that year, Combs promoted a concert and celebrity basketball game at City College of New York (CCNY). The event drew more people than the school's gym could hold, and a crowd stampede killed nine people. Soon afterward, the *New York Post* blamed the disaster on "a fool named Puff Daddy." But those deaths didn't end Combs's career. Harrell hired lawyers for his young protégé, and he also assigned Combs to guide the career of Uptown's latest signing, the young Yonkers-born R&B singer Mary J. Blige. Combs produced some of Blige's 1992 debut album, *What's the 411?*, and he persuaded Blige to sing over rap beats, marketing her as the queen of the new hybrid genre hip-hop soul. The concept worked brilliantly. *What's the 411?* went triple platinum, and "Real Love," the single that featured Blige wailing about romantic need over the drums from Audio Two's 1987 underground hit "Top Billin'," reached #7 on the Hot 100. Combs's career didn't just survive the CCNY stampede. He thrived in its wake.

Flush with success, Combs started making plans to launch his own label. On the recommendation of the *Source* columnist Mateo "Matty C" Capoluongo, Combs listened to a demo tape from an unsigned rapper who called himself Biggie Smalls, and he quickly set off on a quest to sign Biggie to Uptown. Christopher "Biggie Smalls" Wallace was a small-time drug dealer who rapped on street corners while working.

Biggie's friends, impressed with his ability, convinced him to record that demo with Brooklyn producer Easy Mo Bee. Combs signed Biggie, and Easy Mo Bee produced Biggie's 1993 debut single, "Party and Bullshit," which appeared on the soundtrack of the Uptown-produced film *Who's the Man?* The movie was a flop, but Biggie's single sold five hundred thousand copies. Combs also used Biggie's booming, commanding voice on a remix of Mary J. Blige's single "What's the 411?" and also added a thundering Biggie verse to his "Bad Boy Remix" of the Jamaican dancehall artist Super Cat's single "Dolly My Baby." On that remix, Combs also tried his own hand at rapping, but his verse was clumsy and inept. For all his skills as a record man, Sean Combs was clearly not a rapper.

In 1993, Andre Harrell fired Sean Combs from Uptown Records. The boastful and flamboyant Combs was getting harder and harder to manage, and Harrell had grown tired—or, to hear some tell it, jealous—of Combs. Combs, who was still living in Harrell's house at the time, was crushed, but he quickly regrouped. That same year, Combs founded his own label, Bad Boy Records, and he signed a deal with Clive Davis, the music-business legend who'd shepherded the career of Whitney Houston. As a flashy and ego-driven young executive, Davis himself had been fired from Columbia Records before rebounding with his own label, Arista. Davis made Bad Boy a subsidiary of Arista, and he also bought Biggie Smalls's contract out from Uptown. Biggie's 1994 debut album, *Ready to Die*, was the first LP released on Bad Boy.

By disposition, Biggie Smalls—who changed his name to the Notorious B.I.G. when an unknown white rapper known as Biggy Smallz threatened a lawsuit—was a street rapper. He possessed unearthly gifts for talking tough and telling crime-life stories. After the success of Dr. Dre and Snoop Doggy Dogg, that kind of hardcore rap had vast new commercial possibilities. Combs and Biggie used the sonic sweep of Dre's Death Row records as a model for *Ready to Die*, and Combs pushed Biggie to adapt lush R&B hooks and smooth sex-symbol lyrics.

Biggie was dubious about Combs's commercial instincts, and *Ready to Die* presents a tug-of-war between those aesthetics. The album features tons of good-life triumphalism, but it ends with Biggie's fictional suicide. Biggie vacillates wildly between bloodthirsty nihilism and laid-back party raps. That combination could've easily come off schizophrenic and incoherent, but thanks to Biggie's towering charisma and writing skills, it worked. Rather than sinking the album artistically, Combs's pop concessions simply provided fresh new ways for Biggie to showcase what he could do.

The use of samples on *Ready to Die* became a trademark for Sean Combs. Combs wasn't a rap producer in the traditional sense; he didn't splice together beats himself. Instead, he worked with a staff of producers—a team that would later be known as the Hitmen—and he suggested samples and tweaks and changes in tone. In the wake of the lawsuits that followed hits like "Ice Ice Baby," rap producers in the mid-nineties generally tried to disguise the records that they sampled—using tiny shards of music from old records, then layering or distorting those sounds so that copyright holders wouldn't recognize them. Combs had other ideas. He wanted to use instantly recognizable chunks of music, clearing those samples with lawyers and riding the goodwill that audiences had for those older records. For Biggie's heartfelt single "Juicy," for instance, Combs wanted to use an undisguised loop of Mtume's 1983 R&B hit "Juicy Fruit." When Combs brought the idea to Easy Mo Bee, Mo Bee blanched at the idea: "If you were looping, you weren't really working." But Combs insisted, and the resulting track, which Mo Bee did not produce, became Biggie's breakout hit.

In *GQ* years later, Sean Combs explained his whole philosophy when it came to sampling. An ideal sample, to Combs, wasn't an artful and obscure chop. Instead, it was a way of triggering an audience's affection for an older record: "I remember watching *Soul Train* and dancing in my living room with my mother. I wanted to fuse those elements with what was going on at the time with 'gangsta rap,' or reality rap. 'Juicy

Fruit' was a record that always felt like summertime in the city." Soon enough, Biggie's "Juicy" felt like summertime in the city, too.

Ready to Die was an artistic triumph, and it was also a commercial smash. Within a little more than a year, the album was double platinum. "Big Poppa," its smoothest single, reached #6 on the pop charts. After the album had been out for a year, Combs remixed Biggie's "One More Chance," adding the vocals of R&B singers Mary J. Blige and Aaliyah, as well as Faith Evans, a young Bad Boy discovery who had just married Biggie Smalls; that single made it to #2. Another early Bad Boy hit was "Flava in Ya Ear," an Easy Mo Bee–produced track from the Long Island rapper Craig Mack; that one made it to #9, thanks in part to an all-star remix with a prominent Biggie verse. In the videos for those songs, and even on the songs themselves, Combs was a constant presence, toasting his discoveries and muttering encouragement.

Combs continued to produce tracks for Mary J. Blige, and he worked with TLC, who were signed to Ruffhouse, an Arista sublabel that Clive Davis had cofounded. Combs also signed R&B groups like Total and 112 to Bad Boy. He remixed Staten Island rapper and Wu-Tang Clan member Method Man's gruff love song "All I Need," adding a Mary J. Blige chorus, and the track rose to #3 on the Hot 100 in 1995. The next year, Combs also remixed Mariah Carey's chart-topper "Fantasy," adding Method Man's fellow Wu-Tang member Ol' Dirty Bastard—yet another hugely successful pop fusion of rap and R&B.

While recording *Ready to Die*, Biggie Smalls became friendly with Tupac Shakur. Shakur, born in New York and raised largely in Baltimore, was the son of Black Panther activists. As a teenager, Shakur moved to the Bay Area and broke into the rap scene alongside the group Digital Underground. Shakur's explosive charisma, revolutionary rhetoric, and tough-guy braggadocio made him an instant star. Shakur could act, too; in movies like *Juice* and *Poetic Justice*, he was magnetic. But Shakur was also erratic and short-fused, and he was increasingly drawn to California's gang culture.

When Tupac and Biggie were both ascendant rap stars, they bonded, but their friendship turned sour quickly. In November 1994, Shakur was heading into New York's Quad Studios to record, and a group of gunmen robbed him and his friends in the studio lobby. When Shakur resisted, the gunmen shot him five times. He survived. Biggie was recording upstairs at the studio at the time, and Shakur, convinced that Biggie and Combs had set him up, launched a furious barrage of on-record insults at his former friend. Almost immediately after the shooting, Shakur began serving a jail sentence for sexual assault. Death Row cofounder Suge Knight visited Shakur in prison and persuaded him to sign with Death Row, in exchange for Knight paying Shakur's legal bills and helping him get out of jail. (At the time, Death Row was an Interscope subsidiary, and Shakur already recorded for its parent label.)

When Tupac Shakur moved to Death Row, Knight took his side in the dispute with Biggie and Combs. Onstage at the Source Awards in 1995, when Shakur was still in prison, Knight shouted out Tupac and said that Death Row was "riding with him." He also took an implicit shot at Sean Combs and Bad Boy: "Any artist out there want to be a artist, and wanna stay a star, and don't want to have to worry about the executive producer trying to be all in the videos, all on the records, *dancing*, come to Death Row." The Madison Square Garden crowd, immediately understanding that their hometown heroes were being attacked, rained down boos, and that limited dispute led to rap's fabled and much-hyped East Coast–West Coast conflict.

It also helped sell a lot of records for both Death Row and Bad Boy. Tupac Shakur's Death Row debut, the 1996 double album *All Eyez on Me*, sold millions, and it also made Shakur arguably the first hardcore rapper with a #1 hit on the Hot 100. Before Shakur, a couple of other rappers made it to #1 with tracks that were slightly more serious than "Jump" or "Baby Got Back." In 1995, Compton, California, rapper Coolio rose to #1 with "Gangsta's Paradise," a street-life lament from the soundtrack of *Dangerous Minds*, a movie where

Michelle Pfeiffer played a virtuous inner-city teacher. A year later, the Cleveland melodic-rap pioneers Bone Thugs-N-Harmony topped the Hot 100 for two months with "Tha Crossroads." The track was a mournful elegy for Eazy-E, Dr. Dre's N.W.A colleague turned adversary, who had discovered and signed the group.

By the standards of crossover pop hits, "Gangsta's Paradise" and "Tha Crossroads" were credible rap music. But the songs weren't as furious and profane as the Bad Boy and Death Row tracks that had dominated the rap conversation for two years. So when Shakur replaced "Tha Crossroads" at #1, it signaled a changing-of-the-guard moment. Shakur's one #1 hit was a double-sided single. The track that got the most attention was the rumbling, anthemic Dr. Dre collaboration "California Love," but that song was technically the B-side. Shakur's real #1 hit was "How Do U Want It," a plush and sexual track with an R&B chorus. For the "How Do U Want It" hook, Shakur recruited K-Ci & JoJo, two members of Jodeci, the Uptown Records R&B group whose early career had been guided by Sean Combs. Shakur landed his one #1 hit at the height of his vendetta against Bad Boy. But without the groundwork that Combs had laid with Jodeci, Shakur might've never gotten there.

The same month that Shakur's song was on top, Sean Combs flew the entire Bad Boy production staff to Trinidad for a sort of recording retreat. Those producers weren't allowed to bring wives or girlfriends. Artists weren't invited. Instead, Puff and his Hitmen were there to focus all their energy and attention on making smooth, crowd-pleasing hits. The tracks that those producers crafted on that trip formed the spine of Biggie Smalls's 1997 sophomore album, the double-CD *Life After Death*, as well as the debut album that Combs himself was planning to release. Combs wanted to call it *Hell Up in Harlem*.

In 1996, Combs also signed the good-looking, mushmouthed young Harlem rapper Mase, whom he'd met at an Atlanta convention. Mase had spent his last few dollars on a plane ticket to Atlanta, hoping to find an audience with Jermaine Dupri, the producer who had discovered Kris Kross. Instead, he left Atlanta as a Bad Boy artist. That year, Mase made his Bad Boy debut, rapping on a remix of 112's single "Only You." That's how Bad Boy worked. Combs would use one artist's record to introduce another artist, thus deploying his Bad Boy roster as a sort of promotional web.

Two months after "How Do You Want It" reached #1, Tupac Shakur was shot dead in Las Vegas while riding in a car that Suge Knight was driving. The murder remains unsolved, but at the time rumors flew, and plenty theorized that Shakur's murder was a result of his feud with Bad Boy. Shakur's death left Biggie deeply shaken. A few days after Shakur's death, Biggie got into a car accident that hospitalized him for months, and he considered quitting music altogether. But Combs's rollout plan for Biggie's sophomore album, *Life After Death*, continued, and so did Combs's designs for his own solo career.

Sean Combs had tried rapping under his Puff Daddy alias. It had gone badly. Puff Daddy simply was not a good rapper. By 1997, though, Puff had the benefit of familiarity. As his Bad Boy artists landed hit after hit, Combs made sure that he was always right there, in front of the camera, in all the videos, dancing, and on all the records, playing a nonchalant cheerleader role. In the process, Combs turned himself into a brand. In his new protégé, Mase, Combs found a rapper whose strengths—overwhelming confidence, flashy posing, sleepy delivery— were things that Combs could replicate himself. Mase later told GQ that his verses on Combs's debut album "were records I wrote in that one-bedroom apartment in Harlem before I even got to the label. I gave them to Puff because he was the one with the hot hand."

For "Can't Nobody Hold Me Down," Combs continued with his established practice of repurposing beloved old songs. In the case of his debut single, the choice of samples was so audacious that it was almost subversive. "Can't Nobody Hold Me Down" is built on the beat from "The Message," the classic 1982 hip-hop single credited to Grandmaster Flash & the Furious Five. Flash, the pioneering Bronx DJ, didn't actually have anything to do with "The Message," and he didn't even like the song. Instead, the song was the creation of Furious

Five rapper Melle Mel and Sugar Hill Records producer Ed "Duke Bootee" Fletcher. Melle and Fletcher wrote the song in response to a 1980 transit workers' strike, and they used it to paint a picture of a violent, hopeless, poverty-stricken neighborhood. "The Message" wasn't a huge crossover hit; it reached only #62 on the Hot 100. But the track made it onto the top 10 of the R&B charts, and it became well known as well as historically important. Before "The Message," rap was party music. After "The Message," the music started to document and investigate things like structural racism and economic inequality.

With "Can't Nobody Hold Me Down," Puff and Mase threw away the message of "The Message" but kept its sparse, echoing synth-bleeps and its sticky chorus. They essentially used the music of "The Message" to turn rap back into party music. When Puff and Mase referred back to "The Message," they used its lyrics as simple signifiers, ways to communicate their own moneyed-up magnificence. In turning a beloved text of political rap into something gleefully self-aggrandizing, Puff and Mase essentially baited their critics into hating them more.

On "Can't Nobody Hold Me Down," Puff and Mase describe themselves as triumphant jerks, laughing at anyone who might be jealous of their riches. They also sing the chorus of "Break My Stride," a cheerfully meaningless reggae-flavored track from white pop singer Matthew Wilder that reached #5 in 1984. Wilder, a onetime Clive Davis discovery who never managed another major hit and had become a pop producer, was happily perplexed when Puff and Mase used his song. In a *Songfacts* interview years later, Wilder said, "This was the first I'd ever heard of something like that. They came to us with the finished product and said, 'We've used your song,' followed by, 'Can we use it?' And I was like, 'You're kidding, right?' So it's been kind of an annuity."

As a party song, "Can't Nobody Hold Me Down" is slyly irresistible. The rapping itself isn't too impressive, but the confidence is off the charts. Those samples simply drive home the point of the song: Puff Daddy was willing to spend money to make hits. As he rapped about his soaring record sales and his bulletproof E-Class, he also flaunted his expensive samples. Because of those samples, "Can't Nobody Hold Me Down" has eleven credited songwriters: Puffy, Mase, three different members of Bad Boy's production squad, and the writers of both "The Message" and "Break My Stride." (One of those writers is Sugar Hill Records founder Sylvia Robinson, who gave herself a songwriting credit on "The Message.")

For the "Can't Nobody Hold Me Down" video, Sean Combs recruited director Paul Hunter, one of the showiest stylists of the late-nineties music-video world. The clip opens with Biggie Smalls and comedian Eddie Griffin calling Puffy on a cell phone while making fun of the cops who have just pulled them over. Then it cuts nonsensically to Puff and Mase slow-motion strolling from an abandoned Rolls-Royce and to Puff, open-shirted, striking Jesus Christ poses in a nightclub while women paw at his chest. The video is almost avant-garde in its sheer display of new-money bravado. It makes no sense, and it looks like a blockbuster.

While "Can't Nobody Hold Me Down" raced up the charts, Puff and the rest of the Bad Boy team went to the Soul Train Awards in New York. As Biggie Smalls was leaving an afterparty, a car pulled up next to him at a red light, and a passenger shot Biggie dead. Biggie's murder, like Tupac's, remains unsolved. As with Tupac's murder, rumors have swirled for decades. "Can't Nobody Hold Me Down" reached #1 just two weeks after Biggie's death.

The same week that "Can't Nobody Hold Me Down" began its run atop the Hot 100, Biggie's second album, *Life After Death*, arrived in stores, and Biggie's murder gave it a morbid new significance. The album, which found Biggie operating more in Combs's big-money pop-rap wheelhouse, was a huge success, and its hard-strutting single "Hypnotize" replaced "Can't Nobody Hold Me Down" at #1. In the process, Biggie Smalls joined Otis Redding, Janis Joplin, Jim Croce, and John Lennon on the morbid list of artists who reached #1 after dying. Combs switched up his solo-album plans, changing the album's tone from victorious to mournful but still victorious. With Biggie's widow, Faith Evans, Puff recorded the Biggie elegy "I'll Be Missing You," building the track from a loop of the Police's chart-topping 1983 stalker ballad "Every Breath You Take." With that song—and with the video, where he crashed a motorcycle and danced in the rain—Puff essentially appointed himself Biggie's mourner in chief.

Because of some combination of Bad Boy's shiny-suit flashiness and the sad fascination with Biggie's murder, Puff Daddy productions remained at #1 for almost all of 1997. After six weeks of "Can't Nobody Hold Me Down" and three weeks of "Hypnotize," the teenage Oklahoma trio Hanson made it to #1 with their joyously ebullient "MMMBop," but this was only a brief interruption of Puffy's dominance. After "MMMBop" fell from #1, "I'll Be Missing You" spent eleven weeks atop the Hot 100. Then the late Biggie Smalls reclaimed the spot with the bright, anthemic "Mo Money Mo Problems," which also had Puff, Mase, and a big and bright and obvious Diana Ross loop. After "Mo Money Mo Problems," the #1 spot went to Mariah Carey's "Honey." Puff Daddy was one of that song's producers; Mase and Bad Boy group the Lox rapped on the remix. In the video, Carey escapes from a crime lord—who happens to look a lot like her ex-husband, Tommy Mottola—in a jet-ski chase and then in a helicopter flown by Mase.

During that era of complete Bad Boy dominance, Puff Daddy released his solo debut, *No Way Out*, which sold seven million copies. Two more singles, "It's All About the Benjamins (Remix)" and "Been Around the World," reached #2. Bad Boy's videos became cameo-packed big-budget extravaganzas, mini-versions of Michael Bay action epics. After meeting her on the set of the "Been Around the World" video, Combs started dating Jennifer Lopez, the movie star who would soon record a number of #1 hits on her own. Even after the loss of Biggie Smalls, Sean Combs had reason to celebrate. Nobody had dominated the Hot 100 like that since the Bee Gees in 1977, or maybe even since the Beatles in 1964.

It didn't last. Puff Daddy and Bad Boy made more hits, but they never had another run like what happened in 1997. Rap moved on. DMX, a harsh and guttural Yonkers rapper, emerged with a feverish, desperate style that felt like a rebuke to Bad Boy and all it represented. Combs had passed on signing DMX to Bad Boy even after he'd rapped a standout guest verse on Mase's debut album. The Lox, DMX's Yonkers friends, soon began an ultimately successful street-level campaign to be released from their Bad Boy contracts so that they could join DMX's Ruff Ryders crew instead. In 1999, Mase announced that he was retiring from music to start a ministry. Combs kept making records, but his Sean John fashion label soon became more lucrative than his music.

But even if Bad Boy faded from the charts, its approach didn't. Southern labels like No Limit and Cash Money, following the Bad Boy model, found vast success by launching their own empires, with their own artists showing up on each other's tracks and their own CEOs acting as rap figureheads. As the nineties went on, Will Smith, a teenage eighties rapper who'd become a movie star, returned to rap and scored a couple of #1 hits with glossy party songs built on obvious loops—sanitized versions of the Bad Boy house style. R&B artists like Usher, TLC, and Destiny's Child also reached #1 with bright, clubby hits built on rap-style cadences. In the next decade, St. Louis native Nelly took off running with the cockiness and melodic flair of Bad Boy's past, while former Biggie collaborator Jay-Z built himself up as a lyrical mastermind who was also an avaricious mogul—Biggie and Puff combined into one person. In the early 2000s, two new superstars, 50 Cent and Kanye West, owed clear stylistic debts to Mase (50 even briefly signed a back-from-retirement Mase to his G-Unit label). Bad Boy's model of aspirational flossiness continued to thrive on the charts for a solid decade after its heyday.

More important, though, Bad Boy confirmed something that had been in the works for a long time. Before Bad Boy's takeover, rap music was quickly becoming the sound of young America. When Bad Boy ran the tables on the Hot 100 in 1997, that streak made rap's dominance undeniable. Pop stations stopped worrying about putting too much rap in rotation, and the genre became a global pop lingua franca. Bad Boy's chart-toppers, starting with "Can't Nobody Hold Me Down," were shamelessly irresistible, and they took clear delight in their own subversion of rap's street-level roots. In Puff Daddy's hands, rap music became pop music, and that's what it's been ever since.

CHAPTER 16

Britney Spears–
". . . Baby One More Time"

Released October 23, 1998
Hit #1 January 30, 1999
Two-week reign

WHEN BRITNEY SPEARS SANG "I'M MISS AMERICAN DREAM since I was seventeen" on her 2007 hit "Piece of Me," she wasn't boasting. She was lamenting. "Piece of Me" is a song about living an entire life in the public eye and about the burden of being "an exceptional earner." The lyric is also something of an understatement. Spears released her debut single, ". . . Baby One More Time," a few weeks before her seventeenth birthday, and the song didn't *just* make her Miss American Dream. Instead, ". . . Baby One More Time" made Spears a global phenomenon, or maybe a globally dominant representative of a certain American ideal. ". . . Baby One More Time" topped charts from Norway to New Zealand, and it ensured that Britney Spears would never, ever get a chance to live a normal life.

When she was Miss American Dream at seventeen, Spears didn't seem like someone especially interested in living a normal life. Spears presented herself as a normal American teenager; it was her idea that the ". . . Baby One More Time" video should show her dancing through high school hallways. By that time, though, Spears had already spent more than half of her life performing. She'd had a brief taste of normal life, and she'd decided that it wasn't for her. Instead, she went after stardom with a fierce intensity, and that intensity is all over ". . . Baby One More Time." It's the song's driving force.

Almost immediately, though, Britney Spears's stardom became a runaway monster, a thing that could not be controlled. In the process, Spears became a pivotal popular-culture figure, a symbolic embodiment of all sorts of societal and generational changes. The electric charge of ". . . Baby One More Time," and the attention brought on by both the song and its video, made Spears the central figure in the tabloid economy when it was at its most lucrative and bloodthirsty. Spears's various public breakdowns only made her more famous. They didn't stop Spears from being an exceptional earner, but they did make her a prisoner of her own fame.

". . . Baby One More Time" also helped mark a pop-music sea change. Through most of the nineties, the most culturally dominant genres were thick, guttural alternative rock and flamboyant, nihilistic rap. Alt rock never made much of a dent in the Hot 100, and hardcore rap didn't consistently top charts until the 1997 reign of Bad Boy, but that has more to do with how *Billboard* tabulated the Hot 100 than how ubiquitous those genres were. Throughout most of the nineties, the chart played catch-up to the rest of the cultural sphere. In the late nineties, though, a new form of bright, poppy, unashamed bubblegum pop began to take over. Teenage entertainers who'd come up through the Disney system made flashy, attention-grabbing songs that drew on dance and rap and R&B, and they sold those songs through sparkly videos and athletic dance routines.

These new artists rose up right around the time that MTV debuted *Total Request Live*, a show driven by call-in votes that aired during the weekly after-school hours. The series enabled younger teenagers to take control of the institution of MTV, and that's exactly what they did. In the years after *TRL*'s original broadcast in September 1998, acts targeted directly at teenagers and preteens—people like the Backstreet Boys, NSYNC, and Christina Aguilera—helped spur on one final music-industry boom time, selling vast quantities of CDs before file-sharing services like Napster upended the entire business model approximately three years later.

Britney Spears was the first of those artists to reach #1, and she quickly became the most successful and inescapable of all of them. But "... Baby One More Time" wasn't only a breakthrough for Spears. It was also a coming-out party for Karl Martin Sandberg, the Swedish songwriter and producer known professionally as Max Martin. Martin had his hand in a few hit singles before "... Baby One More Time," but Spears's single became Martin's first chart-topper and his calling card. In the years since "... Baby One More Time," Martin's precision-engineered dance-pop has come to utterly dominate the Hot 100. Martin has written or cowritten dozens of #1 hits. Only Paul McCartney and John Lennon have songwriting credits on more #1 hits, and Martin might still overtake one or both of them. Martin's whole approach—one built more around soaring, language-transcending melody than around any particular genre or sound—has proved massively influential, and many of his protégés have made multiple chart-toppers of their own. All of that starts with "... Baby One More Time."

Max Martin was a product of a particular system. In the early nineties, Stockholm DJ Dag Krister Volle, who went by the name Denniz Pop, formed SweMix, a collective of songwriters based in Cheiron Studios, the Stockholm compound that Pop built. Denniz Pop loved music that was melodically simple and straightforward—synthpop like the Human League, glam metal like Def Leppard—and wanted to combine it with the rhythmic intensity of the American rap and R&B that he played in clubs.

Sweden had a grand tradition of broad, sticky pop music. In 1974, a group called Blue Swede reached #1 in the United States with a giddy, chant-happy cover of the B. J. Thomas song "Hooked on a Feeling." Around the same time, the group ABBA became a global phenomenon with a series of sensational, euphoric pop sing-alongs animated by a half-hidden sense of melancholy. (ABBA reached #1 on the Hot 100 only once, with 1976's "Dancing Queen," but they were stars around the planet, and the United States wasn't immune.) The glam-metal band Europe found early-eighties success with a couple of synth-driven anthems, and the duo Roxette notched four gloriously nonsensical American chart-toppers in the late eighties and early nineties. These acts didn't sound anything like each other, but they all boasted laser-focused eager-to-please melodies. Denniz Pop's big idea was to combine those towering hooks with hard-hitting, body-moving beats.

In the early nineties, Denniz Pop and his SweMix collaborators had some Scandinavian success producing tracks for Swedish artists like Dr. Alban and Leila K. A local group called Ace of Base—two men and two women, just like ABBA—gave Pop a demo tape, and that tape got stuck in the broken tape deck of Pop's car, so he heard it whenever he drove. After half-unwillingly hearing their songs a few hundred times, Pop agreed to work with Ace of Base, and he coproduced their slinky, reggae-informed 1992 single "All That She Wants." The song picked up steam around Europe. Arista Records boss Clive Davis, after hearing "All That She Wants" while on vacation, signed Ace of Base to an American contract. In America, Ace of Base clicked. Working with Ace of Base, Denniz Pop found a sound that was both sugary and hypnotic. It didn't sound like American R&B, but it didn't sound like the endorphin-rush thump of European club music, either. Instead, Ace of Base had a sunny, insinuating grace that helped them stand out on the American pop charts. The group's debut album, *The Sign*, sold nine million copies in the United States alone, and three of its singles made the top 10. One of them, the album's title track, topped the US charts for six weeks in the spring of 1994.

During Ace of Base's run atop the charts, Denniz Pop started to work with his new protégé, Max Martin. Martin had been the frontman of an unsuccessful Swedish glam-metal band called It's Alive, and they'd recorded their 1994 album, *Earthquake Visions*, at Denniz Pop's

Cheiron Studios. Pop recognized that Martin had a gift for hammering, bombastic melodies, and he brought Martin into the fold. Martin cowrote and coproduced a few tracks on Ace of Base's second album, 1995's relatively unsuccessful *The Bridge*. A year later, Denniz Pop and Max Martin went to work with the Backstreet Boys.

The Backstreet Boys were the brainchild of Lou Pearlman, a Queens con man who, in the late eighties, ran a business leasing out blimps and charter jets. In 1989, Pearlman chartered a jet for the overwhelmingly popular boy band New Kids on the Block, and he became fascinated with that group's sudden, dominant success. Pearlman went to work putting together his own boy band. After moving his aviation business to Orlando, Pearlman held auditions and assembled the Backstreet Boys, coming up with a lineup of five good-looking white kids that directly mirrored the five-kid lineup of New Kids on the Block.

Eventually, Pearlman got the Backstreet Boys signed to Jive Records, a New York label founded by South African businessman Clive Calder. Calder had gotten his start playing in Motown cover bands in South Africa, and he envisioned Jive as a self-supporting system like Motown had been in the sixties. When Jive signed the Backstreet Boys, the label was best known for releasing music from rappers like KRS-One and A Tribe Called Quest and R&B singers like R. Kelly and Aaliyah. While planning out the Backstreet Boys' first album, the label connected Pearlman with Denniz Pop and Max Martin. At the time, Pop and Martin were working with a group called 3T. All three members of 3T were sons of Tito Jackson, the former Jackson 5 member. Michael Jackson, the boys' uncle, was an executive producer on the 3T album, and Pop and Martin worked with him on one song. That Michael Jackson connection was intriguing to Pearlman, who paid to send the Backstreet Boys to Sweden in 1995.

The Backstreet Boys' early singles, recorded with the Cheiron brain trust, were a sleek and Scandinavian take on Black American R&B. At first, the group's singles went nowhere in the United States, where actual R&B still held sway over the pop charts. But the Backstreet Boys immediately struck huge in Europe and, thanks in part to a French-language version of their song "We've Got It Going On," in Quebec. In 1996, the New York rock station Z-100 rebranded as a top-40 pop station and started putting Backstreet Boys singles in rotation. Finally, the Backstreet Boys gained steam in the United States. In September 1997, the Backstreet Boys made it to #2 on the Hot 100 with "Quit Playing Games (with My Heart)," a song that Max Martin coproduced and cowrote. (To date, that's the Backstreet Boys' highest-charting single. They've never made it to #1 in the United States.)

The Backstreet Boys were not the only straight-up pop group who took off in 1997. That same year, the Spice Girls, a brash and hyper-active British act whose five members had a cartoonish spectrum of personae, topped the Hot 100 with their dizzily hormone-charged breakout single "Wannabe," while the fresh-faced young Oklahoma trio Hanson briefly interrupted Puff Daddy's summer of dominance with their euphoric gibberish anthem "MMMBop." Lou Pearlman, seeing that the Backstreet Boys were taking off, put together an extremely similar boy band called NSYNC to compete with his own group, and he sent NSYNC to Stockholm to work with the Cheiron Studios team and to recapture the Backstreet magic. That same year, Denniz Pop and Max Martin also worked with the Swedish singer Robyn, who scored a pair of top-10 hits with their songs.

While all of this was happening, Britney Spears was making her own moves. Spears, born in Mississippi and raised in Louisiana, was a talent-show kid. She'd started taking dance lessons at three and began singing soon after, and her working-class parents sent her around the state to compete against other talented little kids. At eight, Spears had auditioned to join the cast of the Disney Channel's recently rebooted *Mickey Mouse Club*. The show's producers thought she was too young, but they were impressed with her voice and her presence, and they suggested that she move to New York. Spears and her mother made the move. Spears found an agent, understudied for an off-Broadway musical, and went to the Professional Performing Arts School. At ten, Spears competed on *Star Search*, singing the Judds' country ballad "Love Can Build a Bridge" with the throaty power of a Broadway veteran at least three times her age. She came in second in the show's competition. A year later, Spears again auditioned for *The Mickey Mouse Club*. This time, she made it.

On *The Mickey Mouse Club*, Spears joined a team of future stars who would sing in front of national TV audiences every week. A couple of her castmates, Justin Timberlake and JC Chasez, would soon join NSYNC. Two others, Ryan Gosling and Keri Russell, would become film and television stars. After Spears found pop stardom, Christina Aguilera, another ex-Mouseketeer, would follow the Britney blueprint closely, with tremendous success. But *The Mickey Mouse Club* didn't launch any of those young talents directly to fame. Instead, Disney canceled the show in 1994. Spears moved back to Mississippi, where she played high school basketball and found that the life of a regular teenager was much too boring for her. Lou Pearlman was putting together a girl group called Innosense, and Spears came close to joining. Instead, while weighing the Innosense offer, Spears took her shot at a solo career. Larry Rudolph, the entertainment lawyer who later became Spears's manager and conservator, made a demo tape of Spears singing an unreleased song from the R&B star Toni Braxton. In 1996, Spears returned to New York to audition for four record labels. Three of them said no. The odd one out was Jive Records, which was flush from the success of the Backstreet Boys.

At her auditions, Spears sang grown-up ballads from R&B singers like Whitney Houston and Mariah Carey. Jive initially planned to market Spears as an adult-contemporary artist; the label didn't even know that she loved to dance until they'd already signed her. Jive arranged for Spears to meet Max Martin. An impressed Martin thought that maybe Spears could be an American Robyn. Spears, initially intimidated by Martin, loved "Hit Me Baby One More Time," a new song that Martin had written. Jive flew Spears to Stockholm, where she went to work with Martin and the Cheiron Studios brain trust. Spears never met Cheiron founder Denniz Pop. When Spears arrived in Stock-holm, Pop was sick with stomach cancer, and he couldn't go to the stu-dio. Pop died in August 1998 at the age of thirty-five. On Spears's debut album, Pop is credited as executive producer. After Pop's death, Max Martin took over as the head of Cheiron Studios.

As with most Max Martin songs, the track that would become ". . . Baby One More Time" started with a melody. Martin sang the chorus into his Dictaphone one night, and when he'd finished writing the entire song, he brought it to coproducer Rami Yacoub, a Palestin-ian Swedish remix specialist who'd only just joined the Cheiron team. Martin later said that Yacoub "is much more urban and R&B-based than me. I'm more of a melody man. So he's a big reason that the song turned out the way it did."

Max Martin calls his songwriting process "melodic math." The lyr-ics are always secondary to the melody. Martin rarely gives interviews, but in 2019, he explained his priorities to the *Guardian*: "Growing up, I listened to songs by ABBA, Elton John, the Beatles, and I had no idea what they meant, so to me the phonetics have always been important. I felt something hearing this music, and it meant something to me. If you can have a great lyric that also phonetically sounds amazing, then you're golden. But it's also kind of cool if you can write a song and peo-ple are emotionally moved without understanding what's being said. That, to me, is as powerful."

When he first wrote "Hit Me Baby One More Time," Martin thought he'd come up with an R&B song, and he initially offered the track to the phenomenally successful Atlanta girl group TLC. But the song that would become ". . . Baby One More Time" is not R&B. It's too stark and hard and direct, and it carries no echoes of the Black gos-pel tradition that grounds virtually all American R&B. TLC turned the song down. Later, TLC member Tionne "T-Boz" Watkins told MTV, "I was like, 'I like the song, but do I think it's a hit? Do I think it's TLC?' . . . Was I going to say, 'Hit me, baby, one more time'? Hell no!" Martin also pitched the song to Robyn, but she didn't record it, either.

The lyric was a problem. Max Martin was writing his own interpretation of American slang. Martin did not intend the "hit me" part
as a reference to abuse or sadomasochism. Instead, Martin's song is all
about romantic desperation, about postbreakup infatuation. "Hit me"
simply meant "call me." Later, Martin said, "To me, it was obvious
that it meant 'so let's do it again' or 'try this once more.' But it was a big
controversy. I was very naive, thinking Americans would accept that
kind of a title." Spears was immediately convinced that the song was a
smash, but Jive, trying to avoid controversy, changed the song's title to
". . . Baby One More Time."

When Britney Spears flew to Stockholm, it was her first time overseas. She was there for a week, and in that week, she recorded half
of her 1999 debut album, also called . . . *Baby One More Time*, at
Cheiron. The night before she laid down her vocal for ". . . Baby One
More Time," Spears played Soft Cell's synthpop hit "Tainted Love"
over and over, late into the night. Later, she told *Rolling Stone*, "I
wanted my voice to be kind of rusty. . . . When I went into the studio,
I wasn't rested. When I sang it, I was just laid back and mellow."

But the Britney Spears of ". . . Baby One More Time" does not
sound laid-back or mellow. Instead, she's fierce, almost predatory.
On the song, Spears uses melisma, but she doesn't use it like an
R&B singer. Instead, her ululations are slight, and she deploys them
with precision. Her southern accent becomes a kind of weapon, too:
"Oww bay-beh, how *was* I supposed to know that somethin' wasn't
raaaaht here?"

". . . Baby One More Time" is a track built with focus and pur-
pose. From its opening three-note piano riff, ". . . Baby One More
Time" radiates total confidence. The song has a lot of little instrumental touches—guitars that growl like Spears's voice, squelchy little keyboards, a few melodramatic piano tinkles on the bridge—but there's
nothing playful or funky about those flourishes. Instead, the entire
track moves with a mechanized force that feels almost alien. Spears
locks in with the track completely. On the chorus, Spears and Martin

sing in harmony together. They're not asking you to hit them, baby, one more time. They're demanding it. Jive Records was right to worry; when the song reached American airwaves, plenty of people thought it was about S&M. But that vague frisson of the illicit only lent the song more power. (Years later, Rihanna would recruit Britney Spears to sing on the remix of a single that was literally called "S&M," and that remix would go straight to #1.)

For the ". . . Baby One More Time" video, Jive paired Spears up with Nigel Dick, a veteran director who'd made videos with rock bands like Guns N' Roses and Oasis and recently worked with the Backstreet Boys. Dick had plans to make the video into a live-action sci-fi cartoon aimed at kids, but Spears vetoed that plan. She wanted to be in a high school, dancing around with cute boys. Spears also shot down the wardrobe that Dick had picked out. Instead, Spears insisted on a Catholic school uniform. Spears also had the idea to knot her shirt and bare her belly button. In the clip, Spears and her backup dancers wear clothes that the video's producers had bought at Kmart. The video immediately marked Spears as an underage sex symbol, but Spears's presence is anything but passive. Instead, Spears stares down the camera with a ferociously confident sense of charisma, and her presence captured the collective imagination of the young and predominantly female fan base that had already turned the Backstreet Boys into stars.

When the ". . . Baby One More Time" single came out, Jive sent Spears on a promotional tour. A decade earlier, teen-pop star Tiffany had made her name by touring shopping malls before landing a pair of #1 hits. Spears did something similar, traveling to different malls and performing her song with a pair of backup dancers. Spears would also visit radio stations, where the program directors could see for themselves that she had star quality. A month later, the ". . . Baby One More Time" video debuted on MTV, where it immediately took hold. *Total Request Live* had debuted earlier that fall, and ". . . Baby One More Time" caught fire on the show. At the end of 1998, viewers voted it the #1 video for *TRL*'s first year. Two weeks into the new year, Spears released her . . . *Baby One More Time* album. It sold a half-million copies in its first day and debuted at #1 on the album charts. A few weeks after that, the ". . . Baby One More Time" single topped the Hot 100.

By the end of 1999, . . . *Baby One More Time* had sold 10 million copies, and Britney Spears was one of the world's most famous musicians. Spears, the Backstreet Boys, and NSYNC dominated *TRL* and became the new faces of MTV. For the next few years, the ensuing teen-pop boom essentially powered the entire music industry. In 2000, Spears released her sophomore album, *Oops . . . I Did It Again*, which sold 1.3 million in its first week, still the biggest one-week sales ever for a solo artist. That same year, the Backstreet Boys and NSYNC also had seven-figure sales weeks, and NSYNC reached #1 with "It's Gonna Be Me," another song written by Max Martin and his Cheiron colleagues. Other young female pop singers like Jessica Simpson and Mandy Moore came along in the immediate wake of Britney Spears, but only her fellow former Mouseketeer Christina Aguilera could even approach Spears's level of success.

Jive Records, in true Motown fashion, used Britney Spears and the Backstreet Boys to promote one another; . . . *Baby One More Time*, for instance, ended with a promotional spot for a forthcoming Backstreet record. NSYNC were initially signed to RCA, but once the members of the group realized how badly Lou Pearlman was exploiting them, they sued him for fraud. RCA backed Pearlman in the legal battle, and after they settled the lawsuit, NSYNC moved to Jive, which meant that the three biggest-selling acts in pop were all recording for the same label. Britney Spears and NSYNC's Justin Timberlake became a couple, and the gossipy hysteria around the two of them cranked up to whole new levels. In 2002, when the teen-pop wave was peaking, Clive Calder sold Jive to Sony BMG for $2.74 billion, making himself the richest record executive in the history of the business. This turned out to be the exact right time to sell. The crash was coming.

For the first few years of the new millennium, *Total Request Live* became a battlefield. The young people who couldn't stand those teen-pop stars would vote for aggro rockers like Limp Bizkit or Kid Rock, or for Eminem, the gleefully trolling white rapper who effectively pitched himself as an enemy of the teen-pop establishment. This whole setup was hugely lucrative for everyone involved. The file-sharing service Napster went online in June 1999, months after the release of . . . *Baby One More Time*. Before long, it had tens of millions of users, many of whom were young music fans who were sick of paying eighteen dollars for CDs. The major labels reacted angrily, suing Napster and many of the service's users, seemingly at random. This was a public-relations disaster for the record business, and even though Napster shut down in 2002, more file-sharing sites sprang up to replace it. In the early 2000s, CD sales took a nosedive.

For the first few years of the decade, teen pop—and the rap and nu-metal records that benefited from the backlash against teen pop— helped keep the music industry's bubble expanding. Many of those Britney Spears, Backstreet Boys, and NSYNC CDs sold to kids who were too young to figure out how to use Napster. These teen-pop artists, for a brief stretch of time, were cash cows, exceptional earners. But once their wave crashed, many of the stars suffered. The Backstreet Boys, like NSYNC before them, realized that Lou Pearlman had taken millions and paid them barely anything, and they also sued their former Svengali. Other members of Pearlman-assembled boy bands accused Pearlman of sexual misconduct. Eventually, federal investigators realized that Pearlman was running a Ponzi scheme and using his access to his boy bands to snare investors. Pearlman went on the run, but he was arrested in Indonesia in 2007. After being convicted of bank fraud, Pearlman died in prison in 2016.

NSYNC's Justin Timberlake went solo in 2002, making the transition out of teen pop by rebranding himself as a club-friendly, Michael Jackson–style R&B singer. Timberlake used his tabloid notoriety to his advantage, implicitly accusing Britney Spears, his ex, of cheating on him on the hit "Cry Me a River." Spears herself continued to sell records, releasing five more multiplatinum albums after . . . *Baby One*

More Time. It took nearly a decade for Spears to return to #1 on the Hot 100, but she made it back to the top spot with the dance-pop track "Womanizer" in 2008. Three more #1 singles followed; Max Martin cowrote and coproduced two of them. But Spears was more famous for her constant tabloid appearances than for her music. Magazines like *US Weekly* and bloggers like Perez Hilton noisily covered every new Britney Spears story, and she lashed out at all the attention, shaving her head and attacking a paparazzo with an umbrella. In 2008, Spears's family placed her in an involuntary conservatorship, an arrangement usually intended for elderly or infirm people. Under the new arrangement, Spears's father and her management would have total control of every part of her life.

For years, Spears maintained a successful career under that conservatorship. She made hit records. She toured. She played a years-long Las Vegas residency. Eventually, though, Spears fought back against that conservatorship, accusing her conservators of financial exploitation and emotional abuse. Legal records of Spears's battle against her conservators remained sealed for years, but the story came out in a slow-drip series of investigative reports. Spears herself had been quietly lobbying for a court to end that conservatorship, and after a widespread fan outcry, she went public with her fight. In November 2021, a judge finally ended the conservatorship, finally allowing Spears to take control of her life and career. Within a few months, Spears had signed an eight-figure book deal.

As Britney Spears suffered under that conservatorship, Max Martin thrived. During the teen-pop boom, Martin also made hits with people like Bon Jovi and Celine Dion. Then, in 2004, after the end of the teen-pop wave, Clive Davis paired Max Martin with Kelly Clarkson, the winner of the first season of the new TV-ratings bonanza *American Idol*. With Martin as cowriter and coproducer, Clarkson recorded the howling, rock-influenced breakup anthem "Since U Been Gone," and that single made it to #2. "Since U Been Gone" is grittier and less synthetic than the hits that Martin made with Britney Spears and NSYNC, but it's still got the scientific rigor of Martin's teen-pop work. When "Since U Been Gone" blew up, the song opened up a whole new lane for Martin.

Over the years, Max Martin continued to tweak his bright, gleaming ultrapop style to fit changing times, and his sound became even more dominant than it had been during the Britney/Backstreet heyday. In 2008, Martin returned to #1, cowriting Katy Perry's breakout hit, "I Kissed a Girl." In the years that followed, Perry and Martin made seven more chart-toppers together. Martin also had a hand in #1 hits from Clarkson, Pink, Maroon 5, and Justin Timberlake. When Taylor Swift wanted to move out of country and into mainstream pop, she teamed up with Max Martin. When the Weeknd wanted to move out of critically acclaimed atmospheric R&B decadence, he teamed up with Max Martin. Max Martin became the world's most dependable hitmaker.

Martin closed Cheiron Studios in 2000, but he started a new production company called Maratone shortly thereafter, and he continued to work with many of his Cheiron colleagues. Just as Denniz Pop had mentored Martin, Martin served as a collaborator and mentor figure for pop producers like Rami Yacoub, Savan Kotecha, and Shellback. Martin's best-known collaborator is Lukasz Gottwald, known professionally as Dr. Luke. Before getting in with Max Martin, Dr. Luke was a New York weed dealer and a member of the *Saturday Night Live* band, and he made beats for the underground rap label Rawkus. Martin brought in Luke as a collaborator, and the two started working together on Clarkson's "Since U Been Gone." Since then, Dr. Luke has worked on #1 hits for artists like Avril Lavigne, Flo Rida, Miley Cyrus, and Kesha.

Kesha, once Dr. Luke's protégée, started out the 2010s with a series of #1 hits that Luke cowrote and coproduced. A few years later, though, Kesha accused Luke of harassment and sexual assault, which led to a long legal battle. Many of Kesha's peers joined her in speaking out against Dr. Luke, but that didn't end Luke's career. In 2020, Luke coproduced rapper and singer Doja Cat's chart-topper "Say So."

The career of Dr. Luke is not exactly a shining jewel in Max Martin's legacy, but it illustrates a strange sort of behind-the-scenes continuity that Martin has helped propagate. Dr. Luke served as a mentor and collaborator for Benny Blanco, a Virginia producer who's gone on to make #1 hits with people like Justin Bieber and Maroon 5. Benny Blanco, meanwhile, has served a similar role for Cashmere Cat, a Norwegian producer who's been involved in making big songs for Halsey and for the team of Shawn Mendes and Camila Cabello. Maybe Cashmere Cat will go on to serve as someone else's mentor, keeping this behind-the-scenes lineage of hitmaking apprenticeship alive.

In the years since ". . . Baby One More Time," Max Martin and his various protégés and imitators have never left the charts. They've built an unbroken legacy of merciless, machine-tooled digital pop music—high-impact ear candy that continues to adapt to a changing environment. For young stars like Britney Spears, it can be disastrous, on a human level, to get involved with that machinery. For the people who keep the gears whirring behind Spears and her successors, though, that machine has been hugely lucrative. ". . . Baby One More Time" stands as a mythmaking moment, an introduction to a whole new kind of assembly-line efficiency. We're still living in its aftermath.

CHAPTER 17

T-Pain–
"Buy U a Drank (Shawty Snappin')"
(Featuring Yung Joc)

Released February 20, 2007
Hit #1 May 26, 2007
One-week reign

W HEN FLORIDA SINGER T-PAIN TURNED THE MOST EXTREME setting of the pitch-correction program Auto-Tune into a signature style, he was working within a grand tradition. From the early days of recorded popular music, mad-scientist tinkerers have been attempting to warp the human voice into unnatural new shapes, moving beyond the expressive limits of bodily capability in the never-ending search for new sounds and new frequencies. In 1939, for example, jazz bandleader and amateur radio operator Alvino Rey, grandfather of Arcade Fire members Win and Will Butler, invented an early talk-box effect that would enable him to modulate the sound of his steel electric guitar through the mouth of his wife, singer Luise King. The effect sounded strange and robotic, so Rey invented a mechanical guitar-shaped figure, almost like a ventriloquist doll, named Stringy who would mouth along with those effects at his big-band performances. At the time, Rey's talking-guitar effect was sheer novelty.

Novelties have a way of transforming into other things. Over the decades, various different forms of vocal manipulation wove themselves into the DNA of pop music itself. At the same time as Rey invented his singing guitar, Les Paul was using reel-to-reel tapes to develop a technique that he called Sound on Sound. Paul, the pioneering guitarist, would layer different sounds over each other, letting musicians harmonize with themselves. In 1951, Paul and his wife, singer Mary Ford, hit #1 on the pre–Hot 100 *Billboard* charts with "How High the Moon," a jaunty track that used Ford's double-tracked voice to eerie, uncanny effect.

At Sun Studios, Sam Phillips discovered his own tape-delay vocal effect, and he used it on early records from Elvis Presley and Buddy Holly. In 1958, actor and musician David Seville used the sound of his own sped-up voice to create the Chipmunks, a trio of squeaky cartoon characters. Seville duetted with the Chipmunks on "The Witch Doctor," a song that reached #1 in 1958 three months prior to the institution of the Hot 100, and again a few months later on "The Chipmunk Song (Christmas Don't Be Late)," only the eighth song to reach #1 on the Hot 100. Throughout their careers, the Beatles and the Beach Boys doubled their own voices, sometimes to psychedelic effect.

In pop music, then, the human voice has never been sacred. Instead, it's a tool, or maybe a toy. It's a thing to be altered and garbled and manipulated. A new vocal-distortion technique could lead to a hit record—even, or especially, if that new technique changed the way the technology was supposed to be used in the first place. The vocoder, for one, was not invented as a musical tool. Instead, the vocoder was simply a technique to compress and distort the human voice, and its first applications were military. Bell Labs engineer Homer Dudley started developing the vocoder in 1929, and he got the patent on his contraption nine years later, just in time for the US government to use the vocoder to send encoded signals during World War II. In 1948, just after the war ended, German scientist Werner Meyer-Eppler gave a paper on how a vocoder could be used in electronic music, but it took years for that technique to cross over.

In 1968, composer Wendy Carlos came out with *Switched-on Bach*, an album of Bach compositions performed on a modular Moog synthesizer, and the LP became an unexpected hit, selling a million copies. Two years later, Carlos worked with synthesizer pioneer Robert Moog to invent a solid-state musical vocoder. Carlos used that vocoder on her score for Stanley Kubrick's transgressive sci-fi film *A Clockwork Orange* a year later. In *A Clockwork Orange*, the vocoder transformed a Beethoven symphony into something mysterious and detached. In 1975, experimental German art-pop act Kraftwerk did something similar with the vocoder, using it to create a sense of unnatural distance on their twenty-three-minute odyssey "Autobahn." That single became an international hit, reaching as high as #25 on the Hot 100. Progressive-rock acts picked up on the vocoder, too, and its robotic effects appeared on seventies records from Emerson, Lake & Palmer; the Alan Parsons Project; and Pink Floyd.

As the vocoder trickled into pop music, so did the talk box. Using new versions of the technology behind Alvino Rey's talking guitar, musicians could stick tubes connected to their instruments into their mouths, and then they could effectively transform their own bodies into amplifiers, using their mouths to shape the reverberating sounds coming out. The effect was strange and alien, neither fully human nor fully electronic. Stevie Wonder and Pink Floyd's David Gilmour used talk boxes on seventies records, and Peter Frampton memorably played a couple of talk-box solos on the live double-LP *Frampton Comes Alive!*—the biggest-selling album of 1976.

For Black American musicians in the seventies and eighties, the vocoder and the talk box became sci-fi tools, techniques to evoke brighter futures. Underground electro-funk masterminds like Afrika Bambaataa and Egyptian Lover chanted hip-hop cadences through vocoders, making themselves sound otherworldly, while Roger Troutman, leader of the Dayton funk band Zapp, turned the electro-distorted robo-rumble talk-box voice into his signature, using its robotic rumble-gurgle as a call to the dance floor. Roger Troutman never sounded natural, and he never tried to fool anyone into thinking that his voice was supposed to sound like that. The interplanetary weirdness was central to the appeal. That appeal had legs, too. In 1996, just three years before his brother and former Zapp bandmate murdered him, Roger Troutman layered his gooey talk-box vocals all over 2Pac and Dr. Dre's massive hit "California Love."

In the eighties, future-minded artists used vocoders on big hits: Styx on "Mr. Roboto"; Phil Collins on "In the Air Tonight"; Earth, Wind & Fire on "Let's Groove"; Michael Jackson on "PYT (Pretty Young Thing)." As the newness of the vocoder faded, it came to represent the retro futurism of that early-eighties moment. But in the late nineties, a whole new kind of electronic vocal distortion crashed its way onto the pop charts, using new studio tools in ways that they were not meant to be used.

Andy Hildebrand, the inventor of Auto-Tune, had been a classical flute virtuoso as a young man, but he'd put away music for science. Working first for Exxon and then for his own firm Landmark Graphics, Hildebrand used sound waves to map the earth's subsurface. This information was hugely important to the oil industry, which could use Hildebrand's work to locate underground oil deposits, and this made Hildebrand a very rich man. Hildebrand retired from the oil industry at forty and went on to work in music, inventing a sampling synthesizer that could more naturally replicate the sound of an orchestra. Then a friend's wife asked him, "Why don't you invent a box that would have me sing in tune?" Hildebrand realized that the same mathematical techniques he'd used in seismic data processing could also work for music. Through his company Antares, Hildebrand introduced Auto-Tune, a piece of software that could shift vocals, bending notes to reach the desired pitch. Within the music industry, where an invention like this could significantly reduce the labor of recording vocals, Auto-Tune made an instant impact.

Auto-Tune was meant to be subtle, to shift vocal pitches slowly enough that they could sound natural. But when he introduced Auto-Tune, almost as a goof, Hildebrand included what he called the zero setting—a filter that would change pitches instantly, without hiding what was happening. The effect sounded truly unnatural, a disorienting vocal warp not altogether dissimilar from the robo-voice sound of the vocoder or the talk box. It wasn't long before pop producers realized that this unnatural quality could itself work as a tool.

Auto-Tune first hit the market in September 1997. Just over a year later, long-faded pop star Cher released "Believe," the woozy and futuristic dance track that would become an unlikely comeback smash. Cher had already lived three or four different public lives before "Believe," the Euro-house smash that introduced Auto-Tune's voice-distorting power to the world. A twenty-one-year-old Cher first reached #1 in 1965, when she and then husband, Sonny Bono, sang the dewy-eyed love song "I Got You, Babe." (Actually, Cher's voice had first appeared on a #1 single a year earlier; she'd sung backup on the Righteous Brothers' Phil Spector–produced opus "You've Lost That Lovin' Feeling.") In the thirty-four years after that first hit, Cher had been an acid-tongued variety-show comedian, an Oscar-winning actor, a butt-baring eighties rocker, and an infomercial pitchwoman. She'd sung folk-rock, exoticist pop, disco, and power ballads. But when she recorded "Believe," Cher hadn't made a #1 hit in more than two decades.

Cher recorded "Believe" with Mark Taylor and Brian Rawling, two British dance-pop producers who'd only enjoyed middling success beforehand. Cher agreed to work with the two producers because their sound reminded her of the disco records she'd made in the late seventies. "Believe," the title track from the album that Cher made with the two producers, is basically a house song—a robotic thump with a relentless electronic beat and a wailing, passionate vocal about postbreakup survival. The song would've been a striking, futuristic move for Cher even without the Auto-Tune. But in using Hildebrand's zero setting, Taylor and Rawling made Cher sound like a heartbroken cyborg for a few lines on "Believe." For years, Taylor denied that he'd used Auto-Tune, claiming that they'd achieved the effect with a vocoder. Before long, though, the rest of the music world caught up. Within a few years, the Auto-Tune users' manual was referring to the zero setting as the "Cher effect." That sound set "Believe" apart.

Early in 1999, "Believe" spent a month at #1, making the fifty-two-year-old Cher the oldest woman ever to top the Hot 100. In the years after "Believe," plenty of other pop singers used Auto-Tune, but none of them were anywhere near as blatant about it—at least until T-Pain took that zero setting and built a whole style out of it. T-Pain was born Faheem Rasheed Najm in a working-class Bahamian Muslim family in Tallahassee. Najm dropped out of school in eighth grade, and he pursued a deep love of music, joining a local rap group called Nappy Headz and making regional hits like "Robbery." But T-Pain also wanted to sing, and using a computer that a friend had stolen from a CompUSA store, he turned his bedroom into an amateur studio.

In 2001, while making music in that bedroom, T-Pain became fascinated with the choppy, distorted sound of the zero setting of Auto-Tune—not because of "Believe" but because of a remix of Jennifer Lopez's 1999 chart-topper "If You Had My Love." The sound of that zero-effect setting spoke to something within T-Pain. Years later, trying to describe the appeal of that Auto-Tune sound to writer Ben Westhoff, T-Pain said, "I don't know, man, it's weird. I think it might be because it makes your voice an instrument. It's like a jazz song, with a saxophone solo over it the whole time. The shit is so soothing, it just makes you feel better."

For a solid year, T-Pain experimented with different computer plug-ins, looking for the effect he'd heard on that Jennifer Lopez remix. He figured out how to replicate that sound with a pirated version of Auto-Tune. In a 2021 episode of the Netflix documentary series

This Is Pop, T-Pain says, "Oh boy, when I found that Auto-Tune, I cried a little bit because I had finally found the thing that was going to make me different."

T-Pain didn't get his first contract because of Auto-Tune. Instead, as a mixtape track, T-Pain recorded his own version of "Locked Up," a 2004 hit from the Senegalese American singer Akon. Akon used Auto-Tune, though not as aggressively as T-Pain, and he sang in a chirpy high-pitched tone that worked with the software. "Locked Up," a song about Akon's time in prison for auto theft, became his first hit, reaching #8 on the Hot 100. T-Pain, singing in a timbre similar to Akon's, called his version "I'm Fucked Up." T-Pain's revision got Akon's attention. T-Pain wrote a song called "I'm Sprung" with Akon in mind. Akon didn't want to record the song, but he liked it enough to sign T-Pain to Konvict Muzik, the record-label imprint that Akon had just founded in 2004. (Akon had an ear for talent. Later, he'd also sign Lady Gaga to Konvict.)

"I'm Sprung" is a love song inspired by T-Pain's wife, Amber, whom he'd married in 2003, and it became his first single. Like Cher's "Believe" before it, "I'm Sprung" was a big-bang moment for Auto-Tune in pop. Where "Believe" had used zero-setting Auto-Tune fleetingly, "I'm Sprung" was fully built around the effect. T-Pain piled his voice into woozy psychedelic layers. On "I'm Sprung" and the singles that followed, T-Pain sounded endlessly excited about falling in love, but he also came off fragile, like a corrupted computer program starting to glitch out.

T-Pain's debut, *Rappa Ternt Sanga*, became the first album released on Konvict Muzik. Akon boosted "I'm Sprung" by appearing in the video, and the single reached #8. Shortly thereafter, T-Pain made it to #6 with "I'm 'n Luv (wit a Stripper)," a profoundly goofy song with a guest verse from Houston rapper Mike Jones. That year, T-Pain also sang hooks on singles like E-40's "U and Dat" and Bow Wow's "Outta My System." In those songs' videos, T-Pain established a flamboyant visual style—white sunglasses, oversize top hats—that made it clear that he didn't take himself too seriously. Both vocally and visually, he was a distinctive presence.

T-Pain's rise on the charts coincided with a big shift in rap and R&B. Early in the 2000s, the center of the two intertwined genres moved from New York and Los Angeles to Atlanta. That process might've started as early as 1992, when the kiddie-rap duo Kris Kross reached #1 with the boisterous anthem "Jump." Kris Kross had been masterminded by nineteen-year-old producer Jermaine Dupri, who went on to help make #1 hits for young Atlanta singers like Usher and Monica. At the same time, Atlanta production crew Organized Noize helped their protégés OutKast and Goodie Mob become artistic and commercial forces, and they also produced TLC's 1995 smash "Waterfalls." Early in the 2000s, Atlanta artists like Usher and OutKast utterly dominated the Hot 100. Then, around 2005, snap music happened.

Snap music came out of crunk, which in turn developed from the simplistic and chant-heavy late-eighties regional rap style known as Miami bass. As Miami bass became commercially successful in the early nineties, the Memphis underground group Three 6 Mafia slowed its tempo, making the music shadowy and sinister and violent. Around 2000, Atlanta producer Lil Jon popularized a brighter, more accessible form of crunk, using it to craft hits for R&B singers like Usher and Ciara and also for his own group the East Side Boyz. While Lil Jon took over the charts in the early 2000s, Dem Franchize Boyz and D4L, two groups from the Atlanta neighborhood Bankhead, developed a spacier, quieter version of crunk, and that became known as snap music.

Snap kept the vivid hedonism of crunk, but it reduced the music to total minimalism: one-finger keyboard riffs, singsong hooks, rhythm tracks built from the sampled sound of snapping fingers. Snap music was cheap to produce, and it was often infernally catchy. Outside the South, plenty of critics and rap peers dismissed it as "ringtone rap," and the sales of cell-phone ringtones certainly helped the commercial fortunes of snap. (The songs tended to sound good even on tinny cell-phone speakers.) But snap had its own form of strange energy, and that energy became an Atlanta rap wellspring.

At the beginning of 2006, D4L reached #1 with their out-of-nowhere strip-club smash "Laffy Taffy," while Dem Franchize Boyz made it to #7 with their snap-dancing instructional "Lean wit It, Rock wit It." Other snap tracks, like Unk's "Walk It Out" and Yung Joc's "It's Goin' Down," lodged in the upper reaches of the charts. Lil Jon got in on it, reaching the top 10 with his 2006 single "Snap Yo Fingers." These sparse, sticky songs had flamboyant videos and easy-to-learn dances. T-Pain didn't come from Atlanta, but he was savvy enough to tap into that sound with the lead single of his second album, *Epiphany*.

T-Pain produced "Buy U a Drank (Shawty Snappin')" himself, building the track on the same kind of melodic minimalism that had come into vogue with the rise of snap music. His beat has the finger snaps and the dinky keyboard riffs of snap, but it also has rich and echo-drenched keyboard melodies that sound like strip-club takes on eighties Prince. T-Pain slathers on layer after layer of his own voice, making a luxuriant bed for his boilerplate club-rap lyrics. He sings about buying a girl a drink and taking her back to his crib, but he sounds slightly lost and desperate. Almost every lyric is a pickup line or a dance instruction, but there's a touch of pathos to T-Pain's computerized pickup routine. His modulated squeak comes out sounding like a sex-starved yelp trapped in a machine.

T-Pain's "Buy U a Drank" lyrics are made up almost entirely of references to snap and crunk hits: Lil Jon's "Snap Yo Fingers," Lil Boosie's "Zoom," Unk's "Walk It Out." One quote from Lil Scrappy's "Money in the Bank" is enough of a lift that both Scrappy and "Money in the Bank" producer Lil Jon got songwriting credits on "Buy U a Drank." Newly minted Atlanta hitmaker Yung Joc drawls out a guest verse, helpfully referencing his own #3 hit "It's Goin' Down," possibly saving T-Pain the trouble of one more shout-out to another club anthem. But amid all these slightly sweaty callbacks to the hits of the moment, T-Pain weaves an oddly sad and pretty ode to the fraught practice of trying to meet someone special in a nightclub. It's a hypnotic little twinkle-blues about sexual need.

T-Pain later told *USA Today* that "Buy U a Drank" was his "first record where I was trying to make a hit song." The playful Auto-Tune experiments of "I'm Sprung" and "I'm 'n Luv (wit a Stripper)" had given way to a commercial vocation. T-Pain knew that there was an audience for his wounded-computer-wizard style, and he was going to serve that audience. He was specifically making the song for nightclubs, but the gambit was unfulfilling. At first, T-Pain didn't like "Buy U a Drank": "That's not really making music to me. That's making hit songs to get some money real quick." But as he layered on more and more Auto-Tuned harmonies, T-Pain came around to liking the song. Those harmonies gave "Buy U a Drank" a sense of softness, of vulnerability, that hints at the depths that the lyrics themselves never express.

"Buy U a Drank" came out ahead of T-Pain's *Epiphany* album, and it rose slowly up the Hot 100, boosted by remixes that featured verses from Kanye West and from the cult-beloved Texas duo UGK. Around the time that the song reached #1, the floodgates opened. In 2007, T-Pain's smeared electronic sing-squeak became inescapable. T-Pain duetted with Akon on the follow-up single "Bartender"—which, like "Buy U a Drank," chronicled a night out on the prowl—and it reached #5. T-Pain also sang hooks on hits from DJ Khaled, Plies, and Baby Bash, among many others. For two weeks in 2007, T-Pain was on four of the top-10 singles on the Hot 100. In short order, he appeared on two more #1 hits, Chris Brown's "Kiss Kiss" and Flo Rida's "Low." T-Pain had briefly become a one-man assembly line for pop hits.

As T-Pain's profile rose, so did the backlash against his whole style. In his *Pop Life* episode, T-Pain tells a story about how Usher once took him aside on a plane and told him that he had ruined music. Other artists complained bitterly about the widespread use of Auto-Tune, despairing the way it made actual musical talent obsolete. Use of Auto-Tune had become industry standard by 2007, but T-Pain had made himself the face of that practice by building his whole aesthetic around it. So he became a target.

On his 2009 single "D.O.A. (Death of Auto-Tune)," Jay-Z lodged a protest against all the computer-addled melodic rap that he was hearing. On that track, Jay called for the "death of the ringtone" and admonished rappers to "get back to rap, you T-Paining too much." When Jay debuted "D.O.A." at Hot 97's Summer Jam concert that year, T-Pain surprised Jay by walking onstage and defiantly posing next to him. Jay walked offstage without acknowledging T-Pain except to yell the phrase "Good riddance." But "D.O.A." wasn't the game changer that Jay wanted; it stalled out on the charts at #24. (Shortly thereafter, Jay finally reached #1 as a lead artist with "Empire State of Mind," an Alicia Keys collaboration with no noticeable Auto-Tune but plenty of melody.)

Jay might've regarded Auto-Tune as an obnoxious fad, but it was something else. After "Buy U a Drank" and T-Pain's 2007 hitmaking run, other artists started to pick up on what Auto-Tune could do. In 2008, the surging New Orleans rapper Lil Wayne finally reached #1 with "Lollipop," a sung-not-rapped erotic fantasia that owed T-Pain a serious artistic debt. Terius Nash, the hitmaking songwriter who called himself The-Dream, launched a singing career that essentially sounded like an extended T-Pain impression, and he landed a couple of top-20 hits in 2007 and 2008. Veteran rapper Snoop Dogg tapped into the similarities between T-Pain's Auto-Tune and the vocoders that had been so popular in early-eighties soul, and he released "Sensual Seduction," a retro-loverman computer-soul track that reached #7.

At the end of 2008, Kanye West, a towering figure who'd started off as one of Jay-Z's producers, released *808s & Heartbreak*, a heavy-hearted and despondent synthpop album. West had already been playing around with vocal filters in the previous year. He'd sampled the retro-futuristic vocoder vocals of Daft Punk's dance hit "Harder Better Faster Stronger" on his own chart-topper "Stronger," and he'd worked with T-Pain on the top-10 hit "Good Life." For *808s & Heartbreak*,

West stopped rapping altogether, delving deep in the emotional possibilities of the robot voice.

808s & Heartbreak was hugely influenced by T-Pain, and the album became influential on plenty of others. In the early 2010s, rappers embraced melody wholeheartedly, adapting T-Pain's zero-filter Auto-Tune style. At first, plenty of those vocal-manipulation songs, like the T-Pain hits that they imitated, were essentially sci-fi party music; the Black Eyed Peas topped the Hot 100 for twelve weeks with the hovering-spacecraft bacchanal "Boom Boom Pow." But for plenty of younger rappers, Auto-Tune wasn't a gimmick; it was a whole new vehicle for expression. Drake, who never saw a useful distinction between singing and rapping, used Auto-Tune liberally. He first crashed his way into the pop charts with the 2009 #2 hit "Best I Ever Had," and then he never left. Others, like Future and Travis Scott, used Auto-Tune to darker and more atmospheric ends, using it to howl about drugs and depression. Those darker Auto-Tune tracks often became hits, too.

By the beginning of the 2010s, it was clear that Auto-Tune wasn't a fad; it was a new state of being. More than a decade after "Buy U a Drank," rappers were regularly racking up #1 hits that would've been unthinkable without the gluey and uncanny Auto-Tune style that T-Pain introduced. T-Pain's Auto-Tune sensibility drifted from genre to genre, but it was there in practically every big hit of 2020, from the bitterly intense street rap of Roddy Ricch's "The Box" to the snotty singsong pop-punk of 24kGoldn and Iann Dior's "Mood." At this point, it's hard to think of a recent #1 single without heavy and obvious Auto-Tune. T-Pain's sound has become part of the landscape.

While his influence never faded from the charts, T-Pain himself eventually did. At the time of this writing, he hasn't appeared on a top-10 hit since 2011. In the years since his hitmaking run, T-Pain has had something of a tortured relationship with his own signature style. In 2009, he stopped using Auto-Tune, and he developed his own competing vocal-filter software, the iPhone app I Am T-Pain. Millions downloaded it. Two years later, T-Pain sued Auto-Tune creator Andy

Hildebrand's company Antares, alleging that Antares had made unauthorized use of his name. (Hildebrand countersued, and they settled out of court.)

In recent years, T-Pain has made a point of showing the world that he can actually sing without filters, recording a widely celebrated *Tiny Desk Concert* video for NPR in 2014 and then winning the first season of Fox's absurdist competition show *The Masked Singer* in 2019. T-Pain is now a fixture on the music-festival circuit and a popular source of memes. In 2021, he published a book of liquor recipes called *Can I Mix You a Drink?* T-Pain appears to be doing fine.

More than a decade after "Buy U a Drank (Shawty Snappin')," plenty of people still complain about Auto-Tune, but that software has become firmly entrenched as a fundamental part of the pop-music process—as potentially expressive as a guitar and a whole lot more commercially relevant. Talking to *Priceonomics* in 2016, Andy Hildebrand offered a concise defense of his creation: "If you're going to complain about Auto-Tune, complain about speakers, too. And synthesizers. And recording studios. Recording the human voice, in any capacity, is unnatural." T-Pain essentially taught every other pop musician how to steer into that unnatural quality, and those pop musicians have been doing it ever since.

CHAPTER 18

Soulja Boy Tell'em–
"Crank That (Soulja Boy)"

Released May 2, 2007
Hit #1 September 15, 2007
Seven-week reign

I N OCTOBER 1966, A GROUP OF MEXICAN AMERICAN TEENAGERS fluked their way to #1 with a song so simple and amateurish that it almost sounded deranged. The members of ? and the Mysterians were sons of migrant farmworkers whose parents had found jobs at a General Motors plant in Bay City, Michigan. The band ? and the Mysterians started in the early sixties as an instrumental combo, playing surf-music covers at parties. After a little while, the group recruited Rudy Martinez, the best dancer in town, as their new singer. Martinez started calling himself ?, and the band recorded their half-improvised heartbreak rage-out "96 Tears" in a local living room.

The song "96 Tears" is undeniably catchy, and it's also frantic and sloppy and horny. (The original title was "69 Tears.") A local indie label pressed five hundred copies of the band's single, and the Mysterians took the record to stores in the region and to their local radio station, promising to play any and all promotional events as long as the station would spin "96 Tears" every so often. The song spread through

Michigan—from Bay City to Saginaw to Detroit and then into Canada, where it became a big hit in Windsor. At the time, future disco mogul Neil Bogart ran Cameo-Parkway Records, the same label that had launched Chubby Checker's "The Twist" to #1 years earlier. Cameo-Parkway had fallen on hard times, but when Bogart picked up "96 Tears" for national distribution, the song's strange, amateurish edge touched a nerve. In an era dominated by folk-rock and Motown, "96 Tears" eked out a week at #1.

The band ? and the Mysterians never made another major hit, and they broke up in 1969, shortly after Cameo-Parkway shut down. But the raw simplicity of "96 Tears" helped inspire a growing garage-rock movement, a whole wave of young bands who made fast, ugly, catchy, intense singles and usually disappeared after a year or two. Some of those singles became local hits, and a few, like "96 Tears," even went national. Years later, that whole sound helped inspire punk rock. A couple of generations later, something similar happened with the sudden rise of a sixteen-year-old rapper and producer named DeAndre Way, who called himself Soulja Boy Tell'em. But when Soulja Boy's "Crank That (Soulja Boy)" reached #1 in 2007, the song didn't need to slowly catch on in local markets before going national. Instead, Soulja Boy had the Internet, and the Internet changed everything.

Way understood the Internet earlier and better than any of his elders. Way, born in Chicago in 1990, moved to Atlanta at the age of six, and he spent his childhood bouncing between his mother's house in Atlanta and his father's in Batesville, Mississippi. In Atlanta, Soulja absorbed all the regional rap subgenres like crunk and snap that were growing and mutating there. While staying with his father in Batesville, Soulja started making music on his own.

When he was fourteen, Way's uncle Justin gave him a demo version of FL Studio, the digital audio workstation once known as Fruity-Loops. FruityLoops, launched in Belgium in 1998, quickly became popular among amateur musicians. It had a simple interface, and it could be pirated easily. Way didn't need anything more than the sounds included in the FL Studios demo pack. Years later, Way told *Vice*, "It wasn't even a full, registered purchased program." Using that demo program, Way made beats every day after coming home from school: "I could make any type of beat that I wanted, pretty fast." Those beats were rough, energetic takes on existing Atlanta rap sounds. Soulja would crudely record his own vocals over those beats, delivering his raps in a simplistic and vaguely mocking chant style. Once he had some songs, he started posting them online.

Soon after getting his first laptop, Way discovered SoundClick, a briefly popular social-media platform that allowed listeners to post their own songs. Way's music was built for SoundClick. Calling himself Soulja Boy Tell'em, Way registered his SoundClick account in July 2005, a few weeks before he turned fifteen, and he posted his first track, a raw dance song called "Leap Frog," shortly thereafter. The tracks that Soulja posted in those early days were catchy and memorable. Often, those songs were also funny, in a distinctly puerile teenage sort of way. Soulja Boy knew how to make a novelty song.

Talking to *Vulture*, Soulja later described how he used Sound-Click: "You'd post MP3s, and people would rate your music, and you'd get put on charts. I had this song called 'Doo Doo Head.' It was this stupid comedic song, and after a few weeks, it went #1 on the charts, and everyone started coming to my page, looking for new music." Soon afterward, Way discovered other social-media platforms. MySpace and YouTube were both relatively new, and Soulja Boy jumped on them right away. He used all of his accounts to promote each other: "Really, all my MySpace views came from SoundClick, and all my YouTube views came from MySpace. They fed off each other."

Long before he became famous, Soulja Boy was a relentless and shameless self-promoter. On his SoundClick page, Soulja included links to all his other accounts, as well as his cell-phone number and the info for his iChat and his Xbox Live tag. Internet-borne social networks were new things, but Soulja was young and smart enough to understand and embrace them right away. He might have been only a serviceable musician, but he was a genius-level early adopter.

Soulja would do anything in his power to get his music out to other teenagers. He even saw an opportunity in illicit music-download sites like LimeWire, which in the wake of Napster had effectively destroyed the music-business economy in the early twenty-first century. On those sites, Soulja would post his own music, mislabeling it so that users would think they were downloading whatever was popular at the moment. Later, Soulja told the *Daily Beast*, "I was on LimeWire, and I was like, 'Shit, I'm going to blow up my own song.' I'd put it on there but change the title so they clicked on it. I would just take a name— Britney Spears, 50 Cent, Michael Jackson. Anything that was on the radio, anything that people wanted to hear at the time, I would just upload it and change the title. After I did that, it just started getting millions of downloads. It was so fast, like overnight. . . . I was always tricking people, just to get my name out there."

Most of the people who downloaded those mislabeled songs presumably weren't too happy about being tricked into dropping this teenager's snap songs into their libraries, but maybe a few of them at least remembered Soulja Boy's name. Soulja understood the Internet as a way to get his name out; he was among the first wave of enterprising artists who wrote their own Wikipedia bios, boasting of his own not-yet-existent buzz. All of Soulja's Internet tactics started to build him an audience. Soulja figured out a visual trademark: white plastic-frame sunglasses with the name Soulja Boy written across the lenses in Wite-Out. Eventually, Soulja booked enough club gigs that he could afford to quit his part-time job at Burger King.

In 2007, at the age of fifteen, Soulja Boy recorded a simple, infectious dance song called "Crank That (Soulja Boy)," building a simple beat out of stock FL Studios sounds. There's very little to the backing track other than an echoing snap, a few stomps and hi-hats, and a maddeningly repetitive and memorable steel-drum riff. Over his own beat, Soulja switches back and forth between a deadpan drawl and an excitable bellow: "Yoooouuuulll!" This is not sophisticated music, but it has its own hypnotic force. Even without knowing the backstory, you can tell that this is a kid at work, making something that can effectively worm its way into as many heads as possible.

Soulja Boy's "Crank That" lyrics are all low-stakes boasting and lines about Soulja doing his own dance. In that sense, then, "Crank That (Soulja Boy)" is one more entry in the age-old dance-craze tradition, a direct descendant of "The Twist." Soulja Boy's dance instructions are vague and open to interpretation. When the song became popular, one of those lyrics became the subject of widespread speculation. On the chorus, Soulja says, "Watch me crank that Soulja Boy, then superman that ho." The immediate urban legend was that he was joking about ejaculating on a girl's back and then using the jism to stick a bedsheet to her, so that it would look like a superhero's cape. Soulja himself played dumb: "It was just something that I was saying. . . . The song blew up in the mainstream, and people started making up all kinds of crazy definitions on the internet. It's really nothing that you can actually do." Whether there was anything to the "superman that ho" story or not, the rumor, and the presumed crassness of it, didn't hurt the song's popularity.

But before "Crank That (Soulja Boy)" could become established enough for people to have the time to read into its lyrics, the song had to reach beyond Soulja Boy's MySpace fan base. "Crank That (Soulja Boy)" is very much a product of its time. In producing the song, Soulja relied on the spaced-out, minimal production of Atlanta's snap music, the same genre that T-Pain referenced so liberally on his own chart-topper "Buy U a Drank (Shawty Snappin')." But previous snap hitmakers like D4L and Dem Franchise Boyz had come up through Atlanta's vast and insular rap scene, which is deeply connected to the city's drug trade and to its strip-club network. Soulja Boy was never a part of any of that, and he bypassed Atlanta rap networks by bringing "Crank That (Soulja Boy)" directly to the Internet.

To sell this dance song, Soulja Boy needed to come up with a dance. In an instructional video that he posted on YouTube, Soulja Boy, his name written across his sunglasses, stands in an empty swimming pool, with five friends flanking him in matching oversize Soulja Boy T-shirts. Talking directly to the camera, Soulja says, "We gonna show you step by step. This the instructional DVD." (It's not a DVD.) He then walks the audience through all the steps of the dance. At the "superman that ho" part, he leans forward, like he's taking off through the air. During the "*Yoooouuuulll!*" chant, he jumps three times to the side, his hands out like he's revving a motorcycle. The dance works a bit like the electric slide—simple enough that anyone can learn it, complicated enough that anyone can make fun of their friends for messing it up.

In 2007, "Crank That (Soulja Boy)" became a kind of Internet-underground sensation. Teenagers posted videos of themselves doing the Soulja Boy dance or doing the many answer-song versions: "Crank That Spiderman," "Crank That Batman," "Crank That Silver Surfer," "Crank That Spongebob." In the early days of YouTube, those dances made for a fascinating rabbithole. Anyone who clicked on enough links could behold a whole universe of young people, in driveways and kitchens and dens, inventing their own universes of vaguely linked dances, almost all of which referenced one pop-culture hero or another.

Soon enough, the music business came calling. Michael Antoine Crooms, a rap producer first known as DJ Smurf and then as Mr. Collipark, had become a budding mogul in southern rap. In 2000, Collipark had produced some hits for the Atlanta crunk duo Ying Yang Twins, and he'd set himself a mission to discover any new rap phenomenon that was ripe for the mainstream. When Collipark first encountered Soulja Boy's MySpace page, he was skeptical, later telling writer Ben

Westhoff, "I didn't understand how it worked. When I saw those millions of hits, I thought that shit was fake." Collipark consulted with a friend, Atlanta radio veteran Greg Street, who reported that he'd been getting a ton of requests for Soulja Boy and that he had no idea who this kid was.

Eventually, Collipark signed Soulja Boy to his Collipark Music imprint, and he resolved to change nothing about what Soulja Boy was doing: "I allowed him to be who he is. His first album was literally just us going in and re-recording songs he had on MySpace." That album is just as sloppy and unpolished as "Crank That (Soulja Boy)" itself. Soulja Boy gave it the self-promotional title *souljaboytellem.com*, and Collipark brokered a deal with the major label Interscope. At his first meeting with Interscope boss Jimmy Iovine, Soulja Boy demonstrated how he sold downloads through SoundClick.

The video for "Crank That (Soulja Boy)" tells a stylized version of the whole origin story. Mr. Collipark, wearing a suit in his office, is completely baffled that his kids are singing the song and doing the dance. His kids are baffled that Collipark doesn't know who Soulja Boy is. As Collipark seeks out Soulja Boy and signs him to a deal, kids all over Atlanta do Soulja's dance and watch his videos on their flip phones. When Soulja signs his deal, the news goes word-of-mouth viral, and kiddie-rap luminaries like Bow Wow and Omarion show up to do the Soulja Boy dance. It's a sunny, concise visual summary of how Soulja Boy took his Internet stardom mainstream.

Soulja Boy's timing was good. In 2007, a struggling music industry had found a new temporary savior: the ringtone, the insistent and obnoxious burst of melody that would sound whenever your cell phone rang. Ringtones were cheap and easy routes to self-expression for anyone with a phone. The first iPhone was released in 2007, and its speakers were relatively advanced. But most cell-phone speakers were crude and tinny, and they demanded crude, tinny music. If you were picking a piece of music that would play anytime your phone rang, you'd want something loud and obvious and instantly recognizable. In 2007, ringtone sales peaked, bringing in more than $700 million. The "Crank That" ringtone alone sold millions.

"Crank That" also sold millions of single-track iTunes downloads, which pushed it to #1 in September 2007, little more than a month after Soulja Boy's seventeenth birthday. "Crank That (Soulja Boy)" dominated the Hot 100 for most of that fall, with only Kanye West's "Stronger" briefly interrupting its reign. In the process, Soulja Boy became the youngest artist ever to write and produce his own #1 hit. (Debbie Gibson, the previous record holder, had been eight months older when her song "Foolish Beat" topped the Hot 100 in June 1988, two years before Soulja Boy was born.)

Naturally, Soulja Boy had his detractors. To an older generation, Soulja became a symbol of all the things that were wrong with rap music in 2007: the mumbled monotonal delivery, the goofy dances, the utter lack of a social message, the focus on ringtone sales, the sudden primacy of southern rap. *Entertainment Weekly* named *souljaboytellem.com* the worst album of 2007. Nineties rap greats like Snoop Dogg and Method Man expressed their disapproval. Fifty-year-old gangsta rap originator Ice-T, who'd been starring on *Law & Order: SVU* for nearly a decade at that point, made his total disgust for Soulja Boy clear. In an interlude on his *Urban Legend* mixtape, Ice claimed that Soulja had "singlehandedly ruined hip-hop" and advised him to "eat a dick."

Soulja Boy did not create a generation gap in rap music. A year earlier, when Wu-Tang Clan member Ghostface Killah snarled about D4L's hit "Laffy Taffy" on record, D4L figurehead Fabo talked in interviews about how surprised and hurt he was over the rejection. Soulja Boy, however, steered right into that generation gap. In an instantly viral YouTube video, Soulja Boy, talking into a webcam for seven straight minutes, mercilessly clowned Ice-T while two friends guffawed behind him: "Real talk, dawg, I'll let you fight my grandaddy! The n***a knock your ass out! You was born before the internet was created! How the fuck did you even find me?" Then, in between jokes, Soulja got serious: "Think about it in my shoes. This time last year, I was poor as fuck. I was in the hood. I was in the ghetto. If what you living is true, you would understand where I'm coming from. . . . You should be congratulating me."

Plenty of Soulja's older peers did congratulate him. Soulja's chart rival Kanye West wrote in praise of Soulja on his blog: "He came from the hood, made his own beats, made up a new saying and a new dance with one song. He had all of America rapping this summer. If that ain't Hip Hop then what is?" Rapper 50 Cent interviewed Soulja on BET's *Rap City* and only lightly clowned him. Travis Barker, the star drummer of the massive pop-punk band Blink-182, put together a rock remix of "Crank That (Soulja Boy)." But nobody has ever been a more tireless advocate for Soulja Boy than Soulja Boy himself.

In the years after "Crank That," Soulja Boy displayed an impressive staying power. Soulja never returned to #1 after "Crank That," but he came close when the 2008 love-rap "Kiss Me thru the Phone" peaked at #3. Other Soulja tracks missed the top 10, but they were hits on rap radio and, more important, on the Internet: "Turn My Swag On," "Pretty Boy Swag," "Gucci Bandana." Soulja kept recording, cranking out dozens of mixtapes that might as well have been recorded in his bedroom. He produced songs for Bow Wow, Lil Wayne, and Nicki Minaj, and his protégé V.I.C. Soulja collaborated with younger rappers whose Internet rises mirrored his own: Lil B, Chief Keef, Odd Future. He also kicked off a series of increasingly shady business ventures: a brand of hookah pens, a short-lived sneaker line, a couple of knockoff gaming consoles. In the summer of 2020, Soulja claimed that he had bought the video game company Atari; Atari was quick to release a statement denying that claim. Soulja Boy has also gotten into legal trouble, including a 2021 lawsuit claiming that he had raped, imprisoned, and physically abused a former personal assistant. Soulja Boy is not a reliable narrator.

When Soulja Boy talks about his own influence, he's particularly grandiose. In 2019, Soulja Boy went viral again for a *Breakfast Club* radio interview where he screamed about Drake, then the biggest star in the world: "He copied my whole fucking flow! Word for word, bar for bar!" Talking to *Complex* in 2021, Soulja continued to argue that he was more influential than Drake or Jay-Z or, for that matter, any other rapper in history: "I motherfuckin' showed you how to get famous from your bedroom on the internet! That should go down in history, for any record label, any kid! Now, you got all these new artists, all they gotta do is go on YouTube and now they claiming millions of views, go viral, to get signed to a million-dollar record contract. I did that!" He's not wrong. (In that same *Complex* interview, Soulja also said, "They'll talk about it in history books later, later, years later." And now here I am, talking about it in a history book.)

"Crank That (Soulja Boy)" sounds like a cruder, more amateurish example of the sort of rap songs that were exploding on the charts in 2006 and 2007. (Many of those were already plenty crude and amateurish.) But the groups who made those songs followed established trajectories. The popular rappers of the early 2000s came up under the tutelage of other popular rappers, or they built grassroots audiences in local and regional scenes before going nationwide. Soulja Boy had a grassroots audience, but it wasn't specifically based in Atlanta. Instead, Soulja Boy bypassed any and all gatekeepers by going straight to the Internet. He did this, at least at first, without established advisers or major-label money behind him. When Collipark and Interscope signed Soulja Boy, they were simply glomming onto an organic Internet phenomenon that was already happening. This was new.

Before anything else, Soulja Boy understood that virality wasn't merely a component of success in an Internet era; it was the entire story. Soulja Boy knew how to put himself into the position where he could go viral. In the years after "Crank That," he did it again and again, for reasons both musical and not. He transformed himself into a living meme before "meme" was a word that everyone understood. Before trolling was an established strategy for getting attention online, Soulja Boy knew how to troll.

The rappers who rose to fame after Soulja Boy followed his example closely, often to the point where they recycled his musical ideas. Nicki Minaj's 2009 mixtape hit "Itty Bitty Piggy" used the beat from Soulja Boy's 2007 album track "Donk," and when Nicki rose to fame, she did it in part by stoking feuds with established rap figures like Lil' Kim. On "Miss Me," a single from his own 2009 breakout mixtape *So Far Gone*, Drake borrowed the hook from "What's Hannennin," a 2008 Soulja Boy mixtape track. (That's what Soulja Boy was yelling about in that *Breakfast Club* interview.) Years later, with the loose 2013 Internet single "We Made It (Remix)," Drake again repurposed a Soulja Boy mixtape track. With that one, though, Drake brought Soulja Boy in to rap on it.

By 2013, Drake had cultivated a reputation as rap's ultimate A&R figure—someone who would spy a regional trend and bless it by posting about it online or even showing up on a remix. In 2013, for instance, Drake was instrumental in the rise of the Atlanta trio Migos, bringing the group attention by rapping on a remix of their mixtape hit "Versace." But Soulja Boy did the Internet-adapter thing before Drake, and "Versace" could've been his song. Two years before Migos recorded "Versace," Soulja Boy rapped over the song's Zaytoven-produced beat on his mixtape track "Teach Me How to Cook: OMG Part 2."

If "Crank That (Soulja Boy)" was the first true Internet-era rap hit, then Drake was the first Internet-era rap superstar. Unlike Soulja Boy, Drake actually did have the backing of a major rap star: Lil Wayne, who signed Drake to his Young Money label and took Drake on tour before he was famous. Like Soulja, though, Drake carefully curated his online persona, documenting virtually every part of his own rise. *So Far Gone*, a free downloadable mixtape, went Internet viral and made Drake a star, to the point where his hit "Best I Ever Had," which ultimately peaked at #2, was all over the radio long before it was commercially available. (Also, like Soulja Boy, Drake has always understood the value of a dance craze; Drake's instructional single "Toosie Slide" debuted at #1 in 2020.)

Drake took ideas from Soulja Boy, but he refined Soulja's approach by depicting himself as something other than a huckster. Instead, Drake was a vulnerable polymath who sang about his own heartbreak and rapped over sensitive Swedish indie-pop tracks from Lykke Li and Peter Bjorn and John. Drake's stint playing the quadriplegic former basketball star Jimmy Brooks on the Canadian teenage soap opera *Degrassi: The Next Generation* had made young audiences that much more likely to sympathize with him, and Drake seized on that sympathy.

In the years ahead, other rap stars rose up by cultivating their own personae online. Nicki Minaj, for instance, was a brash and colorful drama queen. Wiz Khalifa was a languid stoner. Kendrick Lamar was a cerebral crusader. These artists all wound up with #1 hits of their own, and all of them tirelessly promoted themselves online, taking off by releasing free-download albums long before coming out with their major-label debuts. Like Soulja Boy, all of them rose up on the Internet. Unlike Soulja Boy, all of them knew how to self-promote without coming off like they were selling you something. The greatest example of this phenomenon might be the Weeknd, whose strategy was the exact opposite of what Soulja Boy did. In 2011, four years after "Crank That," Toronto singer Abel Tesfaye released the free online album *House of Balloons*. But rather than clumsily seizing the world's attention, Tesfaye cultivated mystique. At first, he kept himself anonymous, hiding his face and identity, refusing interviews and live-show offers. Eventually, Tesfaye stepped further and further into the spotlight, and he started notching #1 hits of his own in 2015.

The Soulja Boy effect extended outside of rap music. Whether they had label machinery working behind them or not, virtually every major star who emerged after Soulja Boy did so online. In 2007, for instance, a twelve-year-old Justin Bieber sang Ne-Yo's hit "So Sick" at a local talent competition in Stafford, Ontario. His mother taped the performance and put it on YouTube. Manager Scooter Braun saw the video, flew Bieber down to Atlanta, and helped him get signed to Usher's record label. A year later, Bieber was an explosively popular teen idol, thanks in part to the very-online young female fan base that came to be known as the Beliebers. Other young stars like Taylor Swift and Katy Perry learned how to craft their images on the Internet by using social-media platforms to portray themselves as average girls who happened to be supremely famous and talented. Presumably, the Biebers and Swifts and Perrys of the world would've figured out those skills without Soulja Boy's example, but Soulja Boy still got there first.

In the 2010s, as *Billboard* started factoring YouTube views into its chart tabulation, many hits started out as memes. Baauer's 2013 indie dance chart-topper "Harlem Shake," for instance, owed its success to a viral fad; people loved filming themselves acting crazy when the beat dropped. South Korean rapper Psy, who got to #2 with the novelty hit "Gangnam Style," had a memorably cartoonish video and a silly dance, just like Soulja Boy before him. Hits like Rae Sremmurd's "Black Beatles," Migos's "Bad and Boujee," and Drake's "In My Feelings" took off on the strength of the memes that surrounded them.

By the end of the 2010s, the raw and unpolished production style of "Crank That (Soulja Boy)" even experienced a mini-revival of its own. The streaming site SoundCloud, like SoundClick before it, fueled a whole generation of cheap DIY hits. Young artists recorded no-frills rap and pop songs in home studios, capturing wide audiences without having to interact with the larger music business. Some of those artists — Lorde, Desiigner, Billie Eilish — wound up with #1 hits of their own. Others, including SoundCloud stars like XXXTentacion, built entire personae around lo-fi home-recorded immediacy. (XXXTentacion had a #1 hit of his own with 2018's "Sad!" — but it didn't top the Hot 100 until after the young artist's murder.)

Twelve years after "Crank That," Lil Nas X, another bored kid from Atlanta with a gift for social-media self-promotion, uploaded "Old Town Road," his own strange and simple home-recording experiment. Less than a year later, the song became the longest-reigning #1 single in *Billboard* history. Like Soulja Boy before him, Lil Nas X followed his out-of-nowhere hit by gleefully trolling his detractors. Unlike Soulja Boy, Lil Nas X held onto the fame that came with that first smash; Lil Nas X's first #1 hit was not his last.

This century, the Internet has warped and mutated culture in ways that we don't yet fully understand. But while most of us have scrambled to catch up to the disorienting pace of these changes, younger kids have launched themselves into the void, using the confusion to sail past gatekeepers and make names for themselves. Soulja Boy did it first, and all the artists who have followed are, in one sense or another, his children.

CHAPTER 19

Rae Sremmurd–
"Black Beatles"
(Featuring Gucci Mane)

Released September 13, 2016
Hit #1 November 25, 2016
Seven-week reign

"I'VE ALWAYS LOVED JOHN LENNON'S SWAG. I LIKE HIS glasses." This was how Swae Lee, the younger half of the rap duo Rae Sremmurd, described his affinity for the white Beatles while explaining Rae Sremmurd's "Black Beatles" to *Rolling Stone* in January 2017. The woozy, ethereal party song "Black Beatles" barely has anything to do with any previous Beatles. The song sounds nothing like anything that the Beatles ever made. Instead, "Black Beatles" is all about being young and rich and famous, and its reference points begin and end with the world-altering wave of excitement that greeted the white Beatles when they arrived in America. Rae Sremmurd are more interested in the mania part of Beatlemania than in the Beatle part.

On "Black Beatles," Swae Lee and Slim Jxmmi casually refer back to the myth of the Beatles in vague, vaporous terms. Swae Lee invokes them first: "I'm a fuckin' Black Beatle, cream seats in the Regal, rockin' John Lennon lenses, like to see 'em spread-eagle." (He really does like those glasses.) Later, Slim Jxmmi claims that he and Paul McCartney are "related." In the "Black Beatles" music video, Swae and Jxmmi play guitar on a rooftop, visually echoing the Beatles' final 1969 concert in London. But they're pretending, playing dress-up. After all, there are no guitars on "Black Beatles."

The title "Black Beatles" isn't a joke, exactly, but it's not serious, either. For Rae Sremmurd, the Beatles are just a broad cultural reference, a name that everyone will know. Rae Sremmurd did something similar on their 2014 single "Up Like Trump," which invoked a future president's name as a symbol of rich, carefree life. But there's something poetic about how Rae Sremmurd rose to #1 more than fifty years after the Beatles' arrival—and a few weeks after Trump won the presidency—with a song that signaled the arrival of a whole new pop-chart sea change. "Black Beatles" represented a big change in the way people consumed, encountered, and understood pop music, and it also heralded the arrival of a newly dominant genre of pop.

Trap music, a rap subgenre that doesn't have a firm definition or starting point, was an underground phenomenon for years before it conquered the pop charts. As a genre name, "trap" exemplifies the connections between southern rap and the criminal culture that surrounded it for decades. The term "trap" is Atlanta slang for an empty house used to sell drugs. Atlanta rappers had been using the word "trap" in their music decades before anyone was using it as a musical descriptor. (Kilo Ali on 1991's "Keep on Rollin'": "A quarter to three when I hit the trap / A worker fucking up, so I give him the slap.")

Starting in the midnineties, former New Orleans drug dealer Percy Miller, calling himself Master P, built up his homegrown record label, No Limit, as a tremendous commercial force. P and his No Limit associates made raw, unrefined regional music that often drew on their own experiences in illicit trades. They cranked out albums at a dizzying pace, selling tens of millions of them. Other regional southern labels—Rap-a-Lot and Suave House in Houston, Cash Money in New Orleans—had similar stories. People who made money as criminals realized that there was a more stable future in music, whether as rappers, record-label moguls, or both.

In 2003, Clifford "T.I." Harris, an Atlanta rapper whose 2001 Arista debut, *I'm Serious*, had been a commercial flop, released his sophomore album, *Trap Muzik*. At the time, Atlanta's chief musical export was crunk, the harsh, physical, chant-heavy rap subgenre. T.I. sometimes collaborated with crunk overlord Lil Jon, and he was comfortable with the crunk sound. But on *Trap Muzik*, T.I. tweaked the formula, rapping over more laid-back and expansive tracks while glamorizing his own drug-dealing days. Along the way, T.I. inadvertently came up with a name for a whole new wave of underground Atlanta music.

Trap Muzik went platinum and turned T.I. into a star. Over the next decade, he steadily churned out increasingly triumphal hits and became a pop-radio presence. In 2006, T.I. rapped a verse on Justin Timberlake's chart-topper "My Love." In 2008, T.I. cleaned his sound up even further and reached the top of the Hot 100 with a couple of songs that didn't explicitly acknowledge his drug-dealing past.

Soon enough, other Atlanta rappers followed T.I.'s example. In 2005, Young Jeezy rose up from Atlanta's street-rap underground with *Let's Get It: Thug Motivation 101*, a major-label debut album with lyrics that almost exclusively addressed Jeezy's history of selling crack on corners. Jeezy and T.I. had a fiercely local sound, though that sound became more pop-friendly as the rappers' profiles grew. Producers like Shawty Redd and DJ Toomp made tracks with blaring synth melodies, blooming clouds of bass, and insistent digital hi-hat tics. This sound didn't share much in common with crunk or snap, the other two Atlanta sounds that crossed over on the pop charts in that moment. But that new sound was the future.

Atlanta's rappers made music specifically for clubs, and certain local strip clubs like Magic City became famous for breaking songs and artists. When trap crossed over to the mainstream, that combination of lyrical danger and body-moving music proved intoxicating. In 2008, for instance, the supremely popular R&B singer Usher had a #1 hit with "Love in This Club," a Toomp-produced trap-pop song with a Young Jeezy guest verse.

But while Jeezy ascended on the charts, he was locked in a vicious feud with another Atlanta-based rapper who made his own version of trap music. Radric Davis was an Alabama native who'd moved to Atlanta's Zone 6 neighborhood at the age of nine. Davis started selling crack in eighth grade, and he was in that life for years before he first considered making a career out of music. Davis's mostly absent father, a slick-talking con man who bounced between Atlanta and Detroit, was nicknamed "Gucci Man," and Davis eventually took a version of that nickname for himself. He became Gucci Mane.

Gucci and his friends rapped together in their spare time, but Gucci didn't see a path forward in music. In his 2017 memoir, *The Autobiography of Gucci Mane*, Gucci wrote that all the rappers he knew were broke. He looked down on them. Gucci also didn't like the way his voice sounded whenever he heard himself on tape. Because of his "country" Alabama accent and a slight speech impediment, he didn't think anyone could take him seriously as a rapper. Instead, Gucci wanted to become a mogul. After a 2001 arrest, Gucci looked for a way to make his money legally. Inspired by Master P's success, Gucci started managing his fourteen-year-old nephew, who took the rap name Lil Buddy. Gucci wrote Buddy's lyrics and forged a connection with local producer Xavier "Zaytoven" Dotson. When Lil Buddy lost interest in his budding rap career, Zaytoven pushed Gucci to try it himself.

In 2001, Gucci Mane made his first underground CD, and he sold it hand to hand, the same way he sold drugs. Sometimes, he even sold music and drugs together. In his autobiography, Gucci writes, "I was already a hell of a salesman, and I worked my music into my day-to-day hustle, selling n***as a package deal for a dime of smoke and a CD." Gucci started to pick up steam in Atlanta when he teamed with the indie label Big Cat and released his 2004 song "Black Tee," a crime-themed response to Dem Franchize Boyz' snap hit "White Tee."

The next year, Gucci teamed up with fellow underground stand-out Young Jeezy to release "Icy," the song that became the national breakout hit for both artists. ("Hit" is a relative term for underground artists. "Icy" never made the Hot 100, but it reached *Billboard*'s R&B and hip-hop charts.) But a dispute over the credit and royalties for "Icy" led to a bitter years-long feud between Jeezy and Gucci. On his 2005 mixtape track "Stay Strapped," Jeezy rapped over the beat from T.I.'s hit "ASAP" and promised $10,000 to anyone who could take Gucci's chain: "I got a bounty on that chain, n***a, ten stacks." Soon after-ward, four men attacked Gucci while he was at a lady friend's house, and Gucci shot at them, killing one. Later, police discovered the body of Pookie Loc, a rapper signed to Jeezy's record label, buried behind a middle school. Police arrested Gucci and charged him with murder, but he claimed self-defense, and prosecutors dropped the charges.

In the early days, that sort of violent lore was key to the appeal of trap music, and it inspired a huge cult audience. Gucci Mane fed that cult. While T.I. and Jeezy became pop stars, Gucci remained underground, but became a prolific force. He released a few retail albums in the late 2000s, but those were just the tip of the iceberg. In that same stretch, Gucci also cranked out dozens of street-level mixtapes—albums that could be bought on the street for a few dollars or downloaded on the Internet for free. Mixtapes had started off as lit-eral cassettes; DJs would put together mixes, sometimes with exclusive tracks or cameos from popular artists, and sell them directly to fans. Later, mixtapes became a semi-illicit arm of the music industry. Rap-pers would record themselves rapping over popular beats and assem-ble those tracks into ad-hoc albums, and bootleggers, often with the encouragement of the artists, would sell burned CDs of those albums on street corners. The mixtape trade inspired devoted regional follow-ings, and it helped make stars of rappers like 50 Cent.

Gucci Mane was built for mixtapes. He worked quickly and effi-ciently, and he had a gift for funny, memorable turns of phrase. Gucci liked talking about partying and consuming drugs as much as selling

them, and his slurry, bouncing, playful delivery proved hugely influential. Thanks to his prodigious output, Gucci also worked with many
younger artists and producers who'd never collaborated with a well-
known rapper before Gucci. As mixtapes went from burned CDs on
street corners to free downloads on websites like DatPiff and Livemix-
tapes, Gucci's audience expanded far beyond Atlanta.

In 2009, Gucci had a guest verse on "Break Up," a #14 hit from
R&B singer Mario, and he reached #36 with his own single "Wasted."
Gucci also rapped on a remix of the Black Eyed Peas' "Boom Boom
Pow," the year's biggest hit. But Gucci made a much greater impact in
the mixtape world, where he played mentor to a whole new generation
of artists. Gucci founded his own 1017 Records label, signing younger
artists like OJ da Juiceman, Waka Flocka Flame, Young Thug, and
Migos. At the same time, Gucci also released entire collaborative mixtapes with artists like Yo Gotti, Future, Rich Homie Quan, and Chief
Keef. A whole generation of future stars got their starts by working with
Gucci Mane. Plenty of producers also came up under Gucci. Gucci
worked best within a specific musical zone. Gucci continued to work
with Zaytoven, and he rapped over early tracks from young trap beat-
makers like Metro Boomin, Sonny Digital, and Mike Will Made-It. All
of them saw their profiles rise after producing for Gucci.

Mike Will Made-It, a native of the Atlanta suburb of Marietta,
started making music at fourteen, and he was eighteen when Gucci
Mane heard some of that music. Gucci paid Will $1,000 for a few of
the beats that appeared on his 2007 mixtape *No Pad, No Pencil*. In
the next few years, Mike Will established himself as a trap producer
with pop instincts. In the early 2010s, Will produced hits for artists like
Future, Lil Wayne, 2 Chainz, and Kanye West. In 2013, Will went to
work with former Disney star Miley Cyrus, who played around with
trap sounds on her album *Bangerz*, and he produced her #2 hit "We
Can't Stop." That same year, Mike Will also started his EarDrummers record label. A year later, Mike Will introduced the world to Rae
Sremmurd.

Brothers Aaquil and Khalif Brown were both born in Whittier, California, in the early nineties, but they didn't live in any single place for long until their teenage years. The Brown brothers' father wasn't in the picture, and their mother served in the army, moving around the United States before finally settling down in Elvis Presley's hometown of Tupelo, Mississippi. There, the Brown brothers started a rap group called Dem Outta St8 Boyz. In a 2009 video for their self-produced song "Put It in Rotation," you can see the two Brown brothers and a friend wearing enormous matching basketball jerseys and dancing in synchronized lockstep, doing their best Soulja Boy imitations. A few years later, the Brown brothers, like Soulja Boy before them, would move from Mississippi to Atlanta, and they would find viral fame.

In Tupelo, Aaquil and Khalif cared more about music than school, and they skipped enough classes that their mother threw them out. The Browns squatted in an abandoned house and threw huge parties. While working civilian jobs, Dem Outta St8 Boyz performed locally and eventually traveled to New York to compete in a BET talent show. A friend introduced them to P-Nazty, a producer from Tupelo who was living in Atlanta and working for Mike Will's EarDrummers label. For a while, the brothers moved back and forth between Atlanta, where they'd work on music, and Tupelo, where Aaquil held down a day job in a mattress factory and rented an apartment. After a solid year, Mike Will signed the brothers to EarDrummers and changed their name to Rae Sremmurd—"EarDrummers" spelled backward. Aaquil started calling himself Slim Jxmmi, and Khalif took the name Swae Lee.

Working with Mike Will, Rae Sremmurd developed a springy, catchy, melodic take on trap music. The brothers had never sold drugs, though they'd grown up around that world. (In Tupelo, the brothers' stepfather had sometimes worked as a dealer.) So Rae Sremmurd didn't rap about selling drugs. Instead, they rapped about girls and partying. Their giddy energy and Swae Lee's sticky singsong hooks, along with Mike Will's thick and booming production, set them apart. At the SXSW festival in 2014, Rae Sremmurd performed on every available stage, and Mike Will collaborator Future let them perform their debut single, "No Flex Zone," during his sets. "No Flex Zone" eventually took off, peaking at #36, and the horny follow-up "No Type" did even better, reaching #16. The brothers' debut album, *SremmLife*, released at the beginning of 2016, was a shameless collection of sugary hooks and cinematic beats, and it went platinum. Rae Sremmurd played festivals and toured as an opening act for established rappers like Nicki Minaj.

Hook-centric party rappers like Rae Sremmurd don't often have long careers. When they first arrived, a lot of people compared Rae Sremmurd to Kris Kross, the Atlanta kiddie-rap duo who had an out-of-nowhere #1 hit with 1992's "Jump" and faded from the charts soon afterward. Like Kris Kross, Rae Sremmurd were fresh-faced young rappers with short dreadlocks and bouncy music that made a virtue of its own lack of seriousness. (Slim Jxmmi and Swae Lee were both in their early twenties when Rae Sremmurd took off, but they both looked like they were about twelve.) But Rae Sremmurd were also pop craftsmen who knew their way around a hook. The two kids in Kris Kross had been assembled by young producer Jermaine Dupri, who wrote their raps. Rae Sremmurd worked closely with other big-name producers, but they were creative forces, too, and *SremmLife* burst with energy and melodic ideas.

Rae Sremmurd quickly followed their *SremmLife* debut with their 2016 sophomore album, *SremmLife 2*. The new LP debuted in the top 10, but its first two singles fizzled. One missed the Hot 100 entirely, while the other made it only to #72. If *SremmLife 2* had disappeared without leaving a ripple, nobody would've been surprised. Instead, the Mannequin Challenge happened.

In October 2016, a high school student in Jacksonville, Florida, posted a strange and hypnotic video on social media. In the clip, the camera floated through a group of high school students, all of whom were frozen in place. All those frozen bodies created a kind of unsettling, uncanny sci-fi effect, but it was also clearly the work of a group of friends having fun. The stunt caught on with insane speed. More and more groups of teenagers posted their own Mannequin Challenge videos. Celebrities got in on it, too. Basketball, football, and hockey teams posted Mannequin Challenge videos. Beyoncé reunited with Destiny's Child for a Mannequin Challenge. Adele did one, and so did Taylor Swift. Michelle Obama and LeBron James did the Mannequin Challenge. The cast of *Saturday Night Live* did it, too. The night before she lost the presidential election, Hillary Clinton posted a Mannequin Challenge video that involved her ex-president husband, her whole campaign staff, and her prominent supporter Jon Bon Jovi. This whole craze took place within the space of a couple of months—a strange little viral-blip fad that was possible only in the social-media era.

That first Mannequin Challenge video had no music attached. Very quickly, though, Rae Sremmurd's "Black Beatles," the third single from *SremmLife 2*, became the soundtrack of virtually every Mannequin Challenge video. The song fitted the imagery. Mike Will Made-It built "Black Beatles" on a hazy, weightless keyboard melody that recalled the synthpop of eighties and nineties groups like Depeche Mode. Mike Will made the "Black Beatles" beat on a laptop that he'd just bought, and he sent it to Swae Lee, who sent him back an idea for the song's hook. At the time, Will was at Gucci Mane's house, and Gucci liked the in-progress song enough to add a quick verse.

At that point, Gucci Mane was rap's ultimate feel-good story. During his absurdly prolific mixtape run in the late 2000s and early 2010s, Gucci had been deep in the throes of codeine addiction, and his erratic and violent behavior had led to a long and dispiriting string of arrests. For years, Gucci was in and out of jails and psychiatric hospitals, accused of things like beating up fans who'd tried to take pictures of him. Gucci also maintained all of his old rap feuds and started new ones, breaking contentiously from all of his former protégés. Finally, in 2014, Gucci pleaded guilty to the crime of possessing a firearm as a convicted felon, and he spent nearly three years in prison. (Gucci had recorded so much music that new mixtapes kept arriving even after he'd been incarcerated.) While in prison, Gucci kicked his codeine habit and lost more than a hundred pounds. When he emerged from prison, Gucci seemed like a different person. The newly clean-living Gucci was slimmed down and buffed up, and he had turned his life around.

After being freed from prison in May 2016, Gucci got back to work, and "Black Beatles" was one of the many songs he recorded during that run. Gucci, more than a decade older than either of the Rae Sremmurd brothers, fitted smoothly in between their verses. Gucci had never rapped on a big mainstream hit before "Black Beatles." The song gave him the chance to play a sort of wise-elder role, conferring credibility on Rae Sremmurd while capitalizing on their pop instincts. Gucci Mane was sober at this point, but he was still happy to rap about lean and weed and cocaine, whether he still consumed those substances or not. This, after all, was what the world wanted from Gucci. Trap, the genre that Gucci had helped to create, had become party music, and Gucci Mane was never above party music.

The striking thing about "Black Beatles" is how warped and spacey it sounds. On paper, Rae Sremmurd and Gucci Mane's lyrics are all good-life exultation: Lamborghinis, money-counting machines in the club, cash slowly falling through the air, crowds losing it when the DJ drops the needle. But the song's tone is withdrawn, even melancholy. Swae Lee, in particular, sings with unspoken longing in his voice. He brings a girl to the club, and she jumps up on the table, screaming that everybody's famous. He blows all his money and gets more. He doesn't believe anything that anyone tells him. When a girl says that she loves him, he thinks that she's trolling.

The sound of "Black Beatles" reflects the influence of new drugs like Xanax, as well as old ones like weed. It's a loose, pretty drift of a song—a sedative, not a stimulant. "Black Beatles" is built more for zoning out than for going crazy on a dance floor. It evokes the feeling of floating in the air, watching yourself from above. Its gauzy, dream-like synths made "Black Beatles" an ideal soundtrack for all those

Mannequin Challenge videos. But the synchronicity between "Black Beatles" and the Mannequin Challenge craze wasn't entirely organic. "Black Beatles" was already racing up the charts before the Mannequin Challenge, and it might've become Rae Sremmurd's biggest hit even without the viral boost. But the marketers at Interscope, Rae Sremmurd's label, worked to attach "Black Beatles" to the Mannequin Challenge—to make sure this hit could capitalize on this viral fad that was already happening.

As the Mannequin Challenge spread, Interscope worked with Pizzaslime, a viral marketing company and streetwear brand that started off as a music website, to link the Mannequin Challenge to "Black Beatles." Interscope vice president Gunner Safron told Pigeons & Planes, "The Mannequin Challenge hashtag started finding its way online, and we saw how it was going to build. There wasn't one song that was associated with that when it first came out, so it was just about taking 'Black Beatles,' knowing that we had a hit song on our hands, and finding ways to associate that song with the Mannequin Challenge." Little more than a week after the first Mannequin Challenge video appeared online, Rae Sremmurd staged their own Mannequin Challenge, getting an entire crowd at a Denver show to freeze in place during the "Black Beatles" intro. "Black Beatles" had already soundtracked some Mannequin Challenge videos, but Rae Sremmurd's Denver video supercharged that trend.

In November 2016, most of the Mannequin Challenge videos that appeared online were set to "Black Beatles." A few days after Rae Sremmurd posted their video, white Beatle Paul McCartney added his own Mannequin Challenge video, freezing in place while listening to the part of the song where Slim Jxmmi brags that he and McCartney are related. As a caption, McCartney wrote, "Love those Black Beatles." ("When you've reached a Beatle, it's the ultimate co-sign," Swae Lee told Rolling Stone.)

Some celebrities tried Mannequin Challenge videos set to songs other than "Black Beatles"; Britney Spears, for instance, tried to promote her own song "Slumber Party" with a Mannequin Challenge video, and it just looked wrong. The Mannequin Challenge needed Swae Lee murmuring sleepily over moody, gurgling synthesizers. The sounds and the images paired beautifully. A song that sounds like getting too stoned to move soundtracked all these videos of people . . . not moving.

A couple of days before "Black Beatles" reached #1, the Atlanta Hawks held a Gucci Mane Night at Philips Arena. During his halftime-show performance, Gucci got the entire arena to make a Mannequin Challenge video with him. That same night, when Gucci and long-time girlfriend Keyshia Ka'oir appeared on the arena's Kiss Cam, Gucci got down on one knee and proposed to her. A year later, BET made a ten-part TV documentary about their wedding. Thanks in part to "Black Beatles," Gucci Mane became a full-on mainstream celebrity. In 2019, Gucci Mane became the face of an ad campaign from the designer Gucci.

The Mannequin Challenge trend was fully and completely over by mid-December 2016, but "Black Beatles" ascended to #1 in late November, and it stayed there for two months. In January, the Weeknd's Daft Punk collaboration "Starboy" debuted at #1, temporarily displacing "Black Beatles." A week later, though, "Starboy" fell from #1, and "Black Beatles" retook the top spot. "Black Beatles" got a boost from the Mannequin Challenge, but it outlasted the boost. Even after the trend was over, the song remained hugely popular.

"Black Beatles" was not the first song to ride a viral trend to #1. Soulja Boy had gate-crashed the charts nearly a decade earlier. In 2013, *Billboard* started using YouTube views in collating the Hot 100, and the immediate beneficiary was Baauer, a New York dance producer whose year-old track "Harlem Shake" had become the soundtrack of another viral challenge. Groups of people filmed themselves acting crazy when the "Harlem Shake" bass-drop hit, and celebrities got in on the action, just as they later would with the Mannequin Challenge. "Harlem Shake," an instrumental with no official music video and no significant radio play, topped the Hot 100 for five weeks.

Baauer had nothing to do with the viral "Harlem Shake" trend; that developed on its own. Rae Sremmurd, by contrast, intentionally attached themselves to the Mannequin Challenge phenomenon, which put them in a better place to capitalize on its success. "Harlem Shake" proved to be a strange little one-off. Instrumental dance music didn't experience a sudden surge of popularity after "Harlem Shake," and Baauer never made another significant hit, even after collaborating with Rae Sremmurd on a 2014 single.

Instead, Bruno Mars's ballad "When I Was Your Man" knocked "Harlem Shake" out of the #1 spot, and smooth, globally minded dance-pop ruled the Hot 100 for the next few years. In 2016, two of the year's biggest hits included the Drake-Rihanna duet "Work" and Drake's own "One Dance." These songs drew on pop genres from around the world—dancehall from Jamaica, afrobeats from Nigeria, funky house from the United Kingdom—but they presented these sounds as frictionless, carefree club music. Just before "Black Beatles" finally rose to #1, the Chainsmokers and Halsey ruled the Hot 100 for three months with "Closer," a sort of coffeehouse-dance track built for festival light shows. "Black Beatles" was slick enough to fit in next to "One Dance" and "Closer" in radio playlists or DJ sets, but it augured new changes to come.

The big change was streaming. In 2015, subscription streaming services like Spotify and the newly launched Apple Music became the single biggest revenue source for the entire music industry. In the years that followed, streaming became only more popular, essentially becoming the default way that most people heard new music. Radio dwindled, and actual record sales became a virtual nonfactor. Since the streaming services' playlists and algorithms constantly updated themselves, a viral fad like the Mannequin Challenge could have an immediate effect on the charts. Rae Sremmurd and their label were smart enough to connect the group to a viral fad, and in the new streaming economy, this was enough to push them to #1.

Rap music was an underdog on the Hot 100 for many years, at least in part because pop radio stations were hesitant to add rap to heavy rotation. Streaming services had no such reservations. Streaming services also didn't have to comply with Federal Communications Commission regulations, so people listening to new-music playlists on Spotify didn't have to contend with the irritating experience of hearing rap singles with all the curse words edited out. In the early 2000s, the rappers who conquered the Hot 100 most often were the artists offering sanitized, lightweight versions of rap music. Often, these artists were white: Macklemore, Iggy Azalea, even the newly sober and slightly less bloodthirsty Eminem. These were the rappers most acceptable to radio stations with white program directors and predominantly white audiences. When streaming services took over the charts, those artists no longer had a leg up.

Instead, the rap music that took over in the middle of the decade was the sort of rap that thrives on streaming—hazy, melody-driven, slightly unfocused party music. Atlanta trap, which emphasizes bleary melody and light psychedelia, proved ideal for this new world. Six months before "Black Beatles" reached #1, Desiigner's "Panda" rode a Kanye West endorsement and a whole lot of streaming to #1. Desiigner was an eighteen-year-old unknown from Brooklyn, but he sounded so much like the Atlanta mainstay Future that plenty of fans were surprised to learn that "Panda" was not a Future song. "Panda" was a warning of things to come, but "Black Beatles" was the moment that trap music truly stormed the gates of the Hot 100.

When "Black Beatles" finally fell from the #1 spot, the song that replaced it was another trap anthem from another Atlanta-based family act. Migos, a trio of two cousins and their uncle, had started off as Gucci Mane protégés, and their song "Bad and Bou-jee" knocked "Black Beatles" from the #1 spot. Lil Uzi Vert, a guest rapper on "Bad and Boujee," was a Philadelphia transplant based in Atlanta, and he was simply the latest new artist to get a big boost from Gucci Mane. The same week that "Black Beatles" rose to #1, Uzi and Gucci Mane released a collaborative mixtape. Like "Black Beatles" before it, "Bad and Boujee" rode a viral meme to #1. (With

"Bad and Boujee," it was Migos member Offset's "raindrop, droptop" line, which became the source material for many Twitter jokes.) Like "Black Beatles," "Bad and Boujee" was a low-key, hypnotic party song that made perfect sense on streaming services.

After "Black Beatles," trap music ruled the Hot 100 for years, and major labels devoted serious marketing muscle to turning songs into memes. The cerebral Los Angeles rapper Kendrick Lamar, for instance, topped the Hot 100 a few months later with "Humble," a Mike Will–produced anthem with a thundering trap beat—one that Mike Will had originally made for Gucci Mane—and an eye-grabbing video that worked as pure meme fuel. Cardi B, wife of Migos member Offset, had been a stripper, an Instagram celebrity, and a reality TV star before becoming a rapper; she was truly built for this new environment. Less than a year after "Black Beatles," Cardi rose to #1 with "Bodak Yellow," a track that she'd originally intended for a mixtape. Many more Cardi B chart-toppers followed.

After "Black Beatles," rap hits grew even more expansive and melodic. Post Malone, a face-tatted white guy from upstate New York, started a rap career while living in Dallas, but he never seemed especially interested in rapping, delivering most of his lines in a kind of Auto-Tuned staccato singsong instead. Post's blurry half-rap first conquered the Hot 100 in the fall of 2017, and it was still a huge presence years later. As with "Black Beatles," a whole lot of streaming-friendly trap hits involved artists comparing their wild lifestyles with those of the mythic rock stars of the past. Two different trap-friendly rappers— Post Malone in 2017 and DaBaby in 2020—topped the Hot 100 with two different songs that were both called "Rockstar."

Swae Lee seemed more interested in singing than rapping in the years after "Black Beatles." Rae Sremmurd followed *SremmLife 2* with *SR3MM*, a wildly ambitious 2018 triple album—a Swae Lee solo album, a Slim Jxmmi solo album, and a Rae Sremmurd group album, all packaged together. *SR3MM* didn't have any hits, but Swae Lee's lonely falsetto kept popping up on big songs, including the massively popular 2018 Travis Scott–Drake team-up "Sicko Mode." In 2019, Post Malone and Swae Lee reached #1 with their duet "Sunflower," a sung-not-rapped duet from the soundtrack of the animated film *Spider-Man: Into the Spider-Verse*. Slim Jxmmi, meanwhile, yelped ad-libs in the background of Childish Gambino's 2018 chart-topper "This Is America," a sort of satirical trap song mostly popular because of its extremely viral music video.

In the late 2010s, even the most mainstream pop artists latched onto trap sounds. Taylor Swift rapped with Future on "End Game." Ariana Grande replicated 2 Chainz cadences on her chart-topper "7 Rings." Maroon 5 had to recruit Cardi B for a guest verse to push their "Girls Like You" to #1. The Internet ruled the pop charts, and trap music ruled the Internet. But the Internet changed things in other ways, too. By the end of the decade, pop stars around the world had developed their own Internet-based fan armies. And in a few cases, those fan armies were powerful enough to push artists from outside the American pop-music system to the top of the Hot 100.

CHAPTER 20

BTS—"Dynamite"

| Released August 21, 2020 |
| Hit #1 September 5, 2020 |
| Three-week reign |

A S WE KNOW, WHEN *BILLBOARD* FIRST INTRODUCED THE HOT 100 in 1958, the #1 song in America was "Poor Little Fool," the lovelorn ditty from rock 'n' roll teen idol Ricky Nelson. The song that knocked "Poor Little Fool" out of the #1 spot two weeks later had nothing to do with teen idols or with rock 'n' roll. That song was "Nel blu dipinto di blu (Volare)," a playful, heavily orchestrated romantic chanson from Italian singer and songwriter Domenico Modugno. Modugno's song had come in third at that year's Eurovision Song Contest, and it had gone on to become a huge hit in Italy before spreading to the rest of Europe and to the United States. In America, "Nel blu dipinto di blu (Volare)" topped the Hot 100 for five weeks. *Billboard* eventually named it 1958's biggest single, and it also won the first-ever Grammy for Record of the Year. Domenico Modugno was eventually elected to the Italian parliament, but he never became a superstar in the United States; "Piove (Ciao, ciao bambina)," his only other charting single, peaked at #97 in 1959.

America's Italian immigrant communities were at least partly responsible for the success of "Nel blu dipinto di blu (Volare)," but they weren't the whole story. The song was too big for that. Instead, American record buyers heard a song in a foreign language, and they liked it enough that the song became a smash. That doesn't happen often, but it does happen every once in a while. In 1961, for example, a toothy Illinois singer named Joe Dowell had a #1 hit with "Wooden Heart (Muss I Denn)," a clumsy polka that was half in German. Elvis Presley had sung "Wooden Heart" in his film *G.I. Blues*, but he didn't want to release the song as a single in the United States because he thought it was too cheesy. Dowell capitalized on Presley's hesitance, and he wound up with his only major hit.

Two years later, a sad Japanese-language ballad from nineteen-year-old singer Kyu Sakamoto reached #1 in the United States. A British label exec heard the song, originally titled "Ue O Muite Arukō," in Japan, without realizing that the track was written as a heartbroken protest against America's military presence in Japan. That British exec released the single in the United States and the United Kingdom under the racist title "Sukiyaki"—named after a beef dish, the rare Japanese word that American record buyers might recognize. The renamed "Sukiyaki" spent three weeks at #1 in the summer of 1963. America's postwar resentments against the Axis powers clearly did not extend to the pop charts. Or the country was just oblivious.

Over the decades, foreign-language hits have generally been received as novelties in the United States. They haven't led to big careers for the artists responsible, and they haven't signaled any huge shifts in American perceptions. That was the case with the Singing Nun's French-language acoustic march "Dominique" in 1963, with Falco's keyboard-heavy German-language dance-pop hit "Rock Me Amadeus" in 1986, and with Los del Río's mostly Spanish dance-craze smash "Macarena (Bayside Boys Mix)" in 1996. These songs might have briefly become radio sensations, but they were one-offs, discrete cultural blips. With American radio programmers reluctant to play records that might alienate potential audiences, foreign-language performers never had much of a chance to make more impact than that. But in the 2010s, that barrier started to bend.

In the summer of 2017, Luis Fonsi and Daddy Yankee's reggaeton ballad "Despacito" was already rising up the Hot 100 when Justin Bieber sang an English verse on a remix of the song. With that Bieber verse, "Despacito" became a dominant smash, topping the Hot 100 for an astonishing sixteen weeks. The song led to a burst of interest in reggaeton on the American pop charts. Unlike previous waves of Latin pop excitement in the United States, this one centered around artists who sang in Spanish. A year after "Despacito," the half-Dominican Bronx rapper Cardi B teamed up with two reggaeton artists, Puerto Rico's Bad Bunny and Colombia's J Balvin, on the half-Spanish chart-topper "I Like It." Bunny and Balvin both made top-10 hits of their own, and American record labels rushed to invest in the loose web of Spanish-language genres that became known as urbano.

It's probably not a coincidence that both "Despacito" and "I Like It" became huge hits under the presidency of Donald Trump, a figure who made his political name by railing against Spanish-speaking immigrants. (In a nice little twist of fate, Spanish songs sat at #1 during the first two Independence Days of the Trump administration.) But those songs, anthemic as they were, didn't just take off because of America's large Spanish-speaking population. They took off because the Internet had atomized America into smaller and more segmented audiences. Without any real center, pop music's rigid rules meant less. Radio programmers had a harder time determining what counted as pop and what didn't, and sounds from outside the anglophone mainstream could charge their way up the Hot 100. That, more or less, is what happened with the South Korean genre known as K-pop.

Before the 2010s, South Korean music barely existed in America. Only one Korean group had any success in the United States at all. The

Kim Sisters were three young women who spoke no English but who phonetically memorized English-language pop songs and sang them at American military bases after the Korean War. In the late fifties, the Kim Sisters became regular performers in Las Vegas casinos and on *The Ed Sullivan Show*, and their 1962 cover version of the Coasters' R&B hit "Charlie Brown" reached as high as #7. But the Kim Sisters never stood as representatives of any kind of Korean pop music. They were simply a foreign group who sang American songs. Their appeal was in how they sang our songs back to us in a different accent.

For decades, popular music was mostly broadcast on two national South Korean networks, and it was subject to tight control from a government that was suspicious of anything resembling rock 'n' roll rebellion. On those two networks, the dominant genres were sentimental ballads and the traditional Korean gospel music known as trot. But after a wave of democratic reforms in 1987, Korean networks started to open up and liberalize. Western genres made their way into South Korea's pop music, though the Korean pop industry was still built around a few televised talent competitions.

In 1992, Seo Taiji, a Korean musician who had previously played bass in the heavy metal band Sinawe, formed a boy band called Seo Taiji & Boys. The group took inspiration from American rock and R&B, as well as the hugely popular American boy band New Kids on the Block. On their debut single, "I Know," the trio rapped and sang over crunchy rock guitars, house-music drum loops, and Public Enemy samples. The group got terrible scores when they debuted "I Know" on a televised talent show, but the song became a smash anyway, topping the South Korean charts for seventeen weeks. That TV performance is generally regarded as the big-bang moment for K-pop, the hybridized music genre that eventually became one of South Korea's main cultural exports.

By the time Seo Taiji & Boys broke up in 1996, a whole K-pop system was already in development. In the late nineties, three huge entertainment firms—one of which, YG Entertainment, was founded by former Boys member Yang Hyun-suk—became K-pop's main talent incubators. The primary driving force behind the new system was Lee Soo-man, the American-educated South Korean music producer who founded SM Entertainment, another of the big firms, in 1995. Taking cues from the Japanese pop industry, Lee started recruiting good-looking young people and organizing them into idol groups. SM debuted their first group H.O.T. in 1996, and Lee's methodology quickly became the K-pop industry standard.

In South Korea, young pop idols are trained with military precision. Before these kids get a chance to make any music, they must go through years of lessons in singing, dancing, speaking foreign languages, and interacting with the media. Trainee singers live together and make meager money, and the entertainment firms typically control their music and their images. When those firms decide that the artists are ready, they're presented to the public as fully formed packages. That system leaves plenty of room for abuse and exploitation, and over the years, there have been plenty of cases of both. K-pop stars have spiraled downward, sometimes dying by drug overdose or suicide. But that sleek, hypermodernized take on the old Motown charm-school model has proved hugely lucrative around the world.

In K-pop's system, singers are organized into groups of boys or girls—almost never both—and the standard American five-piece boy-band model isn't necessarily the norm. Entertainment firms seek to attract the widest audiences possible, and they assemble groups like they're casting major motion pictures. Often, in an effort to appeal to international audiences, they'll include Thai or Chinese or Korean American members. In the so-called second generation of K-pop, which started around 2000, groups got bigger and bigger. Girls' Generation, established in 2007, has nine members, while Super Junior, originated in 2005, has twelve. Eventually, the groups came to resemble entertainment agencies themselves, with metaphorical corporate departments and subcommittees. The SM Entertainment group NCT, for example, has twenty-three members, many of which are split off into various different subgroups. Often, YouTube videos or reality shows document every step of the idol-group process, from auditions to dance practices to predebut backstage jitters.

K-pop isn't a genre of music, exactly. It's a different way of understanding and processing pop music. Imagery has always been a huge part of pop music, and American pop has used TV as a sales tool ever since *American Bandstand*. But K-pop takes the visual to new extremes. By and large, K-pop aims to overwhelm. The music itself is important, but choreography and styling are just as central. The tracks often career furiously from hyperkinetic rap verses to thundering blobs of dubstep bass. In videos, troupes of elfin, androgynous young singers with brightly dyed hair and color-coordinated costumes dance in dazzling pop-and-lockstep.

Ever since the early 2000s, when Korean singer BoA became hugely popular in Japan, South Korea's government has looked at K-pop as a crucial cultural soft-power tool. South Korea's government established the country's Ministry of Culture, Sports, and Tourism in 2008 as a way of emphasizing the country's image around the world, and the government has devoted serious resources to K-pop productions. But even as K-pop flourished around Asia, and later Europe and South America, K-pop artists had a hard time cracking the American market, at least until "Gangnam Style."

The rapper Psy, whose single "Gangnam Style" became an international sensation in 2012, was part of YG Entertainment, but he was never a product of the idol system. Instead, Psy was an old friend of YG founder Yang Hyun-suk, and he'd cut his teeth on Seoul's small rap underground before topping the Korean charts for the first time in 2001. Psy was in his midthirties when he released "Gangnam Style," a fizzy and satirical send-up of South Korean materialism. In the song's video, he mugged frantically, screamed at sexy ladies' butts, and did a booty-slapping horsey-ride dance. The extremely meme-able "Gangnam Style" video was an early YouTube sensation, becoming the first video on the platform with one billion views, and it charted as high as #2 on the Hot 100. If *Billboard* had started counting YouTube views in its chart tabulation, then "Gangnam Style" would've been a surefire #1, but the magazine didn't make YouTube a part of its equation until the next year.

After "Gangnam Style," Psy carried himself as an international rap comedian, and he managed a few more American hits. (The 2013 follow-up single "Gentleman" reached #5.) But "Gangnam Style" was essentially a one-off novelty, much like so many previous foreign-language *Billboard* hits. K-pop idol groups like Girls' Generation and 2NE1 made minor inroads in the United States, performing on talk shows or soundtracking TV commercials, but none of them had the broad appeal of Psy's fluky smash. Five years after "Gangnam Style," though, one South Korean group finally broke through in the United States, and that group eventually came to dominate the Hot 100 in ways that nobody could've predicted.

In South Korea, the seven-member boy band known as BTS started off as an underdog project that rejected many of the K-pop system's practices. BTS aren't a product of one of the big three K-pop agencies. Music producer Bang Si-hyuk founded his own Big Hit Entertainment agency in 2005. Bang had previously worked in-house at the big-three company JYP Entertainment, helping to craft hits for idol groups like g.o.d. and Wonder Girls, but in the first few years of his new agency's existence, he had no big hits.

In 2010, Bang met a fifteen-year-old rapper who called himself Rap Monster, and he hatched the idea of putting together a rap group. Bang recruited two more teenage rappers, Suga and J-Hope, before deciding instead to make this new team into a more traditional idol group. One of the members, Jin, was literally recruited off the street just because he was so good-looking. For most of the members, the charisma of leader Rap Monster, who later shortened his name to RM, was the big draw. Bang spent years developing the new group that he called BTS—short for "Bangtan Sonyeondan," a Korean phrase that roughly translates to "Bulletproof Boy Scouts."

Bang wanted BTS to become a welcoming, protective force for the young people of South Korea, so he made some unconventional decisions with the group. The members of BTS often helped write and produce their own music, a rare thing in K-pop. But the real difference with BTS wasn't in how they operated. After all, Bang had come from the K-pop idol system, and BTS are still essentially a traditional South Korean idol group, one that operates within the established system. But BTS came to stand apart because they offered something other than cheery dazzle.

While BTS sometimes sang about standard fare like love and partying, their main topic was the alienation and anxiety of the young people of Korea. BTS have never explicitly made protest music, but their music sometimes comes close. In vague and sometimes platitudinous ways, BTS have often examined the idea that younger generations in South Korea face unrealistic expectations and exploitative systems. On 2013 songs like "No More Dream" and "N.O," the members of BTS decried the "hellish society" where young people are "living lives as puppets." On 2015's "Dope," RM rapped, "The media and adults say we have no willpower and look at us as if we're investments." BTS essentially used the South Korean pop system to criticize the inequalities of the South Korean pop system, and more broadly the South Korean sociopolitical system.

In 2016, BTS engaged a bit more directly with South Korean politics. This was after the Education Ministry policy maker Na Hyang-wook told reporters that South Korea needed to "solidify a class system. . . . The people should be treated like dogs and pigs. It's enough just to feed them and let them live." Na claimed that these freeloaders made up 99 percent of Korean society, comparing them to "Blacks and Hispanics in the United States who don't even try to enter politics or climb the social ladder." The statement drew huge backlash in South Korea, becoming a point of protest for younger people who felt systematically locked out of success. BTS were part of that backlash. On their song "Am I Wrong," Suga rapped about being "dogs and pigs."

BTS weren't leading marches in the streets or anything, but they were subtly allying themselves with the protesters, rather than with the ruling classes. Partly as a result of those escalating protests, the South Korean National Assembly would vote to impeach President Park Geun-hye, the conservative and corporate-friendly daughter of South Korea's former military dictator Park Chung-hee. Park Geun-hye was convicted on corruption charges and eventually sentenced to twenty-five years in prison.

In a context of widening income inequality and governmental dismissiveness, BTS's rebellious sentiments, however subtle, struck a chord. BTS's international fan base calls itself the ARMY, which supposedly stands for "Adorable Representative MC for Youth." Since its emergence in 2013, the BTS ARMY has served as a force of international evangelism for the group, translating their lyrics into different languages and spreading the word on social media. The concept of a virulent subcultural fan club is nothing new; Kiss had their Army decades before BTS had their own. But the Internet made it a whole lot easier for a fan base like the BTS ARMY to mobilize quickly and decisively.

It took time, however, for the ranks of the BTS ARMY to grow. BTS were a minor chart presence in their first few years in Korea, but "Blood Sweat & Tears" became their first South Korean #1 hit in 2016. A year later, BTS started to become an international phenomenon. The general sense of discontent in BTS's lyrics, it turned out, translated—perhaps subtly if not overtly—to the rest of the world, as well.

BTS's upbeat 2017 single "DNA" charted in Australia, Germany, and the United Kingdom, and it became the group's first single to land on the *Billboard* Hot 100, where it peaked at #67. Later that year, the dance song "Mic Drop," a collaboration with California producer Steve Aoki and Brooklyn rapper Desiigner, reached #28. And in 2018, "Fake Love," a song about struggling with self-esteem and mental health, reached #10, making BTS, after Psy, the second K-pop artist to reach the top 10 in America. It's probably telling that Psy and BTS, two artists who didn't fully operate within the K-pop idol system, were the first to truly break through in America. It might also be telling that both Psy and BTS made music that, in very different ways, criticized certain aspects of South Korean society—criticisms that could apply just as easily to America.

When Bang Si-hyuk assembled BTS, he wasn't imagining success in America. Where other K-pop idol groups have international membership, all seven members of BTS are Korean. Their songs about youth struggles and class divides were seemingly fundamentally Korean, too, though the problems themselves are not. (Bong Joon-ho's *Parasite*, the 2019 black comedy that became the first Korean film to win Best Picture at the Oscars, deals with similar concerns from a specifically South Korean viewpoint, but it turned out to be just as universal.)

BTS recorded Japanese-language versions of their singles, but they didn't record in English. In fact, within the group, only RM was fluent in English; he's claimed that he learned the language by watching *Friends* on DVD as a kid. In 2019, RM told *Time* that BTS felt that they wouldn't be true to themselves if they sang in English, even if doing so would've brought them further Hot 100 success: "We don't want to change our identity or our genuineness to get the #1. Like, if we suddenly sing in full English and change these other things, then that's not BTS." To hear RM tell it, the decision not to sing in English was a matter of artistic integrity.

In any case, BTS didn't need to sing in English to become huge in the United States. Without making that adjustment, the group still racked up career accomplishments in America. They performed at the American Music Awards, sent multiple albums to #1 on the US charts, and became the first K-pop group to headline an American stadium show when they sold out New York's Citi Field in 2018. The next year, BTS teamed with American star Halsey on their single "Boy with Luv," and the track peaked at #8. In 2020, "On," a song about resisting fears, made it to #4. But after the COVID-19 pandemic forced the group to cancel all their touring plans, BTS did the thing they said they'd never do. They recorded a song in English.

"Dynamite," BTS's first-ever English-language single, was created specifically to dominate the American charts. BTS achieved their first few top-10 hits in the United States without any significant radio support; stations were still hesitant to play foreign-language music despite the group's obvious and overwhelming popularity. In essence, BTS were a group with a large and rabid pop audience, and they'd made their hits without fully crossing over. Even without the language barrier, their florid, down-tempo sound and their introspective lyrical themes were far removed from whatever remained of the American pop mainstream. BTS fans often expressed deep frustration with Columbia, the label responsible for distributing their music in America, for failing to put enough promotion behind the group. "Dynamite" was a concession for everyone involved: a bright, sticky, happily meaningless English-language song that directly targeted the American charts.

The scheme worked. It's debatable whether "Dynamite" can even be considered a K-pop song, but it's the song that made BTS the first Korean artists ever to top the Hot 100. The members of BTS themselves had a hand in writing most of their previous singles, but "Dynamite" came from the songwriting duo of David Stewart and Jessica Agombar, two British pop-industry professionals who'd previously worked with American stars like the Jonas Brothers and Hailee Stein-feld. Stewart, who produced "Dynamite," had started out in the UK rapper Example's touring band. Agombar, his songwriting partner, had been a member of Parade, a girl group who'd scored a couple of minor UK hits in the early 2010s. Stewart and Agombar heard that BTS were looking for an English-language single. To hear them tell it, tons of American and British pop songwriters submitted tracks—tellingly, not to BTS or to Bang Si-Hyuk, but to Columbia Records head Ron Perry. With "Dynamite," Stewart and Agombar entered the BTS sweepstakes, and they won.

Stewart later told GQ that Columbia had put out feelers, telling songwriters that this BTS single "just needed to be uptempo, fun, not take itself too seriously, almost a bit like Bruno Mars." For Stewart and Agombar, "Dynamite" needed to grab listeners' attention immediately: "We did the Beatles' method, which is to start with the chorus. That way, you're instantly hooked in. . . . But then there are also little tricks you can do, such as making sure that you've got ear candy coming in every four bars to keep the listener inside the song."

"Dynamite" is full of ear candy, and it sounds more than a bit like Bruno Mars. It's a bright, ingratiating piece of disco-pop, with a strutting bass line, pounding piano notes, and scratchy Chic-style guitar ripples. Stewart played every instrument on the track except for the horns, which came from Johnny Thirkell, the veteran Brit-ish session musician who'd played on hits such as Mark Ronson and Bruno Mars's "Uptown Funk." Stewart and Agombar engineered the "Dynamite" hook to rattle around in brains and evoke vague, neb-ulous good-times feelings. The song is a piece of low-stakes, zero-calorie catchiness, and it was perfectly in tune with its moment on the American pop charts. Earlier in 2020, as the world locked down and tried to come to grips with a new reality, a few other celebra-tory and disco-inflected pop songs—Doja Cat and Nicki Minaj's "Say So," Lady Gaga and Ariana Grande's "Rain on Me," Harry Styles's

"Watermelon Sugar"—had reached #1. As if by design, "Dynamite" fitted right in.

Stewart and Agombar's "Dynamite" lyrics aren't about the anhedonia and uncertainty of being young in the twenty-first century. Instead, they're near-gibberish enjoy-the-moment-no-matter-how-mundane exhortations. "Dynamite" is the safest possible example of the party song—the kind that never makes any reference whatsoever to sex or drugs or even alcohol. Instead, everything is wholesome to an almost hallucinatory degree: "Cup of milk, let's rock and roll." Jessica Agombar later told *Billboard*, "I just wanted anything high-energy. It wasn't a particular lyric, it was a bundle of ideas: explosive, fireworks, dynamite, party, fun, energetic, worldwide takeover." As delivered by seven young men whose first language is not English, those lyrics seem almost satirical, as if they're lampooning the emptiness of Western pop music.

By most accounts, the members of BTS were reluctant to record "Dynamite," but they felt that it was a necessary move. RM told *Billboard* that the group had to record in English to avoid losing its prepandemic momentum: "There was no alternative." Most of the members of BTS had to learn the song's lyrics phonetically, using written Korean characters. Jin told *Billboard*, "The English I learned in class was so different from the English in the song. I had to erase everything in my head first."

Talking to *Rolling Stone*, Bang Si-hyuk claimed that "Dynamite" was BTS's response to the pandemic: "'Dynamite' would not have been released if BTS had been on tour as scheduled. The project was chosen to shift the mood as a response to the pandemic situation. I thought it matched BTS and that the song's trendy vibes would be better expressed if sung in English." Given that "trendy vibes" had never been a big part of the BTS mission, "Dynamite" was a spiritual departure as well as a linguistic one. But the single didn't alienate the fans that BTS had already won. Instead, the ARMY made it their mission to turn "Dynamite" into an American hit. They succeeded.

"Dynamite" achieved BTS's stated objective. The song debuted at #1 on the Hot 100, and it even made inroads with American radio, eventually reaching #10 on *Billboard*'s radio-songs chart. "Dynamite" was the breakthrough that BTS needed in the United States, and over the next year, the group returned to #1 four more times—the fastest that any group had racked up five #1 hits since Michael Jackson in 1987 and 1988. A few weeks after "Dynamite" fell from #1, BTS jumped on a remix of "Savage Luv (Laxed—Siren Beat)," a song with its own twisty history.

Jawsh 685, a teenage producer from New Zealand, had uploaded a loping instrumental track called "Laxed (Siren Beat)" on YouTube in 2019, and it had gone viral on social networks like TikTok. American pop singer Jason Derulo, a Columbia recording artist whose debut single, "Whatcha Say," had been a #1 hit in 2009, sang over that beat, releasing the song as "Savage Love" without attributing the track to Jawsh 685. Jawsh 685 objected. Finally, Columbia agreed to sign Jawsh, and the label released the track as "Savaged Love (Laxed—Siren Beat)." The Jawsh-Derulo version was already a top-10 hit before the members of BTS sang on a remix. When that remix came out, "Savage Luv (Laxed—Siren Beat)" went straight to #1.

Two months after "Savage Love," BTS debuted at #1 with "Life Goes On," a single written entirely in Korean. "Life Goes On" is a moody, downcast ballad about struggling through the COVID-19 pandemic. A few Western songwriters, including Disney-musical veteran Antonina Armato and German pop singer Ruuth, worked on "Life Goes On." But BTS members RM, Suga, and J-Hope also cowrote "Life Goes On," as did South Korean producer and regular BTS collaborator Pdogg. And "Life Goes On" captured the yearning, confused feeling that won BTS its passionate fan base in the first place.

Even more than "Dynamite," "Life Goes On" showed the power of the BTS ARMY. "Life Goes On" barely got any radio play, and it didn't do huge streaming numbers, but enough fans bought the single to push it to #1 in its first week. The song's success didn't last. In its second week, "Life Goes On" plummeted to #28, one of the steepest drops in Hot 100 history.

Even with that drop, though, "Life Goes On" proved a point. If enough fans were actively invested in their favorite group's chart success, then they could guarantee that group a #1 hit, and they might make a difference in that group's continued existence. For BTS, this meant governmental favoritism. Before BTS, South Korean idol groups had built-in expiration dates. Men in South Korea have to serve twenty-one months of compulsory military service, and they have to start it by their twenty-eighth birthday. In previous years, boy bands had gone on hiatus when their oldest members reached that milestone. A day before "Life Goes On" reached #1, Jin, the oldest member of BTS, turned twenty-eight. That month, though, the South Korean government passed a revision of the country's Military Service Act, known widely as the BTS Law. Under the BTS Law, a "pop-culture artist" who has "greatly increased the image of Korea both within Korea and throughout the world" can defer that service until the age of thirty.

After the law passed, Jin told *Rolling Stone*, "I think the country sort of told me, 'You're doing well, and we will give you a little bit more time.'" As a nation, South Korea had institutionally recognized the importance of BTS for years, making the group tourism ambassadors as far back as 2017. BTS may have been lightly critical of South Korean society, but they were also important to South Korea's international image. In 2021, Moon Jae-in, the liberal political figure who became South Korea's president after Park Geun-hye's impeachment, gave diplomatic passports to the members of BTS. Soon afterward, the members of the group accompanied President Moon to New York and spoke to the UN General Assembly about the anxiety that their generation faced during the pandemic.

These days, BTS are directly responsible for a decent chunk of South Korea's economy. Bang Si-hyuk is now worth more than $3 billion, and he's one of the richest people in South Korea. Bang's Big Hit Entertainment rebranded as HYBE and went public in 2020. In 2021, the company bought Ithaca Holdings, the company owned by Justin Bieber–Ariana Grande manager Scooter Braun, for $1 billion. It's a symbolic illustration of what's happening in the pop-music world: a South Korean power player absorbing his American competition. The members of BTS, given a measure of equity in Bang's company, have all become millionaires themselves.

In the summer of 2021, BTS and their fans showed just how well they could play the American pop-chart game. The group released their second and third English-language singles, "Butter" in May and "Permission to Dance" in July. Both are sparkly, lightweight, up-tempo party songs very much within the "Dynamite" mold. For "Butter," Columbia Records CEO Ron Perry got a cowriting and coproduction credit. With "Permission to Dance," one of the four cowriters is British pop star Ed Sheeran. On both songs, the input of the BTS members themselves seems relatively minimal, though RM is one of the seven credited writers of "Butter." Both "Butter" and "Permission to Dance" debuted atop the Hot 100. "Butter" stayed there for ten weeks, and it held that spot almost entirely on the strength of the ARMY.

Every week that summer, the "Butter" single sold hundreds of thousands of downloads, mostly through BTS's own webstore. Many of those sales came from the same crowd of BTS fans, who bought the single over and over. BTS steadily rolled out slightly tweaked remixes of the song, all of which counted toward *Billboard*'s tabulation. Fans from around the world coordinated buying campaigns on social media. In different countries, ARMY members offered to reimburse Americans for purchases of singles. The week that "Permission to Dance" came out, "Butter" fell from #1 to #7. The next week,

"Butter" was back on top—a clear example of the fan base temporarily shifting its focus.

"Butter" and "Permission to Dance" were never more than moderate hits on radio and streaming services, but the charts tell a different story. They tell the ARMY's story. In all the weeks that those two singles were at #1, fans of the artists stuck behind BTS on the Hot 100, including Olivia Rodrigo and Dua Lipa, accused the BTS ARMY of chart manipulation. When "Butter" first hit #1, I complained about chart manipulation in a somewhat ill-considered Stereogum article, and my Twitter mentions were an absolute disaster for weeks. I had incurred the wrath of the ARMY.

In a *Billboard* interview during the #1 reign of "Butter," RM addressed those accusations: "If there is a conversation inside *Billboard* about what being #1 should represent, then it's up to them to change the rules and make streaming weigh more on the ranking. Slamming us or our fans for getting to #1 with physical sales and downloads, I don't know if that's right. . . . It just feels like we're easy targets because we're a boy band, a K-pop act, and we have this high fan loyalty." A few months later, *Billboard* actually did institute one such rule change. In December 2021, the magazine announced that its chart tabulations would count only one single purchase per customer per week. The BTS ARMY was not pleased.

If BTS were playing the chart-manipulation game, they're far from the first pop artists to do that. Pop history is full of shadowy stories about labels bribing chart tabulators or threatening reprisal if their singles don't hold the #1 spot. In the Internet age, labels have made an art out of building social-media campaigns around new singles. In the summer of 2020, *Billboard* changed its rules, deciding that artists could no longer elevate their chart positions by selling singles or albums in bundles with T-shirts or concert tickets, a practice that had helped push singles from artists like Taylor Swift and Travis Scott to #1. BTS, it's worth mentioning, had never relied on bundling for their chart spots.

In 2019, when Lil Nas X's runaway smash "Old Town Road" topped the Hot 100 for a record-breaking nineteen weeks, the song held that position, at least in part, from Lil Nas X's precise strategy of releasing a new remix every time it looked like the song was starting to lose momentum. BTS were part of that strategy. On the "Seoul Town Road" remix, Suga rapped alongside Lil Nas X.

Nobody *deserves* a #1 hit. It's not a distinction awarded on merit. The BTS case is interesting because the people manipulating the charts weren't the artists or the label execs. Instead, it was the fans. The members of the BTS ARMY decided that they wanted to keep BTS at #1 for as long as possible. They showed that they were willing to spend their money to ensure the group's chart success. The BTS ARMY aren't the only ones attempting this strategy; fans of stars like Taylor Swift and Justin Bieber have tried to organize in similar ways. Often, they've been successful, but nobody has been more successful than the BTS ARMY. The fans of BTS weren't doing anything illegal; they were simply using the chart rules as they existed at the time. If a group has a fan base large and organized and dedicated enough to shape the record books—a global Internet community who cares enough about this group to spend actual money—then who's to say that the group they support isn't the biggest thing in the world?

At the time of this writing, the long-term effects of BTS's massive success aren't yet evident. Thus far, there has been no Korean Invasion. As I write this, K-pop is essentially a one-artist phenomenon on the US charts. The second-biggest K-pop act right now, the girl group Blackpink, has landed on the Hot 100 a handful of times, but they haven't yet been in the top 10. Their highest-charting single is 2020's "Ice Cream." That one peaked at #13, and it needed a guest vocal from American star Selena Gomez to do that well. But even if K-pop never gains more of a foothold over here, then BTS's success will still be historically significant. It represents the moment that one fan base firmly established that it can control the Hot 100 for months at a time.

Apparently, the Hot 100 is no longer a historical record of the music that dominates pop culture at any particular moment. Instead, the pop charts look more and more like a battlefield for competing fan armies. A change like that forces a reconsideration of the entire idea of pop stardom. BTS have taken the existing model, and they've blown it up like dynamite. It might be years before we know what's next.

Outro

I N 1988, WHEN I WAS EIGHT YEARS OLD, MY FAMILY MOVED TO London. We rented out our house in Baltimore, and we took a plane across the Atlantic, staying with my parents' friends for a few weeks before renting a small town house in Twickenham. My dad was a history professor, and he'd taken a yearlong sabbatical to research and write a book about British army barracks through the ages. My dad never ended up writing that book. Instead, he found something else.

During a trip to an aviation museum, my dad saw a plane called the Baltimore Bomber. He had no idea that such a plane existed. When our year in London ended, my dad started researching the Martin A-30 bomber and the aircraft plant outside Baltimore where the plane was built. When my dad published his first book in 1996, it was about the Baltimore Bomber. Living in London, I guess I found my own something else. I found *Top of the Pops*.

Every Thursday night, the BBC would air this show where the pop stars of the day—Yazz or Neneh Cherry or De La Soul—would lip-synch their newest singles on a set that was full of dry ice and blinking

neon. It looked like a cheap sci-fi movie, and it enraptured me immediately. In between those pantomimed performances, radio DJs
would count down the top-40 singles in the United Kingdom. I didn't
know how they figured out which songs were the top ones, and I
didn't know most of the songs, but the flood of information activated
something in my brain. I would look forward to Thursday nights every
week, watching favorite songs inch their way up or down the countdown. Before the move, I'd poured all my obsessive number-tracking
energy into baseball cards, but I couldn't get those in England. That
year, *Top of the Pops* replaced baseball. After that year, I never really
cared about baseball again.

When my family got back to Baltimore a year later, I was surprised
to learn that we had no *Top of the Pops* equivalent back home. We had
Soul Train and *Showtime at the Apollo* and Casey Kasem's *American
Top 40* radio show, but there wasn't any one single thing that married
the flash of performance to the stat-based numerical collation of that
chart countdown. Still, the *Baltimore Sun* would publish *Billboard's*
top 10 once a week, and I'd keep track of that chart, even as my musical interests moved far away from whatever was on that list in any given
week. By the time I reached high school, I really only listened to punk
rock and Wu-Tang, and I *still* kept an eye on those charts.

I started reading *Spin* in middle school because they stocked the
magazine at the Rite-Aid that was next to my bus stop and because
they put bands like Nirvana on the cover. The writers at *Spin* would
write dizzily and explosively about music that I'd never heard, and
sometimes they did the same for music that I *did* know. In the back of
the reviews section every month, a guy named Charles Aaron would
write sharp, funny little two-sentence reviews of a handful of new singles, and he'd treat a new Archers of Loaf seven-inch just the same as
a new TLC chart-topper. Before reading that column, I'd never really
considered the idea that those songs could exist on an equal playing
field—that the pop music I'd loved at nine could be as valid as the
scummy noise-rock that I'd gotten into a few years later.

I always wanted to be like those writers in *Spin*, and I got my chance when I was twenty-one. That summer, I interned at the *Baltimore City Paper*, my local alt-weekly, and I eventually got up the nerve to ask Lee Gardner, the music editor, if I could pitch him some stuff. He said okay, and I started writing little capsule reviews of rap and indie rock records. Eventually, Lee got promoted, and the new music editor, Bret McCabe, started sending me to interview local bands like Double Dagger and Meatjack and Charm City Suicides. I also started writing for a few websites, like Pitchfork, which didn't pay anything at the time but let me enthusiastically fulminate on new Lil Scrappy and Hold Steady tracks. At twenty-five, I moved to New York and got a job blogging about music at the *Village Voice*. The *Village Voice* is gone now, and so is the *Baltimore City Paper*, but I've been blogging about music ever since.

At the *Voice*, I spent a lot of time writing about warehouse noise shows or Texan rap mixtapes, but I paid attention to the pop charts, too. If something like the *High School Musical* soundtrack became suddenly, bafflingly popular, I wanted to know all about it. And when someone like Lil Wayne, an artist I'd been breathlessly covering, ascended the pop charts, I felt the same vicarious thrill as I did watching those songs go up and down the *Top of the Pops* charts as a nine-year-old.

To be a good music critic, you can't just write about your favorite stuff. That gets old fast. You have to stay curious, to follow the music that speaks to millions of people even if it doesn't speak directly to you. You have to figure out *why* this music connects when it does, and you have to trace the ongoing chaotic narrative of pop music itself. It's easy to dismiss pop music as baby food, as mindless empty audio calories for the masses. But it's a lot more interesting to figure out where a big pop hit fits into a bigger context and to learn the stories of the people who made that big pop hit. If you do that for long enough, you might find yourself falling in love with pop music all over again. That's what happened to me.

My parents lost all interest in contemporary pop music many years before I was born. To them, my fascination with the stuff was a weird character quirk at best and an active irritant at worst. When I turned that fascination into a side hustle, then a job, then a career, my parents were supportive but bewildered. They were impressed, too. It was a real thing. When I got a book deal, it became a *really* real thing.

The whole time I was writing this book, my dad was dying of Parkinson's disease. Near the end, even as it became harder and harder for him to focus, he kept asking about how the book was going, how I was framing the story, what eras I was researching. The last real conversation that I had with my dad was about this book. He died in February 2022, a few weeks after I sent a finished draft to my editor. I got to read the book to him when he was laying immobile in hospice care. I don't know how much of it he understood, but he knew that I'd found my Baltimore Bomber.

Acknowledgments

THIS BOOK WASN'T MY IDEA. I DIDN'T HAVE ANY INKLING THAT my column could be a book until Jack Gernert, my agent, took me out for coffee and presented me with the idea. When I was writing the proposal and freaking myself out, Jack was helpful and encouraging. There's absolutely no way this thing could exist without him.

This book also couldn't exist without my editor Brant Rumble, who put a whole lot of faith into the endeavor and who sharpened and focused every part of this process. He's also got the coolest name. Thanks also to production editor Amber Morris and copy editor Annette Wenda, who put in tremendous work. I still haven't met any of these people in person, and I owe all of them drinks.

Thanks to Scott Lapatine, my boss at Stereogum. Early in 2018, I told Scott that I wanted to undertake this massive, ridiculous project of reviewing every #1 hit in history and that I wanted to get started that day, and Scott let me dive in without any hesitation. Thanks to Chris DeVille, who suggested the name for the column, and to all my other Stereogum coworkers, who have doubtless had to do a whole lot more work because I was researching Milli Vanilli or whatever: James Rettig, Michael Nelson, Gabriela Tully Claymore, Ryan Leas, Peter Helman, Julia Gray, and Rachel Brodsky. Thanks to past Stereogum buds Amrit Singh, Corban Goble, Claire Lobenfeld, Collin Robinson, and everyone else who has worked at the site during my time there. And thanks to the Stereogum commenters and especially the "Number Ones" commenting community. A website with a warm, supportive, nontoxic comments section is a rare thing indeed, and I don't know how we got so lucky.

Thanks to the people who gave me a shot at writing about music in the first place: Lee Gardner and Bret McCabe at the *Baltimore City Paper*, Chuck Eddy and Rob Harvilla at the *Village Voice*, and Scott Plagenhoef and Amy Phillips at Pitchfork.

Thanks to my friends Chris Molanphy and Jack Hamilton, both of whom know a lot about pop history and generously shared that knowledge. Thanks to all the other music critics who have helped shape my thinking, whether on the page or in bars: Marc Hogan, Mark Richardson, Jon Caramanica, Lindsay Zoladz, Brandon Soderberg, Puja Patel, Larry Fitzmaurice, Chris Ryan, Al Shipley, Jayson Greene, Camille Dodero, Eric Harvey, Ian Cohen, David Drake, Andy Greenwald, and countless others. Extra thanks to the guys who became my crew when we were all still in New York: Nick Sylvester, Zach Baron, Jamin Warren, Pete L'Official, Ryan Dombal, and Sean Fennessey. I miss you all.

Thanks to Tom Ewing for writing "Popular," the column that I ripped off, and for being extremely gracious when I told him that I wanted to rip it off.

Thanks to my dad, who isn't around anymore, and my mom, who is. Thanks to my brother, Jim, and my sister, Margaret.

Thanks, above all, to my wife, Bridget, and my kids, Clara and Finn. To write this book, I had to disappear into my own head for months, and I could do that only because my family gave me the love, support, and energy that I needed. It took a whole lot of sacrifice on their part, and I am forever grateful.

Thanks, also, to anyone who ever made music for any reason. And thanks to you, the person who read this whole book, all the way to the Acknowledgments pages.

Selected Bibliography

Bon Jovi with Phil Griffin. *Bon Jovi: When We Were Beautiful.* New York: HarperCollins, 2009.

Braun, Michael. *Love Me Do! The Beatles' Progress.* Los Angeles: Graymalkin Media, 1964.

Bronson, Fred. *The "Billboard" Book of Number 1 Hits.* New York: Billboard Books, 2003.

Caillat, Ken, with Steven Stiefel. *Making "Rumours": The Inside Story of the Classic Fleetwood Mac Album.* Hoboken, NJ: John Wiley & Sons, 2012.

Capouya, John. *Florida Soul: From Ray Charles to KC and the Sunshine Band.* Gainesville: University Press of Florida, 2017.

Carey, Mariah, with Michaela Angela Davis. *The Meaning of Mariah Carey.* New York: St. Martin's Griffin, 2020.

Carlin, Peter Ames. *Catch a Wave: The Rise, Fall & Redemption of the Beach Boys' Brian Wilson.* New York: Rodale Books, 2006.

Charnas, Dan. *The Big Payback: The History of the Business of Hip-Hop.* New York: New American Library, 2010.

Dannen, Fredric. *Hit Men: Power Brokers and Fast Money Inside the Music Business.* New York: Vintage Books, 1990.

Dawson, Jim. *"The Twist": The Story of the Song and Dance That Changed the World.* London: Faber and Faber, 1995.

DeCurtis, Anthony, and James Henke, with Holly George-Warren, eds. *The "Rolling Stone" Illustrated History of Rock & Roll.* New York: Random House, 1992.

Emerson, Ken. *Always Magic in the Air: The Bomp and Brilliance of the Brill Building Era.* New York: Penguin Books, 2005.

Fleetwood, Mick, and Anthony Bozza. *Play On: Now, Then & Fleetwood Mac, the Autobiography.* New York: Little, Brown, 2014.

Gaines, Steven. *Heroes & Villains: The True Story of the Beach Boys.* Burlington, VT: Da Capo Press, 1995.

George, Nelson. *Thriller: The Musical Life of Michael Jackson.* Burlington, VT: Da Capo Press, 2010.

———. *Where Did Our Love Go? The Rise & Fall of the Motown Sound.* New York: St. Martin's Press, 1985.

Greenman, Ben. *Dig If You Will the Picture: Funk, Sex, God, and Genius in the Music of Prince.* New York: Henry Holt, 2017.

Hahn, Alex, and Laura Tiebert. *The Rise of Prince, 1958–1988.* N.p.: Mat Cat Press, 2017.

Hamilton, Jack. *Just Around Midnight: Rock and Roll and the Racial Imagination.* Cambridge, MA: Harvard University Press, 2016.

Hartman, Ken. *The Wrecking Crew: The Inside Story of Rock and Roll's Best Kept Secret.* New York: Thomas Dunne Books, 2012.

Harvey, Eric. *Who Got the Camera? A History of Rap and Reality.* Austin: University of Texas Press, 2021.

Hillman, Chris. *Time Between: My Life as a Byrd, Burrito Brother, and Beyond.* New York: BMG, 2020.

Holland, Eddie, and Brian Holland, with Dave Thompson. *Come and Get These Memories: The Genius of Holland-Dozier-Holland, Motown's Incomparable Songwriters.* London: Omnibus Press, 2019.

Jackson, John A. *American Bandstand: Dick Clark and the Making of a Rock 'n' Roll Empire.* New York: Oxford University Press, 1997.

Jackson, Michael. *Moon Walk.* London: Arrow Books, 1988.

King, Carole. *A Natural Woman: A Memoir.* New York: Grand Central, 2012.

Knopper, Steve. *Appetite for Self-Destruction: The Spectacular Crash of the Record Industry in the Digital Age.* N.p.: CreateSpace, 2017.

———. *MJ: The Genius of Michael Jackson.* New York: Scribner, 2015.

Lawrence, Tim. *Love Saves the Day: A History of American Dance Music Culture, 1970–1979.* Durham, NC: Duke University Press, 2003.

Light, Alan. *Let's Go Crazy: Prince and the Making of "Purple Rain."* New York: Atria Books, 2014.

Marks, Craig, and Rob Tannenbaum. *I Want My MTV: The Uncensored Story of the Music Video Revolution.* New York: Dutton, 2011.

Matos, Michaelangelo. *Can't Slow Down: How 1984 Became Pop's Blockbuster Year.* New York: Hachette Books, 2020.

———. *"Sign 'O' the Times": 33⅓.* New York: Continuum, 2010.

Myers, Marc. *Anatomy of a Song: The Oral History of 45 Iconic Hits That Changed Rock, R&B, and Pop.* New York: Grove Press, 2016.

Nickson, Chris. *Mariah Carey Revisited: Her Story.* New York: St. Martin's Griffin, 1998.

Norman, Philip. *Shout! The Beatles in Their Generation.* New York: Fireside, 1981.

Ro, Ronin. *Bad Boy: The Influence of Sean "Puffy" Combs on the Music Industry.* New York: Pocket Books, 2001.

Sanneh, Kelefa. *Major Labels: A History of Popular Music in Seven Genres.* New York: Penguin Press, 2021.

Seabrook, John. *The Song Machine: Inside the Hit Factory.* New York: W. W. Norton, 2016.

Sheffield, Rob. *Dreaming the Beatles: The Love Story of One Band and the Whole World.* New York: HarperCollins, 2017.

Stone, Henry, and Jacob Katel. *The Stone Cold Truth on Payola! Cash, Cocaine, and Cars in the Music Biz.* 2013.

Unterberger, Richie. *Jingle-Jangle Morning: Folk-Rock in the 1960s.* N.p.: Richie Unterberger, 2015.

Westhoff, Ben. *Dirty South: Outkast, Lil Wayne, Soulja Boy, and the Southern Rappers Who Reinvented Hip-Hop.* Chicago: Chicago Review Press, 2011.

White, Adam, with Barney Ales. *Motown: The Sound of Young America.* London: Thames & Hudson, 2016.

Wilson, Brian, with Ben Greenman. *I Am Brian Wilson: A Memoir.* Burlington, VT: Da Capo Press, 2016.

Index

325